Taste of Home
slow cooker

2/18

Taste of Home

Visit us at tasteofhome.com for other *Taste of Home* books.

International Standard Book Number: 978-1-61765-684-2
Library of Congress Control Number: 2017941092

Cover Photographer: Jim Wieland
Set Stylist: Melissa Franco
Food Stylist: Leah Rekau
Illustration: robuart/shutterstock

Pictured on front cover: Upside-Down Frito Pie, page 72
Pictured on spine: Sweet Onion Creamed Corn, page 196
Pictured on title page: Carrie's Cincinnati Chili, page 63
Pictured on back cover (from left): Beef Brisket Tacos, page 105; Hot Cranberry Punch, page 27; Southwestern Shredded Beef Sandwiches, page 84

Printed in USA.
1 3 5 7 9 10 8 6 4 2

GET SOCIAL WITH US!

To find a recipe tasteofhome.com
To submit a recipetasteofhome.com/submit
To find out about other *Taste of Home* products shoptasteofhome.com

TABLE OF CONTENTS

PAGE 79

PAGE 19

HOME-COOKED MEALS

Ready When You Are!

What could be better than coming home to a bubbling-hot meal that's ready to devour? Grab your slow cooker or electric pressure cooker, and dig in to a pot of savory goodness tonight!

Between long work hours and full slates of after-school activities, delicious family meals are often sacrificed to the time crunch. But you can enjoy hearty menus and bring back family dinners with just a bit of advance planning.

It's easy! **Load the slow cooker** in the morning and a hearty meal will be ready when you get home. Set the cooker at night, and wake up to the aroma of a scrumptious breakfast wafting through the house. Use the slow cooker to carry dishes to an office party, or to keep a dish warm on a weekend buffet. Sensational soups and stews, impressive roasts, spicy pulled pork or chicken sandwiches, warming hot beverages, even tempting desserts and snacks—whatever you're craving, the slow cooker makes it easy. With more than **400 recipes** to choose from, you'll be sure to find new family favorites in every chapter.

Don't miss the **special bonus chapter** that helps you take advantage of another modern kitchen marvel, the Instant Pot® Electric Pressure Cooker. Can't wait to call the gang to the table? Cut cooking time without cutting flavor with this collection of recipes specially adapted for this appliance.

Speaking of beating the kitchen clock, keep an eye out for the FAST FIX icon. It's your guide to finding recipes that **make the most of your time** and budget. All fast-fix recipes either take no longer than 10 minutes of prep time, or have no more than five required ingredients—not including water, salt and pepper, oil and optional extras. So it's a snap to load your slow cooker or electric pressure cooker, set the timer, and get on with your day.

Dig in to all the comfort, convenience and flavor your kitchen devices offer. Let ***Taste of Home Slow Cooker*** show you how!

PAGE 12

PAGE 82

PAGE 37

BUYING & MAINTAINING
Your Slow Cooker

If you're in the market for a slow cooker, there are a lot to choose from, ranging from about $20 to over $200. You may eventually own slow cookers in different sizes, but to start, think about what you'll be using the cooker for to decide which one is best for you. To learn more about specific models, check out product reviews online or in reputable consumer magazines. Consider:

SIZE: Slow cookers are available in sizes from 1½ to 7 quarts. Choose the size that's appropriate for your family.

SLOW COOKER SIZE

HOUSEHOLD SIZE	SLOW COOKER CAPACITY
1 person	1½ quarts
2 people	2 to 3½ quarts
3 or 4 people	3½ to 4½ quarts
4 or 5 people	4½ to 5 quarts
6 or more people	5 to 7 quarts

SHAPE: If you're going to be using your cooker to make roasts, an oval cooker is probably best. Round cookers are great for soups and stews.

SETTINGS: Almost all slow cookers have at least two settings: low (about 180°) and high (about 280°). Some models also have a keep-warm setting, which is useful if you plan to use it for serving at buffets or potlucks. Some slow cookers will automatically switch to the keep-warm setting after the cooking time has elapsed; this provides added convenience and helps you avoid overcooking the food while you're away from home.

INSERT: Most slow cooker inserts are ceramic, but some pricier models have aluminum inserts that let you brown meats without dirtying an extra pan. For convenience, look for inserts that are dishwasher-safe.

A range of cooking times is provided in most recipes to account for variables such as the thickness of a cut of meat, the fullness of the slow cooker, and the desired finished temperature of the food. As you grow familiar with your new slow cooker, you'll be able to judge which end of the range to use.

CLEANING A SLOW COOKER

- Removable stoneware inserts make cleanup a breeze. Be sure to cool the insert before rinsing or cleaning with water to avoid cracking. Do not immerse the metal base unit in water. Clean it with a damp sponge.
- Wash the insert in the dishwasher or in warm soapy water. Avoid using abrasive cleansers since they may scratch the stoneware.
- To remove mineral stains on a ceramic insert, fill the cooker with hot water and 1 cup white vinegar; cover. Set the control to high and allow to "cook" for 2 hours. Discard liquid, and when cool, wash with hot, sudsy water. Rinse well and dry.
- To remove water marks from a highly glazed crockery insert, rub the surface with vegetable oil and allow to stand for 2 hours before washing with hot, sudsy water.

SLOW COOKER TEMPERATURE CHECK

New slow cookers heat up more quickly than older ones. If you have an older model and a recipe directs you to cook on low, try cooking on high for the first hour to ensure food safety. Older cookers may lose their efficiency, so it's a good idea to run regular checks to make sure they're reaching safe cooking temperatures.

To be considered safe, a slow cooker must be able to cook slowly enough that it can be left unattended, yet fast enough to keep the food at a proper temperature. Here's how to check your slow cooker:

1. Fill the slow cooker ½ to ⅔ full with room-temperature water.
2. Cover; heat on low for 8 hours.
3. Use a thermometer to check the temperature of the water. (Work quickly—the temperature can drop once the lid is removed.)
4. The temperature should be at least 185°. If it's too hot, a meal cooked for 8 hours would likely be overdone. If the temperature is below 185°, the slow cooker is not safe to use and should be discarded.

PREPARING FOODS
For the Slow Cooker

BEANS. Soak dried beans prior to cooking. Soak them overnight or place them in a Dutch oven and add water to cover by 2 inches. Bring to a boil; boil for 2 minutes. Remove from heat, cover, and let stand for 1-4 hours. Drain and rinse beans, discarding the liquid. Lentils and split peas do not need soaking. Add any sugar, salt and acidic ingredients (such as vinegar) after the beans are fully cooked; these interfere with the beans' ability to cook.

DAIRY. Milk-based products tend to break down during slow cooking. Add items like milk, cream, sour cream or cream cheese during the last hour of cooking. Add cheese near the very end of the cooking time.

FISH & SEAFOOD. Fish and seafood can break down if cooked too long. Add them to the slow cooker toward the end of the cooking time.

MEAT. It's not necessary to brown meat before adding it to the slow cooker, but it does add to the meat's flavor and appearance and allows you to drain off the fat. Cut roasts over 3 pounds in half to ensure even cooking. Trim excess fat from the outside of the meat. Fat retains heat, and large amounts of fat could raise the temperature of the cooking liquid, causing the meat to overcook.

OATS. Quick-cooking and old-fashioned oats are often interchangeable in recipes, but old-fashioned oats hold up better in the slow cooker.

PAGE 121

PASTA. If added to a slow cooker when dry, pasta gets sticky. Instead, cook pasta according to package directions and stir into the slow cooker just before serving. Small pastas (such as orzo and ditalini) may be cooked in the slow cooker; to keep them from becoming mushy, add during the last hour of cooking. Couscous is best cooked on the stovetop.

RICE. Converted rice is ideal for all-day cooking. If using instant rice, add it during the last 30 minutes of cooking.

VEGETABLES. Firm vegetables like potatoes and carrots tend to cook more slowly than meat. Cut these into uniform pieces and place on the bottom and around the sides of the slow cooker. Place the meat over vegetables. Tender vegetables, like peas and zucchini, shoudl during the last 15-60 minutes of cooking.

PAGE 28

PAGE 27

CONVERTING RECIPES
For the Slow Cooker

Almost any recipe that bakes in the oven or simmers on the stovetop can be converted for the slow cooker. Here are some guidelines:

- Select recipes that simmer for at least 45 minutes. Good choices are soups, stews, pot roasts, chili and one-dish meals.
- Look for a slow cooker recipe that's similar to the one you want to convert. Note the quantity and size of the meat and vegetables, heat setting and cooking time.
- There is no evaporation from a slow cooker, so if a recipe calls for liquid, you'll need to use less. If a recipe calls for 6 to 8 cups of water, start with 5 cups. If the recipe doesn't call for any liquid, add about ½ cup of water, broth or juice—all slow cooker recipes should call for some liquid.

COOK TIMES

CONVENTIONAL OVEN	SLOW COOKER
15 to 30 minutes	Low: 4 to 6 hours High: 1½ to 2 hours
35 to 45 minutes	Low: 6 to 8 hours High: 3 to 4 hours
50 minutes or more	Low: 8 to 10 hours High: 4 to 6 hours

10 TOP TIPS FOR SLOW COOKING

CHOOSE THE RIGHT CUT OF MEAT. Lower-prestige cuts work better than lean cuts. Trim excess fat from the outside, but look for good marbling on the inside—that will break down during cooking and make the meat tender.

DON'T PEEK! Each time you open the cooker, you'll need to add 15-30 minutes of cooking time. Open only when instructed to add ingredients.

MAKE SURE THE LID FITS. Be sure the lid is secure, not tilted or askew. Steam during cooking creates a seal.

AVOID TEMPERATURE SHOCKS. If your cooker has a ceramic insert, put a dishtowel on a cold work surface before setting the hot insert down. Do not preheat your cooker. A cold insert should always be put into a cold base.

THAW THE FROZEN BITS. Unless the recipe instructs otherwise, or you're using a prepackaged meal kit, thaw frozen food before adding it to the slow cooker. Frozen ingredients lower the temperatures inside the cooker and increase the chance of bacteria growing.

GO EASY ON THE ALCOHOL. Alcohol won't evaporate from the slow cooker, so use sparingly. If you brown the meat, use wine to deglaze the pan, then pour the liquid into the slow cooker. This will burn off the alcohol but leave the flavor.

DON'T OVERFILL OR UNDERFILL. Fill the slow cooker between ½ and 2/3 full. Less than ½ full and the food may burn. More than 2/3 full and the food may not cook completely.

DON'T LET IT GET COLD. If you won't be home when the cooking time is up, be sure the cooker will switch itself to Warm. Temperatures between 40-140° are where bacteria thrive. Do not use your slow cooker to reheat food.

HALVE THE TIME BY DOUBLING SETTING. On most models, Low is 170° and High is 280°. For many recipes, cranking up the heat will cut down the cook time.

ADJUST COOK TIME AS NEEDED. If you live at a high altitude, add about 30 minutes for each hour of cooking the recipe calls for; legumes will take roughly twice as long.

ASIAN WRAPS, PAGE 20

SNACKS & BEVERAGES

A slow cooker works wonders when it comes to party time! Use it to make appetizers and snacks, or to keep drinks and dips warm on the buffet. It's magic!

SLOW COOKER KEY LIME FONDUE

FAST FIX

SLOW COOKER KEY LIME FONDUE

Love fondue but want to dip into something other than milk chocolate? Try my white chocolate key lime fondue using graham crackers, fresh fruit and cookies.

—**ELISABETH LARSEN** PLEASANT GROVE, UT

PREP: 5 MIN. • **COOK:** 50 MIN.
MAKES: 3 CUPS

- **1 can (14 ounces) sweetened condensed milk**
- **12 ounces white baking chocolate, finely chopped**
- **½ cup Key lime or regular lime juice**
- **1 tablespoon grated lime peel**
- **Graham crackers, macaroon cookies, fresh strawberries and sliced ripe bananas**

1. In a 1½-qt. slow cooker, combine milk, white chocolate and lime juice.
2. Cook, covered, on low for 50-60 minutes or until chocolate is melted. Stir in lime peel. Serve with graham crackers, cookies and fruit.

FAST FIX

SALTY-SWEET PEANUT TREAT

Who knew slow cooking could transform chocolate, peanuts and pretzels? Once it's cooked, we drop the mix into mini muffin papers for a takeaway treat.

—**ELIZABETH GODECKE** CHICAGO, IL

PREP: 10 MIN. • **COOK:** 1 HOUR + CHILLING
MAKES: ABOUT 6 DOZEN

- **24 ounces milk chocolate, coarsely chopped**
- **2 cups salted peanuts**
- **¼ cup packed brown sugar**
- **1 teaspoon vanilla extract**
- **2 cups crushed pretzels**

In a 3-qt. slow cooker, combine chocolate, peanuts and brown sugar. Cook, covered, on low, stirring halfway through cooking, until chocolate is melted, about 1 hour. Stir in vanilla. Add pretzels; stir to combine. Drop by tablespoonfuls onto waxed paper-lined baking sheets. Refrigerate until set, 10-15 minutes. Store in an airtight container.

FAST FIX

CARAMEL APPLE CIDER

A delectable combination of cinnamon sticks, allspice and caramel, this warm-you-up sipper is sure to chase away winter's chill. Serve brimming mugs alongside a platter of festive cookies at your next holiday gathering.

—**TASTE OF HOME TEST KITCHEN**

PREP: 5 MIN. • **COOK:** 2 HOURS
MAKES: 12 SERVINGS

- **8 cups apple cider or juice**
- **1 cup caramel flavoring syrup**
- **¼ cup lemon juice**
- **1 vanilla bean**
- **2 cinnamon sticks (3 inches)**
- **1 tablespoon whole allspice**
- **Whipped cream, hot caramel ice cream topping and cinnamon sticks, optional**

1. In a 3-qt. slow cooker, combine apple cider, caramel syrup and lemon juice. Split vanilla bean and scrape out the seeds; add the seeds to the cider mixture. Place the vanilla bean, cinnamon sticks and allspice on a double thickness of cheesecloth; bring up corners of cloth and tie with string to form a bag. Add to cider mixture.
2. Cover and cook on low for 2-3 hours or until heated through. Discard the spice bag. Pour cider into mugs; garnish with whipped cream, caramel topping and additional cinnamon sticks if desired.
Butterscotch Mulled Cider: Combine the cider with 1 cup butterscotch schnapps liqueur and 4 cinnamon sticks; heat as directed.
Harvest Cider: Substitute 4 cups pineapple juice for half of the cider. Stud an orange slice with 8 whole cloves; add to juices with 1 cinnamon stick and 1 tea bag. Heat as directed.
Note: This recipe was tested with Torani brand flavoring syrup. Look for it in the coffee section.

FAST FIX

PEACHY SPICED CIDER

I served this spiced cider at a party and received so many compliments. Everyone enjoys the subtle peach flavor and warm spices.

—**ROSE HARMAN** HAYS, KS

PREP: 5 MIN. • **COOK:** 4 HOURS
MAKES: ABOUT 1 QUART

- **4 cans (5½ ounces each) peach nectar or apricot nectar**
- **2 cups apple juice**
- **¼ to ½ teaspoon ground ginger**
- **¼ teaspoon ground cinnamon**
- **¼ teaspoon ground nutmeg**
- **4 fresh orange slices (¼-inch thick), halved**

In a 1½-qt. slow cooker, combine the first five ingredients. Top with the orange slices. Cover and cook on low for 4-6 hours or until heated through. Stir before serving.

CHICKEN SLIDERS WITH SESAME SLAW

These tangy, spicy chicken sliders have an Asian style that tingles the taste buds. At our potlucks, they quickly vanish.

—**PRISCILLA YEE** CONCORD, CA

PREP: 25 MIN. • **COOK:** 6 HOURS
MAKES: 20 SERVINGS

- **1 medium onion, coarsely chopped**
- **3 pounds boneless skinless chicken thighs**
- **½ cup ketchup**
- **¼ cup reduced-sodium teriyaki sauce**
- **2 tablespoons dry sherry or reduced-sodium chicken broth**
- **2 tablespoons minced fresh gingerroot**
- **½ teaspoon salt**

SESAME SLAW

- **¼ cup mayonnaise**
- **1 tablespoon rice wine vinegar**
- **1 tablespoon sesame oil**
- **1 teaspoon Sriracha Asian hot chili sauce**
- **3 cups coleslaw mix**
- **⅓ cup dried cherries or cranberries**
- **2 tablespoons minced fresh cilantro**
- **20 slider buns or dinner rolls, split**

1. Place onion and chicken in a 4-qt. slow cooker. In a small bowl, mix the ketchup, teriyaki sauce, sherry, ginger and salt. Pour over the chicken. Cook, covered, on low for 6-7 hours or until a thermometer reads 170°.

2. Remove chicken; cool slightly. Skim fat from cooking juices. Shred chicken with two forks. Return meat to the slow cooker. Meanwhile, in a small bowl, whisk mayonnaise, vinegar, sesame oil and Sriracha sauce until blended. Stir in coleslaw mix, cherries and cilantro. Using a slotted spoon, place ¼ cup chicken mixture on each bun bottom; top with about 2 tablespoons slaw. Replace tops.

PORK PICADILLO LETTUCE WRAPS

Warm pork and cool, crisp lettuce are a combination born in culinary heaven. My spin on a lettuce wrap is chock full of scrumptious flavor and spice.

—**JANICE ELDER** CHARLOTTE, NC

PREP: 30 MIN. • **COOK:** 2½ HOURS
MAKES: 2 DOZEN

- **3 garlic cloves, minced**
- **1 tablespoon chili powder**
- **1 teaspoon salt**
- **½ teaspoon pumpkin pie spice**
- **½ teaspoon ground cumin**
- **½ teaspoon pepper**
- **2 pork tenderloins (1 pound each)**
- **1 large onion, chopped**
- **1 small Granny Smith apple, peeled and chopped**
- **1 small sweet red pepper, chopped**
- **1 can (10 ounces) diced tomatoes and green chilies, undrained**
- **½ cup golden raisins**
- **½ cup chopped pimiento-stuffed olives**
- **24 Bibb or Boston lettuce leaves**
- **¼ cup slivered almonds, toasted**

1. Mix garlic and seasonings; rub over pork. Transfer to a 5-qt. slow cooker. Add onion, apple, sweet pepper and tomatoes. Cook, covered, on low for 2½ to 3 hours or until the pork is tender.

2. Remove pork; cool slightly. Shred into bite-size pieces; return meat to slow cooker. Stir in raisins and olives; heat through. Serve in lettuce leaves; sprinkle with almonds.

CREAMY ONION DIP

Caramelized onions team up with Gruyere cheese for a rich appetizer fit for a classic cocktail party.

—**REBECCA TAYLOR** MANTECA, CA

PREP: 20 MIN. • **COOK:** 5 HOURS
MAKES: 5 CUPS

- 4 cups finely chopped sweet onions
- ¼ cup butter, cubed
- ¼ cup white wine or chicken broth
- 6 garlic cloves, minced
- 1 bay leaf
- 2 cups shredded Gruyere or Swiss cheese
- 1 package (8 ounces) cream cheese, softened
- ¼ cup sour cream
- Assorted crackers or breadsticks

1. In a 3-qt. slow cooker, combine the onions, butter, wine, garlic and bay leaf. Cover and cook on low for 4-5 hours or until the onions are tender and golden brown.

2. Discard bay leaf. Stir in the Gruyere cheese, cream cheese and sour cream. Cover and cook for 1 hour longer or until the cheese is melted. Serve warm with crackers.

SOUTHWESTERN PULLED PORK CROSTINI

For a distinctly different take on crostini, these hearty appetizers are great for tailgating and other casual parties. Everyone enjoys these spicy, sweet and salty bites.

—**RANDY CARTWRIGHT** LINDEN, WI

PREP: 45 MIN. • **COOK:** 6 HOURS
MAKES: 32 APPETIZERS

- 1 boneless pork shoulder butt roast (about 2 pounds)
- ½ cup lime juice
- 2 envelopes mesquite marinade mix
- ¼ cup sugar
- ¼ cup olive oil

SALSA

- 1 cup frozen corn, thawed
- 1 cup canned black beans, rinsed and drained
- 1 small tomato, finely chopped
- 2 tablespoons finely chopped seeded jalapeno pepper
- 2 tablespoons lime juice
- 2 tablespoons olive oil
- 1½ teaspoons ground cumin
- 1 teaspoon chili powder
- ½ teaspoon salt
- ¼ teaspoon crushed red pepper flakes

SAUCE

- 1 can (4 ounces) chopped green chilies
- ⅓ cup apricot preserves
- ⅛ teaspoon salt

CROSTINI

- 32 slices French bread baguette (¼ inch thick)
- ¼ cup olive oil
- ⅔ cup crumbled queso fresco or feta cheese
- Lime wedges, optional

1. Place roast in a 3-qt. slow cooker. In a small bowl, whisk lime juice, marinade mix, sugar and oil until blended; pour over roast. Cook, covered, on low 6-8 hours or until meat is tender.

2. For salsa, in a small bowl, combine the corn, beans, tomato and jalapeno. Stir in the lime juice, oil and seasonings. In a small saucepan, combine the sauce ingredients; cook and stir over low heat until blended.

3. For crostini, preheat broiler. Brush bread slices on both sides with oil; place on ungreased baking sheets. Broil 3-4 in. from heat 1-2 minutes on each side or until golden brown.

4. Remove roast from slow cooker; cool slightly. Shred pork with two forks. To serve, layer toasts with salsa, pork and cheese. Top with sauce. If desired, serve with lime wedges.

SOUTHWESTERN PULLED PORK CROSTINI

TURKEY-MUSHROOM EGG ROLLS

TURKEY-MUSHROOM EGG ROLLS

I slow-cook ground turkey and mushrooms in a hoisin, soy and sesame sauce and add fresh veggies for a finger-licking filling for my egg rolls. They are a favorite appetizer with guests—I never have any leftovers.

—**SARAH HERSE** BROOKLYN, NY

PREP: 1¼ HOURS • **COOK:** 4 HOURS
MAKES: 3½ DOZEN

- **1½ pounds ground turkey**
- **½ pound sliced fresh mushrooms**
- **2 medium leeks (white portion only), thinly sliced**
- **3 celery ribs, thinly sliced**
- **½ cup hoisin sauce**
- **2 tablespoons minced fresh gingerroot**
- **2 tablespoons rice vinegar**
- **2 tablespoons reduced-sodium soy sauce**
- **1 tablespoon packed brown sugar**
- **1 tablespoon sesame oil**
- **2 garlic cloves, minced**
- **½ cup sliced water chestnuts, chopped**
- **3 green onions, thinly sliced**
- **42 egg roll wrappers**
- **Oil for frying**
- **Sweet-and-sour sauce or Chinese-style mustard, optional**

1. In a large skillet, cook turkey over medium heat for 8-10 minutes or until no longer pink, breaking into crumbles. Transfer to a 5-qt. slow cooker.

2. Stir in mushrooms, leeks, celery, hoisin sauce, ginger, vinegar, soy sauce, brown sugar, sesame oil and garlic. Cook, covered, on low 4-5 hours or until vegetables are tender. Stir water chestnuts and green onions into the turkey mixture; cool slightly.

3. With one corner of an egg roll wrapper facing you, place 2 tablespoons filling just below the center of the wrapper. (Cover remaining wrappers with a damp paper towel until ready to use.) Fold the bottom corner over the filling; moisten remaining wrapper edges with water. Fold the side corners toward the center over the filling. Roll the egg roll up tightly, pressing at the tip to seal. Repeat.

4. In an electric skillet, heat ¼ in. of oil to 375°. Fry the egg rolls, a few at a time, for 3-4 minutes or until golden brown, turning occasionally. Drain on paper towels. If desired, serve with sweet-and-sour sauce.

To freeze: Cover and freeze unfried egg rolls on waxed paper-lined baking sheets until firm. Transfer to resealable plastic freezer bags; return to freezer. To use, fry egg rolls as the recipe directs, increasing the cooking time to 4-5 minutes.

BACON-RANCH SPINACH DIP

During the hectic holiday season, my slow cooker works overtime. I fill it with a savory bacon dip and watch everyone line up for a helping. Keep the recipe in mind for tailgating, too.

—**CRYSTAL SCHLUETER** NORTHGLENN, CO

PREP: 15 MIN. • **COOK:** 2 HOURS
MAKES: 24 SERVINGS

- **2 packages (8 ounces each) cream cheese, softened**
- **1½ cups bacon ranch salad dressing**
- **¼ cup 2% milk**
- **2 cups shredded sharp cheddar cheese**
- **1 can (14 ounces) water-packed artichoke hearts, rinsed, drained and chopped**
- **1 package (10 ounces) frozen chopped spinach, thawed and squeezed dry**
- **2 plum tomatoes, seeded and finely chopped**
- **½ cup crumbled cooked bacon**
- **4 green onions, thinly sliced**
- **Assorted crackers and fresh vegetables**

1. In a large bowl, beat cream cheese, salad dressing and milk until blended. Stir in cheese, artichokes, spinach, tomatoes, bacon and green onions. Transfer to a 4- or 5-qt. slow cooker.

2. Cook, covered, on low for 2-3 hours or until heated through. Serve with crackers and vegetables.

PULLED PORK NACHOS

While home from college, my daughter made these tempting pork nachos, her first recipe ever. My son and I couldn't get enough.

—**CAROL KURPJUWEIT** HUMANSVILLE, MO

PREP: 30 MIN. • **COOK:** 8 HOURS
MAKES: 16 SERVINGS

- **1 teaspoon garlic powder**
- **1 teaspoon mesquite seasoning**
- **¼ teaspoon pepper**
- **⅛ teaspoon celery salt**
- **3 pounds boneless pork shoulder butt roast**
- **1 medium green pepper, chopped**
- **1 medium sweet red pepper, chopped**
- **1 medium onion, chopped**
- **1 can (16 ounces) baked beans**
- **1 cup barbecue sauce**
- **1 cup shredded cheddar cheese**
- **Corn or tortilla chips**
- **Optional toppings: chopped tomatoes, shredded lettuce and chopped green onions**

1. In a small bowl, mix seasoning ingredients. Place roast in a 5- or 6-qt. slow cooker; rub with seasonings. Add peppers and onion. Cook, covered, on low for 8-10 hours.

2. Remove the roast; cool slightly. Strain cooking juices, reserving vegetables and ½ cup juices; discard remaining juices. Skim fat from reserved juices. Shred pork with two forks.

3. Return meat, reserved juices and vegetables to the slow cooker. Stir in beans, barbecue sauce and cheese; heat through. Serve over chips with toppings as desired.

To freeze: Freeze cooled pork mixture in freezer containers. To use, partially thaw in refrigerator overnight. Heat through in a saucepan, stirring occasionally; add broth or water if necessary.

CRANBERRY HOT WINGS

CRANBERRY HOT WINGS

Cranberry wings remind me of all the wonderful celebrations and parties we've had over the years. My daughter's friends can't get enough of them.

—**NOREEN MCCORMICK DANEK** CROMWELL, CT

PREP: 45 MIN. • **COOK:** 3 HOURS
MAKES: ABOUT 4 DOZEN

- 1 can (14 ounces) jellied cranberry sauce
- ½ cup orange juice
- ¼ cup hot pepper sauce
- 2 tablespoons soy sauce
- 2 tablespoons honey
- 1 tablespoon packed brown sugar
- 1 tablespoon Dijon mustard
- 2 teaspoons garlic powder
- 1 teaspoon dried minced onion
- 1 garlic clove, minced
- 5 pounds chicken wings (about 24 wings)
- 1 teaspoon salt
- 4 teaspoons cornstarch
- 2 tablespoons cold water

1. Whisk together first 10 ingredients. For chicken, use a sharp knife to cut through two wing joints; discard wing tips. Place wings in a 6-qt. slow cooker; sprinkle with salt. Pour the cranberry mixture over top. Cook, covered, on low until tender, 3-4 hours.
2. To serve, remove wings to a 15x10x1-in. pan; arrange in a single layer. Preheat broiler.
3. Transfer cooking juices to a skillet; skim fat. Bring juices to a boil; cook until the mixture is reduced by half, 15-20 minutes, stirring occasionally. Mix cornstarch and water until smooth; stir into juices. Return to a boil, stirring constantly; cook and stir until thickened, 1-2 minutes.
4. Meanwhile, broil wings 3-4 in. from heat until lightly browned, 2-3 minutes. Brush with glaze before serving. Serve with remaining glaze.

NACHO RICE DIP

Spanish rice mix adds an interesting twist to this effortless appetizer. Every time I serve this dip at get-togethers, my guests gobble it up.

—**AUDRA HUNGATE** HOLT, MO

PREP: 20 MIN. • **COOK:** 15 MIN.
MAKES: ABOUT 8 CUPS

- 1 package (6.8 ounces) Spanish rice and pasta mix
- 2 tablespoons butter
- 2 cups water
- 1 can (14½ ounces) diced tomatoes, undrained
- 1 pound ground beef
- 1 pound (16 ounces) process cheese (Velveeta), cubed
- 1 can (14½ ounces) stewed tomatoes
- 1 jar (8 ounces) process cheese sauce
- Tortilla chips

1. In a large saucepan, cook rice mix in butter until golden brown. Stir in water and diced tomatoes; bring to a boil. Reduce heat; cover and simmer for 15-20 minutes or until the rice is tender.
2. Meanwhile, in a large skillet, cook beef until no longer pink. Drain and add to the rice. Stir in cheese, stewed tomatoes and cheese sauce; cook and stir until cheese is melted.
3. Transfer to a slow cooker set on low. Serve with tortilla chips.

TEST KITCHEN TIP
To substitute home-canned tomatoes for a 14½-ounce can of stewed tomatoes, add 3 tablespoons finely chopped celery, 2 tablespoons finely chopped onion, 1 tablespoon finely chopped green pepper, ½ teaspoon sugar and ⅛ teaspoon salt to 14½ ounces of home-canned tomatoes.

CILANTRO & LIME CHICKEN WITH SCOOPS

I came up with this recipe when I was preparing for a large party, and I wanted a healthy Tex-Mex chicken to serve in tortilla cups. This can made ahead of time to free up yourself for time-sensitive dishes. Serve it in tortilla chip cups or any other savory crispy cup. Leftovers are great over salad greens or wrapped up in a tortilla as a burrito.

—**LORI TERRY** CHICAGO, IL

PREP: 15 MIN. • **COOK:** 3½ HOURS
MAKES: 16 SERVINGS

- **1 pound boneless skinless chicken breasts**
- **2 teaspoons chili powder**
- **2 tablespoons lime juice**
- **1½ cups frozen petite corn (about 5 ounces), thawed**
- **1½ cups chunky salsa**
- **1½ cups finely shredded cheddar cheese**
- **1 medium sweet red pepper, finely chopped**
- **4 green onions, thinly sliced**
- **Baked tortilla chip scoops**
- **Minced fresh cilantro**

1. Place chicken in a 1½-qt. slow cooker; sprinkle with chili powder and lime juice. Cook, covered, on low until tender, 3-4 hours.
2. Remove chicken; discard the cooking juices. Shred chicken with two forks; return meat to slow cooker. Add corn and salsa; cook, covered, on low until heated through, about 30 minutes, stirring occasionally.
3. Transfer to a large bowl; stir in cheese, pepper and green onions. Serve with tortilla scoops; sprinkle with cilantro.

ASIAN WRAPS

This recipe is just like any other Asian wrap, but with even more delicious and healthy flavor. Instead of ordering Chinese food, you'll be making these yourself!

—**MELISSA HANSEN** MILWAUKEE, WI

PREP: 30 MIN. • **COOK:** 3½ HOURS
MAKES: 1 DOZEN

- **2 pounds boneless skinless chicken breast halves**
- **¼ cup reduced-sodium soy sauce**
- **¼ cup ketchup**
- **¼ cup honey**
- **2 tablespoons minced fresh gingerroot**
- **2 tablespoons sesame oil**
- **1 small onion, finely chopped**
- **2 tablespoons cornstarch**
- **2 tablespoons water**
- **12 round rice papers (8 inches)**
- **3 cups broccoli coleslaw mix**
- **¾ cup crispy chow mein noodles**

1. Place chicken in a 3-qt. slow cooker. In a small bowl, whisk soy sauce, ketchup, honey ginger and oil; stir in onion. Pour over the chicken. Cook, covered, on low 3-4 hours or until the chicken is tender. Remove chicken; shred with two forks and refrigerate until assembly.
2. Meanwhile, in a small bowl, mix cornstarch and water until smooth; gradually stir into the honey mixture. Cook, covered, on high 20-30 minutes or until sauce is thickened. Toss chicken with ¾ cup sauce; reserve the remaining sauce for serving.
3. Fill a large shallow dish partway with water. Dip a rice paper wrapper into water just until pliable, about 45 seconds (do not soften completely); allow excess water to drip off.
4. Place wrapper on a flat surface. Layer ¼ cup coleslaw, ⅓ cup chicken mixture and 1 tablespoon noodles across the bottom third of the wrapper. Fold in both sides of the wrapper; fold bottom over the filling, then roll up tightly. Place wrap on a serving plate, seam side down. Repeat with remaining ingredients. Serve with reserved sauce.

ASIAN WRAPS
Melissa Hansen
Milwaukee, WI

FAST FIX

SLOW COOKER CANDIED NUTS

I like giving spiced nuts as holiday gifts. This slow cooker recipe with ginger and cinnamon is so good, you just might use it all year long.

—**YVONNE STARLIN** WESTMORELAND, TN

PREP: 10 MIN. • **COOK:** 2 HOURS
MAKES: 4 CUPS

- **½ cup butter, melted**
- **½ cup confectioners' sugar**
- **1½ teaspoons ground cinnamon**
- **¼ teaspoon ground ginger**
- **¼ teaspoon ground allspice**
- **1½ cups pecan halves**
- **1½ cups walnut halves**
- **1 cup unblanched almonds**

1. In a greased 3-qt. slow cooker, mix butter, confectioners' sugar and spices. Add nuts; toss to coat. Cook, covered, on low 2-3 hours or until the nuts are crisp, stirring once.

2. Transfer nuts to waxed paper to cool completely. Store in an airtight container.

HAWAIIAN KIELBASA

Savory sausage teams up with juicy, tangy pineapple for a winning combination that you can prep in a flash. The sweet barbecue-style sauce is a tasty way to tie them together.

—**LOUISE KLINE** FORT MYERS, FL

PREP: 15 MIN. • **COOK:** 3 HOURS
MAKES: 12 SERVINGS

- **2 pounds smoked kielbasa or Polish sausage, cut into 1-inch pieces**
- **1 can (20 ounces) unsweetened pineapple chunks, undrained**
- **½ cup ketchup**
- **2 tablespoons brown sugar**
- **2 tablespoons yellow mustard**
- **1 tablespoon cider vinegar**
- **¾ cup lemon-lime soda**
- **2 tablespoons cornstarch**
- **2 tablespoons cold water**

1. Place sausage in a 3- or 4-qt. slow cooker. Drain pineapple, reserving ¾ cup juice; set the pineapple aside. In a small bowl, whisk together ketchup, brown sugar, mustard and vinegar. Stir in soda and the reserved pineapple juice. Pour over the sausage; stir to coat. Cover and cook on low for 2-3 hours or until heated through.

2. Stir in the pineapple. In a small bowl, combine cornstarch and water until smooth. Stir into the slow cooker. Cover and cook 30 minutes longer or until sauce is thickened. Serve with toothpicks.

NO-GUILT BEEFY NACHOS

Nachos you can feel good about! This meaty topping has less fat and sodium than typical nacho beef because you use lean meat and make your own seasoning. The versatile dish is great for a party.

—**CAROL BETZ** GRAND RAPIDS, MI

PREP: 15 MIN. • **COOK:** 4 HOURS
MAKES: 20 SERVINGS (2½ QUARTS)

- **2 pounds lean ground beef (90% lean)**
- **1 can Ranch Style beans (pinto beans in seasoned tomato sauce), undrained**
- **2 tablespoons chili powder**
- **1 tablespoon brown sugar**
- **2 teaspoons ground cumin**
- **2 teaspoons ground coriander**
- **1 teaspoon dried oregano**
- **1 teaspoon cayenne pepper**
- **1 tablespoon cider vinegar**
- **¾ teaspoon salt**
- **Baked tortilla chips**
- **Shredded cheddar cheese, lettuce, sour cream and guacamole, optional**

Combine the first eight ingredients in a 4-qt. slow cooker. Cook, covered, on low until the meat is crumbly, 4-6 hours. Stir in vinegar and salt. Serve with tortilla chips and, if desired, nacho toppings.

To freeze: Freeze the cooled meat mixture in freezer containers. To use, partially thaw in the refrigerator overnight. Heat through in a saucepan, stirring occasionally and adding a little water if necessary. Serve with chips and toppings.

FAST FIX

WARM FETA CHEESE DIP

We're huge fans of appetizers, and this super-easy baked dip is a mashup of some of our favorite ingredients. It goes so well with a basket of crunchy tortilla chips or slices of a French bread baguette.

—**ASHLEY LECKER** GREEN BAY, WI

START TO FINISH: 30 MIN.
MAKES: 2 CUPS

- **1 package (8 ounces) cream cheese, softened**
- **1½ cups crumbled feta cheese**
- **½ cup chopped roasted sweet red peppers**
- **3 tablespoons minced fresh basil or 2 teaspoons dried basil**
- **Sliced French bread baguette or tortilla chips**

In a small bowl, beat cream cheese, feta cheese, peppers and basil until blended. Pour into a greased 1½-qt. slow cooker; cook, covered, on low for 2-3 hours or until heated through. Serve with baguette slices or chips.

Note: To prepare in an oven, mix the ingredients as directed. Transfer to a greased 3-cup baking dish. Bake at 400° for 25-30 minutes or until bubbly.

FAST FIX

PEAR CIDER

Our perfectly spiced, pear-flavored beverage is a wonderful alternative to traditional apple cider.

—**TASTE OF HOME** TEST KITCHEN

PREP: 5 MIN. • **COOK:** 3 HOURS
MAKES: 20 SERVINGS

- **12 cups unsweetened apple juice**
- **4 cups pear nectar**
- **8 cinnamon sticks (3 inch)**
- **1 tablespoon whole allspice**
- **1 tablespoon whole cloves**

1. In a 6-qt. slow cooker, combine juice and nectar. Place cinnamon sticks, allspice and cloves on a double thickness of cheesecloth; bring up corners of cloth and tie with string to form a bag. Place bag in slow cooker.

2. Cover and cook on low for 3-4 hours or until heated through. Discard the spice bag. Serve warm.

FAST FIX

QUINOA GRANOLA

This is a healthy and tasty snack that I feed to my kids often. They love it!

—**CINDY REAMS** PHILIPSBURG, PA

PREP: 5 MIN. • **COOK:** 1 HOUR + COOLING
MAKES: 6 CUPS

- **¼ cup honey**
- **2 tablespoons coconut or canola oil**
- **1 teaspoon ground cinnamon**
- **3 cups old-fashioned oats**
- **1 cup uncooked quinoa**
- **1 cup sweetened shredded coconut**
- **1 cup chopped mixed dried fruit**
- **1 cup chopped pecans**

1. In a 3- or 4-qt. slow cooker, combine honey, oil and cinnamon. Gradually stir in oats and quinoa until well blended. Cook, covered, on high for 1 to 1½ hours, stirring well every 20 minutes.

2. Stir in coconut, dried fruit and pecans. Spread evenly on waxed paper or baking sheets; cool completely. Store in airtight containers.

QUINOA GRANOLA

HEALTHY GREEK BEAN DIP

HEALTHY GREEK BEAN DIP

This crowd-pleasing dip is a fresh alternative to hummus—and healthy to boot! Folks will love to eat their veggies when they have this zesty, distinctive dip served alongside.

—**KELLY SILVERS** EDMOND, OK

PREP: 15 MIN. • **COOK:** 2 HOURS
MAKES: 3 CUPS

- **2 cans (15 ounces each) cannellini beans, rinsed and drained**
- **¼ cup water**
- **¼ cup finely chopped roasted sweet red peppers**
- **2 tablespoons finely chopped red onion**
- **2 tablespoons olive oil**
- **2 tablespoons lemon juice**
- **1 tablespoon snipped fresh dill**
- **2 garlic cloves, minced**
- **¼ teaspoon salt**
- **¼ teaspoon pepper**
- **1 small cucumber, peeled, seeded and finely chopped**
- **½ cup fat-free plain Greek yogurt**
- **Additional snipped fresh dill**
- **Baked pita chips or assorted fresh vegetables**

Process beans and water in a food processor until smooth. Transfer to a greased 1½-qt. slow cooker. Add the next eight ingredients. Cook, covered, on low until heated through, 2-3 hours. Stir in cucumber and yogurt; cool slightly. Sprinkle with additional dill. Serve warm or cold with chips or assorted fresh vegetables.

To freeze: Omitting cucumber, yogurt and additional dill, freeze the cooled dip in freezer containers. To use, thaw in refrigerator overnight. Serve dip cold or, to serve warm, heat through in a saucepan, stirring occasionally. Stir cucumber and yogurt into finished dip; sprinkle with additional dill. Serve with chips or vegetables.

FAST FIX

HOT CRANBERRY PUNCH

I serve this rosy spiced beverage at parties and family gatherings during the winter. Friends like the tangy twist it gets from the Red Hots. It's a nice change from the usual hot chocolate.

—**LAURA BURGESS** BALLWIN, MO

PREP: 10 MIN. • **COOK:** 2 HOURS
MAKES: 3½ QUARTS

- **8 cups hot water**
- **1½ cups sugar**
- **4 cups cranberry juice**
- **¾ cup orange juice**
- **¼ cup lemon juice**
- **12 whole cloves, optional**
- **½ cup Red Hot candies**

In a 5-qt. slow cooker, combine water, sugar and juices; stir until the sugar is dissolved. If desired, place cloves in a double thickness of cheesecloth; bring up the corners of the cloth and tie with string to form a bag. Add the spice bag and Red Hots to the slow cooker. Cover and cook on low for 2-3 hours or until heated through. Before serving, discard the spice bag and stir the punch.

CHILI BEEF DIP

No last-minute party prep needed! Just put this creamy dip together a couple hours before your shindig, and let your slow cooker do the work.

—**PAT HABIGER** SPEARVILLE, KS

PREP: 25 MIN. • **COOK:** 2 HOURS
MAKES: 8 CUPS

- 2 pounds lean ground beef (90% lean)
- 1 large onion, chopped
- 1 jalapeno pepper, seeded and chopped
- 2 packages (8 ounces each) cream cheese, cubed
- 2 cans (8 ounces each) tomato sauce
- 1 can (4 ounces) chopped green chilies
- ½ cup grated Parmesan cheese
- ½ cup ketchup
- 2 garlic cloves, minced
- 1½ teaspoons chili powder
- 1 teaspoon dried oregano
- Tortilla chips

1. In a large skillet, brown beef, onion and jalapeno until the meat is no longer pink; drain. Transfer to a 3- or 4-qt. slow cooker. Stir in cream cheese, tomato sauce, chilies, Parmesan cheese, ketchup, garlic, chili powder and oregano.
2. Cover and cook on low for 2-3 hours or until heated through. Stir; serve with chips.
Note: Wear disposable gloves when cutting hot peppers; the oils can burn exposed skin. Avoid touching your face.

TEST KITCHEN TIP

To chop an onion, peel it and cut it in half from the root to the top. Place a half flat-side down and cut vertically through the onion, leaving the root end uncut. Then cut across the onion; discard the root end. Repeat to chop the second onion half.

CARIBBEAN CHIPOTLE PORK SLIDERS

One of our favorite pulled pork recipes combines the heat of chipotle peppers with cool tropical coleslaw. The robust flavors make these sliders a big hit with guests.

—**KADIJA BRIDGEWATER** BOCA RATON, FL

PREP: 35 MIN. • **COOK:** 8 HOURS
MAKES: 20 SERVINGS

- 1 large onion, quartered
- 1 boneless pork shoulder butt roast (3 to 4 pounds)
- 2 finely chopped chipotle peppers in adobo sauce plus 3 tablespoons sauce
- ¾ cup honey barbecue sauce
- ¼ cup water
- 4 garlic cloves, minced
- 1 tablespoon ground cumin
- 1 teaspoon salt
- ¼ teaspoon pepper

COLESLAW

- 2 cups finely chopped red cabbage
- 1 medium mango, peeled and chopped
- 1 cup pineapple tidbits, drained
- ¾ cup chopped fresh cilantro
- 1 tablespoon lime juice
- ¼ teaspoon salt
- ⅛ teaspoon pepper
- 20 Hawaiian sweet rolls, split and toasted

1. Place onion in a 5-qt. slow cooker. Cut roast in half; place over onion. In a small bowl, combine chipotle peppers, adobo sauce, barbecue sauce, water, garlic, cumin, salt and pepper; pour over roast. Cook, covered, on low for 8-10 hours or until the roast is tender.
2. Remove roast; cool slightly. Skim fat from the cooking juices. Shred pork with two forks. Return meat to slow cooker; heat through.
3. For coleslaw, in a large bowl, combine cabbage, mango, pineapple, cilantro, lime juice, salt and pepper. Place ¼ cup of the pork mixture on each roll bottom; top with 2 tablespoons of the coleslaw. Replace tops.

SNACKS & BEVERAGES

HAM & CHEDDAR BREAKFAST CASSEROLE, PAGE 39

BREAKFAST & BRUNCH

A slow cooker in your kitchen means that you can have breakfast waiting for you when you wake up. With a little planning, you can put one of these dishes on the table without losing out on precious sleep!

SLOW-COOKED BREAKFAST APPLE COBBLER

SLOW-COOKED BREAKFAST APPLE COBBLER

This is a great recipe to serve on Christmas morning or any other cold morning. You can peel the apples, or leave the peel on, as you prefer.

—**MARIETTA SLATER** JUSTIN, TX

PREP: 15 MIN. • **COOK:** 6 HOURS
MAKES: 6 SERVINGS

- **6 medium apples, cut into ½-inch wedges**
- **1 tablespoon butter**
- **3 tablespoons honey**
- **½ teaspoon ground cinnamon**
- **¼ cup dried cranberries**
- **2 cups granola without raisins**
- **Milk and maple syrup, optional**

1. Place apples in a greased 3-qt. slow cooker. In a microwave, melt butter; stir in honey and cinnamon. Drizzle over the apples. Sprinkle cranberries and granola over top.
2. Cook, covered, on low until the apples are tender, 6-8 hours. If desired, serve with milk and syrup.

FAST FIX

CHEESY HASH BROWN POTATOES

I adapted this recipe for my slow cooker so I could take these cheesy potatoes to a potluck. They're delicious, and so easy to assemble!

—**BECKY WESEMAN** BECKER, MN

PREP: 5 MIN. • **COOK:** 4 HOURS
MAKES: 8 SERVINGS

- **2 cans (10¾ ounces each) condensed cheddar cheese soup, undiluted**
- **1⅓ cups buttermilk**
- **2 tablespoons butter, melted**
- **½ teaspoon seasoned salt**
- **¼ teaspoon garlic powder**
- **¼ teaspoon pepper**
- **1 package (32 ounces) frozen cubed hash brown potatoes**
- **¼ cup grated Parmesan cheese**
- **1 teaspoon paprika**

In a 3-qt. slow cooker, combine the first six ingredients; stir in hash browns. Sprinkle with cheese and paprika. Cook, covered, on low 4 to 4½ hours or until potatoes are tender.

OLD-FASHIONED PEACH BUTTER

Who says peaches are just for summer? Cinnamon and ground cloves give this toast and biscuit topper a wintery, cozy flavor, perfect for the holidays.

—**MARILOU ROBINSON** PORTLAND, OR

PREP: 25 MIN. • **COOK:** 9 HOURS + COOLING
MAKES: 9 CUPS

- **14 cups coarsely chopped peeled fresh or frozen peaches (about 5½ pounds)**
- **2½ cups sugar**
- **4½ teaspoons lemon juice**
- **1½ teaspoons ground cinnamon**
- **¾ teaspoon ground cloves**
- **½ cup quick-cooking tapioca**

1. In a large bowl, combine the peaches, sugar, lemon juice, cinnamon and cloves. Transfer to a 5-qt. slow cooker. Cover and cook on low for 8-10 hours or until the peaches are very soft, stirring occasionally.
2. Stir in tapioca. Cook, uncovered, on high for 1 hour or until thickened. Pour into jars or freezer containers; cool to room temperature. Cover and refrigerate up to 3 weeks or freeze up to 1 year.
To use frozen peach butter: Thaw in the refrigerator for 1-2 days; use within 3 weeks.

SLOW-COOKED BIG BREAKFAST

We make this during holidays or on mornings when we know we're going to have a busy day. Set this to cook overnight on low for an early breakfast, or for three hours on high for a leisurely brunch.

—**DELISHA PARIS** ELIZABETH CITY, NC

PREP: 30 MIN. • **COOK:** 3 HOURS
MAKES: 12 SERVINGS

- **1 pound bulk pork sausage**
- **2 pounds potatoes (about 4 medium), peeled and cut into ½-in. cubes**
- **¼ cup water**
- **1 large onion, finely chopped**
- **1 medium sweet red pepper, chopped**
- **2 cups fresh spinach**
- **1 cup chopped fresh mushrooms**
- **1 pound cubed deli ham**
- **1 cup shredded cheddar cheese**
- **12 large eggs**
- **½ cup 2% milk**
- **1 teaspoon garlic powder**
- **1 teaspoon pepper**
- **½ teaspoon salt**

1. In a large skillet over medium heat, cook and crumble the sausage until no longer pink, 5-7 minutes; drain.

2. Place potatoes and water in a large microwave-safe dish. Microwave, covered, on high until the potatoes are tender, 6 minutes, stirring halfway through the cooking time. Drain and add to the sausage.

3. Stir in the onion, sweet red pepper, spinach, mushrooms, ham and cheese. Transfer to a greased 6-qt. slow cooker.

4. Whisk together the remaining ingredients until blended; pour over the sausage mixture. Cook, covered, on low until the eggs are set, 3-4 hours. Let stand, uncovered, 10 minutes before serving.

FAST FIX

OVERNIGHT CHERRY-ALMOND OATMEAL

Would you like breakfast ready for you when the sun comes up? Just place the ingredients in the slow cooker and turn it on before you go to bed. In the morning, enjoy a healthy, warm and satisfying dish.

—**GERALDINE SAUCIER** ALBUQUERQUE, NM

PREP: 10 MIN. • **COOK:** 7 HOURS
MAKES: 6 SERVINGS

- **4 cups vanilla almond milk**
- **1 cup steel-cut oats**
- **1 cup dried cherries**
- **⅓ cup packed brown sugar**
- **½ teaspoon salt**
- **½ teaspoon ground cinnamon**
- **Additional almond milk, optional**

1. In a 3-qt. slow cooker coated with cooking spray, combine all ingredients. Cook, covered, on low until oats are tender, 7-8 hours.

2. Stir before serving. If desired, serve with additional milk.

Note: Steel-cut oats are also known as Scotch oats or Irish oatmeal. Nutritionally, steel cut oats are about the same as rolled oats. Skip instant oatmeal mixes, which have added sugar.

FAST FIX

SLOW COOKER HONEY GRANOLA

This granola is so simple to put together, and it's a great breakfast for busy mornings. Change up the fruit to fit your preferences or the seasons.

—**ARISA CUPP** WARREN, OR

PREP: 10 MIN. • **COOK:** 2 HOURS + COOLING
MAKES: ABOUT 8 CUPS

- **4 cups old-fashioned oats**
- **1 cup sunflower kernels**
- **1 cup sweetened shredded coconut**
- **½ teaspoon salt**
- **½ cup canola oil**
- **½ cup honey**
- **1 cup chopped dried pineapple**
- **1 cup chopped dried mangoes**

1. In a 3-qt. slow cooker, combine oats, sunflower kernels, coconut and salt. Whisk oil and honey until blended. Stir into oat mixture. Cook, covered, on high for 2 hours, stirring well every 20 minutes.
2. Remove granola to baking sheets, spreading evenly; cool completely. Stir in pineapple and mangoes. Store in airtight containers.

Rustic Granola Omit sunflower kernels, coconut, salt. Add 12 ounces toasted wheat germ; cook as directed. After cooking, stir in 2 cups bran flakes. Omit fruit.

Cinnamon Granola Substitute walnuts for the sunflower kernels. Add 1½ teaspoons cinnamon to oil mixture. Cook as directed. Substitute 1 cup raisins for the pineapple and mangoes.

SLOW COOKER SAUSAGE & WAFFLE BAKE

Here's an easy dish guaranteed to create excitement at the breakfast table. Nothing is missing from this sweet and savory combination.

—**COURTNEY LENTZ** BOSTON, MA

PREP: 20 MIN. • **COOK:** 5 HOURS.
MAKES: 12 SERVINGS

- **2 pounds bulk spicy breakfast pork sausage**
- **1 tablespoon rubbed sage**

- **½ teaspoon fennel seed**
- **1 package (12.3 ounces) frozen waffles, cut into bite-size pieces**
- **8 large eggs**
- **1¼ cups half-and-half cream**
- **¼ cup maple syrup**
- **¼ teaspoon salt**
- **¼ teaspoon pepper**
- **2 cups shredded cheddar cheese**
- **Additional maple syrup**

1. Fold two 18-in.-long pieces of foil into 18x4-in. strips. Line the perimeter of a 5-qt. slow cooker with the foil strips; spray with cooking spray.
2. In a large skillet, cook and crumble sausage over medium heat until no longer pink; drain. Add sage and fennel.
3. Place the waffles in the slow cooker; top with sausage. In a bowl, mix eggs, cream, syrup and seasonings. Pour over the sausage and waffles. Top with cheese. Cook, covered, on low until set, 5-6 hours. Remove insert and let stand, uncovered, for 15 minutes. Serve with additional maple syrup.

MOCHA MINT COFFEE
Mindie Hilton
Susanville, CA

FAST FIX

MOCHA MINT COFFEE

This doctored-up coffee offers delightful hints of mint, cocoa and cinnamon. The marshmallows on top are a playful addition that brings out the youngster in anyone.

—**MINDIE HILTON** SUSANVILLE, CA

PREP: 10 MIN. • **COOK:** 2 HOURS
MAKES: 8 SERVINGS

- **6 cups hot brewed coffee**
- **2 packets instant hot cocoa mix**
- **½ cup dulce de leche**
- **¼ cup peppermint crunch baking chips or mint chocolate chips**
- **4 teaspoons sugar**
- **1 cup miniature marshmallows**
- **½ teaspoon ground cinnamon**
- **chocolate syrup, optional**

1. In a 3-qt. slow cooker, combine the first five ingredients. Cook, covered, on low until hot, 2-3 hours.

2. Ladle into mugs. Top with marshmallows; sprinkle with cinnamon. Drizzle with chocolate syrup if desired.

Note: This recipe was tested with Nestle La Lechera dulce de leche; look for it in the international foods section. If using Eagle Brand dulce de leche (caramel flavored sauce), thicken according to the package directions before using.

SLOW COOKER CINNAMON ROLL

Wake up to the heavenly aroma of fresh-baked cinnamon rolls! This better-for-you version tastes just as decadent as a regular cinnamon roll, but it smartly sneaks in some whole grains.

—**NICK IVERSON** MILWAUKEE, WI

PREP: 15 MIN. + RISING • **COOK:** 4 HOURS
MAKES: 12 SERVINGS

- **1 package (¼ ounce) active dry yeast**
- **¾ cup warm water (110° to 115°)**
- **½ cup quick-cooking oats**
- **½ cup whole wheat flour**
- **¼ cup packed brown sugar**
- **2 tablespoons butter, melted**
- **1 large egg**
- **1 teaspoon salt**
- **1¾ to 2¼ cups all-purpose flour**

FILLING

- **3 tablespoons butter, softened**
- **⅓ cup granulated sugar**
- **2 teaspoons ground cinnamon**

ICING

- **1 cup confectioners' sugar**
- **2 tablespoons half-and-half cream**
- **4 teaspoons butter, softened**

1. Dissolve yeast in warm water. Add next six ingredients plus 1 cup all-purpose flour. Beat on medium speed until smooth. Stir in enough remaining flour to form a soft dough (dough will be sticky).

2. Turn onto a lightly floured surface; knead until smooth and elastic, about 6-8 minutes. Roll into an 18x12-in. rectangle. For filling, spread dough with butter, then combine sugar and cinnamon; sprinkle over dough to within ½ in. of edges.

3. Roll up dough jelly-roll style, starting with a long side; pinch seam to seal. Cut crosswise in half to form two rolls. Lay rolls side by side; pinch the top ends together to seal. Using a sharp knife, cut each roll lengthwise in half, forming four strips; loosely twist the strips around each other. Pinch the bottom ends together to seal. Shape into a coil; place coil on parchment paper. Transfer to a 6-qt. slow cooker. Let rise until doubled, about 1 hour.

4. Cook, covered, on low until the bread is lightly browned, 4-5 hours. Remove from slow cooker and cool slightly. Beat icing ingredients until smooth. Spread over warm roll.

TEST KITCHEN TIP

To easily test if rising yeast dough has doubled in size, quickly press two fingers into the dough. If the indentation remains, the dough is ready.

SOUTHWESTERN BREAKFAST SLOW COOKER CASSEROLE

This recipe has become a favorite in our family for chilly mornings. Using extra-sharp cheddar cheese instead of mild adds an extra boost of flavor.
—**LISA RENSHAW** KANSAS CITY, MO

PREP: 20 MIN. • **COOK:** 2½ HOURS + STANDING
MAKES: 8 SERVINGS

4 large eggs
8 large egg whites
1⅓ cups fat-free milk
3 teaspoons chili powder
½ teaspoon ground cumin
½ teaspoon pepper
½ teaspoon cayenne pepper
1 can (15 ounces) black beans, rinsed and drained
1 can (7 ounces) Mexicorn, drained
1 cup cubed fully cooked ham
1 cup shredded extra-sharp cheddar cheese
1 can (4 ounces) chopped green chilies, drained
6 slices whole wheat bread, lightly toasted and cubed
Pico de gallo, optional

1. In a large bowl, whisk together the first seven ingredients. Stir in beans, corn, ham, cheese and chilies. Stir in bread to moisten. Transfer to a 5-qt. slow cooker coated with cooking spray.
2. Cook, covered, on low until a knife inserted in the center comes out clean, 2½-3½ hours. Let stand, uncovered, for 10 minutes before serving. If desired, serve with pico de gallo.

APPLE-PEAR COMPOTE

Apples and pears are almost always popular, so this warm, comforting dessert recipe is great for potlucks or other get-togethers. I also like to add raisins or chopped nuts to the compote; for a more adult flavor I add ⅓ cup brandy or rum.
—**NANCY HEISHMAN** LAS VEGAS, NV

PREP: 20 MIN. • **COOK:** 3¼ HOURS
MAKES: 8 CUPS

5 medium apples, peeled and chopped
3 medium pears, chopped
1 medium orange, thinly sliced
½ cup dried cranberries
½ cup packed brown sugar
½ cup maple syrup
⅓ cup butter, cubed
2 tablespoons lemon juice
2 teaspoons ground cinnamon
1 teaspoon ground ginger
5 tablespoons orange juice, divided
4 teaspoons cornstarch
Sweetened whipped cream and toasted chopped pecans, optional

1. In a 4- or 5-qt. slow cooker, combine the first 10 ingredients. Stir in 2 tablespoons orange juice. Cook, covered, on low 3-4 hours or until the fruit is tender.
2. In a small bowl, mix the cornstarch and the remaining orange juice until smooth; gradually stir into the fruit mixture. Cook, covered, on high for 15-20 minutes longer or until sauce is thickened. If desired, top with whipped cream and pecans.
To freeze: Freeze the cooled compote in individual freezer containers. To use, partially thaw in the refrigerator overnight. Heat through in a saucepan, stirring occasionally, adding a little bit of orange juice if necessary.

HAM & CHEDDAR BREAKFAST CASSEROLE

This easy, cheesy casserole has made appearances at holiday breakfasts, potlucks and even my daughter's college apartment to feed her hungry roommates. It's my go-to recipe for action-packed mornings.
—**PATTY BERNHARD** GREENVILLE, OH

PREP: 20 MIN. + CHILLING
COOK: 4 HOURS + STANDING
MAKES: 12 SERVINGS

- **12 large eggs**
- **1 cup 2% milk**
- **1 teaspoon salt**
- **½ teaspoon pepper**
- **1 package (30 ounces) frozen shredded hash brown potatoes, thawed**
- **2 cups cubed fully cooked ham (about 1 pound)**
- **1 medium onion, chopped**
- **4 cups shredded cheddar cheese**

1. Whisk together the first four ingredients. Place a third of the potatoes in a greased 5- or 6-qt. slow cooker; layer with a third of each of the following: ham, onion and cheese. Repeat layers twice. Pour the egg mixture over top. Refrigerate, covered, overnight.

2. Cook, covered, on low until set and the edges begin to brown, 4-5 hours. Turn off slow cooker. Remove insert; let stand, uncovered, 30 minutes before serving.

Note: Avoid temperature shock; either let the insert come to room temperature before cooking, or start with an unheated base.

DENVER OMELET FRITTATA
Connie Eaton
Pittsburgh, PA

DENVER OMELET FRITTATA

Here's the perfect brunch dish to serve company after church or another early outing. Pepper, onion and ham go into this classic breakfast preparation, made simple thanks to the slow cooker.

—**CONNIE EATON** PITTSBURGH, PA

PREP: 25 MIN. • **COOK:** 3 HOURS
MAKES: 6 SERVINGS

- **1 cup water**
- **1 tablespoon olive oil**
- **1 medium Yukon Gold potato, peeled and sliced**
- **1 small onion, thinly sliced**
- **12 large eggs**
- **1 teaspoon hot pepper sauce**
- **½ teaspoon salt**
- **¼ teaspoon pepper**
- **½ pound deli ham, chopped**
- **½ cup chopped sweet green pepper**
- **1 cup shredded cheddar cheese, divided**

1. Layer two 24-in. pieces of aluminum foil; starting with a long side, fold foil to create a 1-in.-wide strip. Shape strip into a coil to make a rack for the bottom of a 6-qt. oval slow cooker. Add water to the slow cooker; set foil rack in water.

2. Heat oil in a large skillet over medium-high heat. Add potato and onion; cook and stir 4-6 minutes or until potato is lightly browned. Transfer to a greased 1½-qt. baking dish (dish must fit in slow cooker).

3. In a large bowl, whisk eggs, pepper sauce, salt and pepper; stir in ham, green pepper and ½ cup cheese. Pour over potato mixture. Top with the remaining cheese. Place dish on foil rack.

4. Cook, covered, on low for 3-4 hours or until the eggs are set and a knife inserted in the center comes out clean.

HEARTY SLOW COOKER BREAKFAST HASH

At the end of summer, it seems like everything in our garden needs to be harvested at the same time. Instead of serving plain ol' steamed vegetables once again, I make them breakfast hash. Serve alongside fresh fruit.

—**COLLEEN DELAWDER** HERNDON, VA

PREP: 25 MIN. • **COOK:** 5 HOURS
MAKES: 4 SERVINGS

- **8 to 10 frozen fully cooked breakfast sausage links**
- **4 cups diced red potatoes (about 1½ pounds)**
- **4 medium carrots, diced**
- **2 green onions, thinly sliced (white and pale green parts only)**
- **2 tablespoons extra virgin olive oil**
- **1 tablespoon red wine vinegar**
- **1¼ teaspoons dill weed, divided**
- **1 teaspoon kosher salt**
- **½ teaspoon coarsely ground pepper, divided**
- **¼ teaspoon crushed red pepper flakes**
- **2 tablespoons crumbled feta cheese**
- **1 tablespoon butter**
- **4 large eggs**
- **2 tablespoons maple syrup**

1. In a large skillet over medium heat, cook the sausage links, turning occasionally, until heated through, 8-9 minutes. Combine the next five ingredients in a 3-qt. slow cooker. Add 1 teaspoon dill, kosher salt, ¼ teaspoon pepper and red pepper flakes. Arrange the sausages on top of the vegetable mixture. Cook, covered, on low until the vegetables are tender, 5-6 hours. Transfer the vegetables to a serving platter; sprinkle with feta cheese. Arrange the sausage links in a ring around the vegetables.

2. In a large skillet, heat butter over medium heat. Break eggs, one at a time, into a small bowl; slip into skillet. Reduce heat; cook until whites are set and yolks have begun to thicken. Flip eggs; cook to desired doneness, 1-2 minutes for over medium. Arrange the eggs over the vegetables. Sprinkle with the remaining dill and pepper; drizzle with maple syrup.

SLOW COOKER BREAKFAST CASSEROLE

Here's a breakfast casserole that is very easy on the cook. I can make it the night before and it's ready in the morning. It's the perfect recipe when I have weekend guests.

—**ELLIE STUTHEIT** LAS VEGAS, NV

PREP: 25 MIN. • **COOK:** 7 HOURS
MAKES: 12 SERVINGS

- **1 package (30 ounces) frozen shredded hash brown potatoes**
- **1 pound bulk pork sausage, cooked and drained**
- **1 medium onion, chopped**
- **1 can (4 ounces) chopped green chilies**
- **1½ cups shredded cheddar cheese**
- **12 large eggs**
- **1 cup 2% milk**
- **½ teaspoon salt**
- **½ teaspoon pepper**

In a greased 5- or 6-qt. slow cooker, layer half of the potatoes, sausage, onion, chilies and cheese. Repeat layers. In a large bowl, whisk the eggs, milk, salt and pepper; pour over top. Cover and cook on low for 7-9 hours or until eggs are set.

TROPICAL FRUIT COMPOTE

Have the taste of summer throughout the year! To make a more adult version of this recipe, use brandy instead of the extra tropical fruit juice.

—**TASTE OF HOME** TEST KITCHEN

PREP: 15 MIN. • **COOK:** 2¼ HOURS
MAKES: 6 SERVINGS

- **1 jar (23½ ounces) mixed tropical fruit**
- **1 jalapeno pepper, seeded and chopped**
- **¼ cup sugar**
- **1 tablespoon chopped crystallized ginger**
- **¼ teaspoon ground cinnamon**
- **1 can (15 ounces) mandarin oranges, drained**
- **1 jar (6 ounces) maraschino cherries, drained**
- **1 medium firm banana, sliced**
- **6 scones or individual round sponge cakes**
- **6 tablespoons sweetened shredded coconut, toasted**

1. Drain tropical fruit, reserving ¼ cup liquid. Combine tropical fruit and jalapeno in a 1½-qt. slow cooker. Combine sugar, ginger, cinnamon and the reserved juice; pour over the fruit. Cover and cook on low for 2 hours. Stir in mandarin oranges, cherries and banana; cook 15 minutes longer.

2. Place scones or cakes on individual plates; top with compote. Sprinkle with coconut.

Note: Wear disposable gloves when cutting hot peppers; the oils can burn exposed skin. Avoid touching your face.

TEST KITCHEN TIP

Candied or crystallized ginger is the root of the ginger plant that has been cooked in a sugar syrup. It's used primarily in dips, sauces and fruit desserts. Larger grocery stores will carry candied ginger in the spice section.

POT ROAST HASH

I love to cook a Sunday-style pot roast for my special hash—it makes a great weekend brunch or a breakfast-for-dinner any night of the week.

—**GINA JACKSON** OGDENSBURG, NY

PREP: 30 MIN. • **COOK:** 6¼ HOURS
MAKES: 10 SERVINGS

- **1 cup warm water**
- **1 tablespoon beef base**
- **½ pound sliced fresh mushrooms**
- **1 large onion, coarsely chopped**
- **3 garlic cloves, minced**
- **1 boneless beef chuck roast (3 pounds)**
- **½ teaspoon pepper**
- **1 tablespoon Worcestershire sauce**
- **1 package (28 ounces) frozen O'Brien potatoes**

EGGS

- **2 tablespoons butter**
- **10 large eggs**
- **½ teaspoon salt**
- **½ teaspoon pepper**
- **Minced chives**

1. In a 5- or 6-qt. slow cooker, whisk water and beef base; add mushrooms, onion and garlic. Sprinkle roast with pepper; transfer to slow cooker. Drizzle with Worcestershire sauce. Cook, covered, on low for 6-8 hours or until the meat is tender.

2. Remove roast; cool slightly. Shred meat with two forks. In a large skillet, cook potatoes according to package directions; stir in shredded beef. Using a slotted spoon, add vegetables from slow cooker to skillet; heat through. Discard the cooking juices.

3. For eggs, in another skillet, heat 1 tablespoon butter over medium-high heat. Break five eggs, one at a time, into the skillet. Sprinkle with half the salt and pepper. Reduce heat to low. Cook until desired doneness, turning after whites are set. Repeat with the remaining butter, eggs, salt and pepper. Serve eggs over hash; sprinkle with chives.

To freeze: Place shredded pot roast and vegetables in a freezer container; top with cooking juices. Cool and freeze. To use, partially thaw in refrigerator overnight. Heat through in a covered saucepan.

Note: Look for beef base near the broth and bouillon.

SLOW COOKER GOETTA

My husband's German grandfather introduced goetta to me when we first got married. I found a slow cooker recipe and changed some of the ingredients to make this the best goetta around. It makes a lot of sausage, but it freezes well.

—**SHARON GEERS** WILMINGTON, OH

PREP: 45 MIN. • **COOK:** 4 HOURS
MAKES: 2 LOAVES (16 SLICES EACH)

- **6 cups water**
- **2½ cups steel-cut oats**
- **6 bay leaves**
- **3 tablespoons beef bouillon granules**
- **¾ teaspoon salt**
- **1 teaspoon each garlic powder, rubbed sage and pepper**
- **½ teaspoon ground allspice**
- **½ teaspoon crushed red pepper flakes**
- **2 pounds bulk pork sausage**
- **2 medium onions, chopped**

1. In a 5-qt. slow cooker, combine water, oats and all the seasonings. Cook, covered, on high for 2 hours. Remove the bay leaves.
2. In a large skillet, cook sausage and onions over medium heat 8-10 minutes or until no longer pink, breaking up sausage into crumbles. Drain, reserving 2 tablespoons drippings. Stir the sausage mixture and the reserved drippings into the oats. Cook, covered, on low for 2 hours.
3. Line two 9x5-in. loaf pans with plastic wrap. Transfer mixture to pans. Refrigerate, covered, overnight.
4. To serve, slice each loaf into 16 slices. In a large skillet, cook goetta, in batches, over medium heat for 3-4 minutes on each side or until lightly browned and heated through.
To freeze: After shaping goetta in loaf pans, cool and freeze, covered, until firm. Transfer goetta to resealable plastic freezer bags or wrap securely in foil; return to freezer. To use, partially thaw in refrigerator overnight; slice and cook as directed.

CINNAMON BLUEBERRY FRENCH TOAST

I like to prep this breakfast in the afternoon, let it chill, then put into the slow cooker before I go to bed. When we wake up in the morning, it's done just right.

—**ANGELA LIVELY** CONROE, TX

PREP: 15 MIN. • **COOK:** 3 HOURS
MAKES: 6 SERVINGS

- **3 large eggs**
- **2 cups 2% milk**
- **¼ cup sugar**
- **1 teaspoon ground cinnamon**
- **1 teaspoon vanilla extract**
- **¼ teaspoon salt**
- **9 cups cubed French bread (about 9 ounces)**
- **1 cup fresh or frozen blueberries, thawed**
- **Maple syrup**

1. Whisk together first six ingredients. Layer half the bread in a greased 5-qt. slow cooker; top with ½ cup blueberries and half the milk mixture. Repeat layers. Refrigerate, covered, 4 hours or overnight.
2. Cook, covered, on low until a knife inserted near the center comes out clean, 3-4 hours. Serve warm with maple syrup.
Note: To increase fiber, swap whole wheat bread for the white French bread.

★★★★★ **READER REVIEW**

"This was a great change from our normal breakfast routine. Definitely what I need for busy mornings!"

ANGEL182009 TASTEOFHOME.COM

CINNAMON BLUEBERRY FRENCH TOAST

GINGER CHICKEN NOODLE SOUP, **PAGE 79**

SOUPS, STEWS & CHILI

Talk about the definition of comfort food! A satisfying, simmering soup is the perfect welcome after a long day. After all, these dishes are hot, hearty and always heartwarming.

MANCHESTER STEW

While in college, I studied abroad at the University of Manchester. I was a vegetarian and was pleasantly surprised at how delicious and diverse vegetarian food in Britain could be. My favorite meal, served at my favorite restaurant, was Beans Burgundy. After returning to the States, I created this version. As it simmers in the slow cooker, the enticing aroma that fills the kitchen reminds me of my time in England!

—**KIMBERLY HAMMOND** KINGWOOD, TX

PREP: 25 MIN. • **COOK:** 8 HOURS • **MAKES:** 6 SERVINGS

2 tablespoons olive oil
2 medium onions, chopped
2 garlic cloves, minced
1 teaspoon dried oregano
1 cup dry red wine
1 pound small red potatoes, quartered
1 can (16 ounces) kidney beans, rinsed and drained
½ pound sliced fresh mushrooms
2 medium leeks (white portion only), sliced
1 cup fresh baby carrots
2½ cups water
1 can (14½ ounces) no-salt-added diced tomatoes
1 teaspoon dried thyme
½ teaspoon salt
¼ teaspoon pepper
Fresh basil leaves

1. In a large skillet, heat oil over medium-high heat. Add onions; cook and stir until tender, 2-3 minutes. Add garlic and oregano; cook and stir for 1 minute longer. Stir in wine. Bring to a boil; cook until liquid is reduced by half, 3-4 minutes.
2. Transfer to a 5- or 6-qt. slow cooker. Add potatoes, beans, mushrooms, leeks and carrots. Stir in water, tomatoes, thyme, salt and pepper. Cook, covered, on low until the potatoes are tender, 8-10 hours. Top with basil.

SHRIMP CHOWDER

I simmer my rich and creamy shrimp soup in the slow cooker. Because the chowder is ready in less than four hours, I can prepare it in the afternoon and serve it to dinner guests that night.

—**WILL ZUNIO** GRETNA, LA

PREP: 15 MIN. • **COOK:** 3½ HOURS
MAKES: 12 SERVINGS (3 QUARTS)

½ cup chopped onion
2 teaspoons butter
2 cans (12 ounces each) evaporated milk
2 cans (10¾ ounces each) condensed cream of potato soup, undiluted
2 cans (10¾ ounces each) condensed cream of chicken soup, undiluted
1 can (7 ounces) white or shoepeg corn, drained
1 teaspoon Creole seasoning
½ teaspoon garlic powder
2 pounds peeled and deveined cooked small shrimp
3 ounces cream cheese, cubed

1. In a small skillet, saute the onion in butter until tender. In a 5-qt. slow cooker, combine the onion, milk, soups, corn, Creole seasoning and garlic powder.
2. Cover and cook on low for 3 hours. Stir in shrimp and cream cheese. Cook for 30 minutes longer or until the shrimp are heated through and the cheese is melted. Stir to blend.
Note: The following spice blend may be substituted for 1 teaspoon Creole seasoning: ¼ teaspoon each salt, garlic powder and paprika; and a pinch each of dried thyme, ground cumin and cayenne pepper.

SHRIMP CHOWDER

AUTUMN SLOW-COOKED BEEF STEW

AUTUMN SLOW-COOKED BEEF STEW

If any dish could taste like a special occasion, it's this one with beef, pears, walnuts and sweet dried apricots. I usually serve a leafy salad and rolls alongside to complete the masterpiece.

—**AMY DODSON** DURANGO, CO

PREP: 35 MIN. • **COOK:** 6 HOURS
MAKES: 8 SERVINGS

- 2 pounds boneless beef chuck roast, cubed
- ½ teaspoon garlic salt
- ½ teaspoon pepper
- 2 tablespoons olive oil
- 2 cups dry red wine (or reduced-sodium beef broth)
- 1 cup reduced-sodium beef broth
- 4 garlic cloves, minced
- 1 teaspoon rubbed sage
- 1 teaspoon dried thyme
- ½ teaspoon salt
- 2½ pounds small red potatoes (about 20)
- 4 medium carrots, cut into 1-inch pieces
- 1 large onion, halved and sliced
- 2 medium pears, quartered
- 1 cup walnut halves
- 1 cup dried apricots
- 2 tablespoons cornstarch
- 3 tablespoons cold water

1. Sprinkle beef with garlic salt and pepper. In a large skillet, heat oil over medium-high heat. Brown beef in batches. Remove with a slotted spoon; transfer to a 6-qt. slow cooker.
2. In a large bowl, combine wine, broth, garlic, sage, thyme and salt; pour over the beef. Top with potatoes, carrots, onion, pears, walnuts and apricots. Cook, covered, on low 6-8 hours or until the meat is tender; skim fat.
3. In a small bowl, mix cornstarch and water until smooth; gradually stir into stew. Cook, covered, on high 20-30 minutes or until the sauce is thickened.

BLACK BEAN, CHORIZO & SWEET POTATO CHILI

Chili is one of my all-time favorite dishes. This recipe takes already great chili to the next level by changing up the flavors and adding a special surprise—sweet potatoes.

—**JULIE MERRIMAN** SEATTLE, WA

PREP: 20 MIN. • **COOK:** 6 HOURS
MAKES: 16 SERVINGS (4 QUARTS)

- 1 pound uncooked chorizo, casings removed, or spicy bulk pork sausage
- 1 large onion, chopped
- 2 poblano peppers, finely chopped
- 2 jalapeno peppers, seeded and finely chopped
- 3 tablespoons tomato paste
- 3 large sweet potatoes, peeled and cut into ½-inch cubes
- 4 cans (14½ ounces each) fire-roasted diced tomatoes, undrained
- 2 cans (15 ounces each) black beans, rinsed and drained
- 2 cups beef stock
- 2 tablespoons chili powder
- 1 tablespoon dried oregano
- 1 tablespoon ground coriander
- 1 tablespoon ground cumin
- 1 tablespoon smoked paprika
- ¼ cup lime juice

1. In a large skillet over medium heat, cook and stir the chorizo, onion, poblanos and jalapenos for 8-10 minutes or until the chorizo is cooked. Using a slotted spoon, transfer to a 6-qt. slow cooker.
2. Stir in tomato paste. Add potatoes, tomatoes, beans, stock and spices; stir to combine. Cover and cook on low for 6-7 hours or until the potatoes are tender. Stir in lime juice.

FAST FIX

BEER BRAT CHILI

My husband and I love this chili—it smells so good as it simmers in the slow cooker all day. I can't think of a better way to use up leftover brats, and he can't think of a better way to eat them!

—**KATRINA KRUMM** APPLE VALLEY, MN

PREP: 10 MIN. • **COOK:** 5 HOURS
MAKES: 8 SERVINGS (2 ½ QUARTS)

- 1 can (15 ounces) cannellini beans, rinsed and drained
- 1 can (15 ounces) pinto beans, rinsed and drained
- 1 can (15 ounces) Southwestern black beans, undrained
- 1 can (14½ ounces) Italian diced tomatoes, undrained
- 1 can (10 ounces) diced tomatoes and green chilies, undrained
- 1 package (14 ounces) fully cooked beer bratwurst links, sliced
- 1½ cups frozen corn
- 1 medium sweet red pepper, chopped
- 1 medium onion, finely chopped
- ¼ cup chili seasoning mix
- 1 garlic clove, minced

Combine all ingredients in a 5-qt. slow cooker. Cook, covered, on low for 5-6 hours.

VEGETARIAN VEGETABLE SOUP

You just have to try this hearty soup for its distinctive blend of flavors and beautiful appearance. I make this soup during the holidays; with all the rich foods being served, it's nice to offer this soup loaded with fiber and vitamins.

—**CHRISTINA TILL** SOUTH HAVEN, MI

PREP: 20 MIN. • **COOK:** 9 HOURS
MAKES: 12 SERVINGS (ABOUT 3 QUARTS)

- ¾ cup chopped onion
- ½ cup chopped celery
- ½ cup chopped green pepper
- 2 tablespoons olive oil
- 1 large potato, peeled and diced
- 1 medium sweet potato, peeled and diced
- 1 to 2 garlic cloves, minced
- 3 cups vegetable broth
- 2 medium fresh tomatoes, chopped
- 1 can (16 ounces) kidney beans, rinsed and drained
- 1 can (15 ounces) garbanzo beans or chickpeas, rinsed and drained
- 2 teaspoons soy sauce
- 1 teaspoon paprika
- ½ teaspoon dried basil
- ¼ teaspoon salt
- ¼ teaspoon ground turmeric
- 1 bay leaf
- Dash cayenne pepper

1. In a large skillet, saute onion, celery and green pepper in oil until crisp-tender. Add potato, sweet potato and garlic; saute for 3-5 minutes longer.
2. Transfer to a 5-qt. slow cooker. Stir in the remaining ingredients. Cover and cook on low for 9-10 hours or until the vegetables are tender. Discard the bay leaf before serving.

BEEF STEW PROVENCAL

BEEF STEW PROVENCAL

When I was young, my favorite food to order in a restaurant was beef stew. When my mother and I decided to create our own, we experimented with ingredients until we came up with this recipe. This stew is now a tradition every time the whole family is together.

—**CHELSEY LARSEN** SPARKS, NV

PREP: 25 MIN. • **COOK:** 6 HOURS
MAKES: 6 SERVINGS

4 medium carrots, chopped
4 celery ribs, chopped
1 cup beef broth
1 jar (7 ounces) julienned oil-packed sun-dried tomatoes, drained
1 can (6 ounces) tomato paste
1 small onion, chopped
⅓ cup honey
¼ cup balsamic vinegar
1 garlic clove, minced
1 teaspoon dried thyme
½ teaspoon onion powder
¼ teaspoon white pepper
1 boneless beef chuck roast (2½ pounds), cut into 2-inch cubes
½ cup all-purpose flour
½ teaspoon salt
½ teaspoon pepper
2 tablespoons olive oil
Hot cooked mashed potatoes or egg noodles

1. In a 4-qt. slow cooker, combine the first 12 ingredients. In a large bowl, combine beef, flour, salt and pepper; toss to coat. In a large skillet, brown the beef in oil in batches. Transfer to slow cooker.
2. Cover and cook on low for 6-8 hours or until beef is tender. Serve with mashed potatoes.

SPICY CHICKEN CHILI
Fred Lockwood
Plano, TX

SPICY CHICKEN CHILI

This easy-to-make chili is loaded with chicken and beans. If the spicy heat is a bit much, tame it a bit with cool sour cream.

—**FRED LOCKWOOD** PLANO, TX

PREP: 25 MIN. • **COOK:** 5 HOURS
MAKES: 10 SERVINGS (3½ QUARTS)

- **4 bone-in chicken breast halves (14 ounces each)**
- **2 medium onions, chopped**
- **2 medium green peppers, chopped**
- **1 cup pickled jalapeno slices**
- **1 can (4 ounces) chopped green chilies**
- **2 jars (16 ounces each) salsa verde**
- **2 cans (15½ ounces each) navy beans, rinsed and drained**
- **1 cup (8 ounces) sour cream**
- **½ cup minced fresh cilantro**
- **Optional toppings: shredded Colby-Monterey Jack cheese, sour cream and crushed tortilla chips**

1. Place chicken, onions, peppers, jalapenos and chilies in a 5- or 6-qt. slow cooker. Pour salsa over top. Cover and cook on low for 5-6 hours or until the chicken is tender.
2. Remove chicken; cool slightly. Shred chicken with two forks, discarding skin and bones; return meat to slow cooker. Stir in beans, sour cream and cilantro; heat through. Serve with toppings of your choice.
To freeze: Before adding sour cream, cilantro and toppings, cool the chili. Freeze in freezer containers. To use, partially thaw in refrigerator overnight. Heat through in a saucepan, stirring occasionally and adding a little water if necessary. Stir in sour cream and cilantro. Serve with toppings if desired.
Note: Wear disposable gloves when cutting hot peppers; the oils can burn exposed skin. Avoid touching your face.

BRAZILIAN PORK & BLACK BEAN STEW

During high school, I spent a year in Brazil and fell in love with the culture and food. One of my favorite dishes was Feijoada, a chili/stew served over white rice. I introduced this recipe to my family and it has become one of our favorite comfort foods.

—**ANDREA ROMANCZYK** MAGNA, UT

PREP: 15 MIN. + SOAKING • **COOK:** 7 HOURS
MAKES: 8 SERVINGS

- **1½ cups dried black beans**
- **1 pound smoked kielbasa or Polish sausage, sliced**
- **1 pound boneless country-style pork ribs**
- **1 package (12 ounces) fully cooked Spanish chorizo links, sliced**
- **1 smoked ham hock**
- **1 large onion, chopped**
- **3 garlic cloves, minced**
- **2 bay leaves**
- **¾ teaspoon salt**
- **½ teaspoon pepper**
- **5 cups water**
- **Hot cooked rice**

1. Rinse and sort beans; soak according to the package directions. Drain and rinse, discarding the soaking liquid.
2. In a 6-qt. slow cooker, combine beans with the next nine ingredients. Add water; cook, covered, on low until the meat and beans are tender, 7-9 hours.
3. Remove pork ribs and ham hock. When cool enough to handle, remove meat from bones; discard the bones and bay leaves. Shred meat with two forks; return to slow cooker. Serve with hot cooked rice.
To freeze: Freeze cooled stew in freezer containers. To use, partially thaw in refrigerator overnight. Heat through in a saucepan, stirring occasionally and adding a little water if necessary.

HEARTY MINESTRONE

I picked up this recipe in California in the '80s and have been making it ever since. I enjoy it partly because it's simple to put together and partly because the flavor is so wonderful!

—**BONNIE HOSMAN** YOUNG, AZ

PREP: 25 MIN. • **COOK:** 6¼ HOURS
MAKES: 7 SERVINGS (ABOUT 2½ QUARTS)

- **2 cans (one 28 ounces, one 14½ ounces) diced tomatoes, undrained**
- **2 cups water**
- **2 medium carrots, sliced**
- **1 medium onion, chopped**
- **1 medium zucchini, chopped**
- **1 package (3½ ounces) sliced pepperoni**
- **2 teaspoons minced garlic**
- **2 teaspoons chicken bouillon granules**
- **½ teaspoon dried basil**
- **½ teaspoon dried oregano**
- **2 cans (16 ounces each) kidney beans, rinsed and drained**
- **1 package (10 ounces) frozen chopped spinach, thawed and squeezed dry**
- **1¼ cups cooked elbow macaroni**
- **Shredded Parmesan cheese**

1. In a 5-qt. slow cooker, combine the first 10 ingredients. Cover and cook on low for 6-8 hours or until the vegetables are tender.
2. Stir in beans, spinach and macaroni. Cover and cook 15 minutes longer or until heated through. Sprinkle with cheese.
To freeze: Cool soup and transfer to freezer containers. Freeze for up to 3 months. To use frozen soup, thaw in the refrigerator overnight. Transfer to a saucepan. Cover and cook over medium heat until heated through. Sprinkle with cheese.

SLOW-COOKED VEGETABLE CURRY

I love the fuss-free nature of the slow cooker, but I don't want to sacrifice flavor for convenience. This cozy, spiced-up dish has both.

—**SUSAN SMITH** MEAD, WA

PREP: 35 MIN. • **COOK:** 5 HOURS • **MAKES:** 6 SERVINGS

- **1 tablespoon canola oil**
- **1 medium onion, finely chopped**
- **4 garlic cloves, minced**
- **3 teaspoons ground coriander**
- **1½ teaspoons ground cinnamon**
- **1 teaspoon ground ginger**
- **1 teaspoon ground turmeric**
- **½ teaspoon cayenne pepper**
- **2 tablespoons tomato paste**
- **2 cans (15 ounces each) garbanzo beans or chickpeas, rinsed and drained**
- **3 cups cubed peeled sweet potatoes (about 1 pound)**
- **3 cups fresh cauliflower florets (about 8 ounces)**
- **4 medium carrots, cut into ¾-inch pieces (about 2 cups)**
- **2 medium tomatoes, seeded and chopped**
- **2 cups chicken broth**
- **1 cup light coconut milk**
- **½ teaspoon pepper**
- **¼ teaspoon salt**
- **Minced fresh cilantro**
- **Naan flatbreads, warmed**
- **Lime wedges**
- **Plain yogurt, optional**

1. In a large skillet, heat oil over medium heat; saute onion until soft and lightly browned, 5-7 minutes. Add garlic and spices; cook and stir 1 minute. Stir in tomato paste; cook 1 minute. Transfer to a 5- or 6-qt. slow cooker.
2. Mash 1 can of beans until smooth; add to the slow cooker. Stir in the remaining beans, vegetables, broth, coconut milk, pepper and salt.
3. Cook, covered, on low until the vegetables are tender, 5-6 hours. Sprinkle with cilantro. Serve with naan, lime wedges and, if desired, yogurt.

SLOW-COOKED VEGETABLE CURRY

SLOW COOKER BUTTERNUT SQUASH SOUP

SLOW COOKER BUTTERNUT SQUASH SOUP

When you're raising two preschoolers, simple but tasty is so important! Much of the work on this soup can be done in advance, and it keeps all day in the slow cooker. This recipe can easily be doubled for potlucks. You can use sage or savory with (or instead of) the thyme, or replace it with nutmeg. Replacing the chicken broth with vegetable broth makes this a great option for vegans.

—**JENNIFER MACHADO** ALTA, CA

PREP: 30 MIN. • **COOK:** 6 HOURS
MAKES: 12 SERVINGS (3 QUARTS)

- **1 tablespoon olive oil**
- **1 large onion, chopped**
- **2 garlic cloves, minced**
- **1 medium butternut squash (about 4 pounds), peeled and cut into 1-inch pieces**
- **1 pound Yukon Gold potatoes (about 2 medium), cut into ¾-inch pieces**
- **2 teaspoons minced fresh thyme or ¾ teaspoon dried thyme**
- **1½ teaspoons salt**
- **¼ teaspoon pepper**
- **5 to 6 cups chicken or vegetable broth**
- **Sour cream, optional**

1. In a large skillet, heat oil over medium heat. Add onion; saute until tender, 4-5 minutes. Add garlic; cook 1 minute longer. Transfer to a 6-qt. slow cooker. Add next five ingredients and 5 cups broth to slow cooker. Cook, covered, on low until vegetables are soft, 6-8 hours.
2. Puree soup using an immersion blender. Or, cool slightly and puree soup in batches in a blender; return to slow cooker. Stir in additional broth to reach desired consistency; heat through. If desired, top servings with sour cream.
To freeze: Freeze cooled soup in freezer containers. To use, partially thaw in refrigerator overnight. Heat through in a saucepan, stirring occasionally and adding a little broth if necessary.

BEEF & POTATO SOUP

Slow-cooker easy, this lightened-up soup is a family tradition at our house after church services.

—**SHEILA HOLDERMAN** BERTHOLD, ND

PREP: 30 MIN. • **COOK:** 6½ HOURS
MAKES: 10 SERVINGS (3 QUARTS)

- **1½ pounds lean ground beef (90% lean)**
- **¾ cup chopped onion**
- **½ cup all-purpose flour**
- **2 cans (14½ ounces each) reduced-sodium chicken broth, divided**
- **5 medium potatoes, peeled and cubed**
- **5 medium carrots, chopped**
- **3 celery ribs, chopped**
- **3 teaspoons dried basil**
- **2 teaspoons dried parsley flakes**
- **1 teaspoon garlic powder**
- **½ teaspoon pepper**
- **12 ounces reduced-fat process cheese (Velveeta), cubed**
- **1½ cups 2% milk**
- **½ cup reduced-fat sour cream**

1. In a large skillet, cook beef and onion over medium heat until meat is no longer pink; drain. Combine flour and 1 can broth until smooth. Add to the beef mixture. Bring to a boil; cook and stir for 2 minutes or until thickened.
2. Transfer to a 5-qt. slow cooker. Stir in potatoes, carrots, celery, seasonings and the remaining broth. Cover and cook on low for 6-8 hours or until the vegetables are tender.
3. Stir in cheese and milk. Cover and cook 30 minutes longer or until the cheese is melted. Just before serving, stir in sour cream.

CREAM OF POTATO & CHEDDAR SOUP

The Yukon Gold potatoes my daughter shares from her garden make this soup incredible. Add some cheddar cheese and crisp croutons, and it's just heavenly. Total comfort with the simplicity of good ingredients!

—**CINDI BAUER** MARSHFIELD, WI

PREP: 25 MIN. • **COOK:** 7½ HOURS
MAKES: 11 SERVINGS (2¾ QUARTS)

- **8 medium Yukon Gold potatoes, peeled and cubed**
- **1 large red onion, chopped**
- **1 celery rib, chopped**
- **2 cans (14½ ounces each) reduced-sodium chicken broth**
- **1 can (10¾ ounces) condensed cream of celery soup, undiluted**
- **1 teaspoon garlic powder**
- **½ teaspoon white pepper**
- **1½ cups shredded sharp cheddar cheese**
- **1 cup half-and-half cream**
- **Optional toppings: salad croutons, crumbled cooked bacon and additional shredded sharp cheddar cheese**

1. Combine the first seven ingredients in a 4- or 5-qt. slow cooker. Cover and cook on low for 7-9 hours or until the potatoes are tender.
2. Stir in cheese and cream. Cover and cook 30 minutes longer or until the cheese is melted. Garnish individual servings with the toppings of your choice.

HARVEST BUTTERNUT & PORK STEW

Cure your craving for something different with this savory stew; it's especially tasty served with warm bread. Edamame adds a protein-packed touch.

—**ERIN CHILCOAT** CENTRAL ISLIP, NY

PREP: 20 MIN. • **COOK:** 8 HOURS
MAKES: 6 SERVINGS (2 QUARTS)

- **⅓ cup plus 1 tablespoon all-purpose flour, divided**
- **1 tablespoon paprika**
- **1 teaspoon salt**
- **1 teaspoon ground coriander**
- **1½ pounds boneless pork shoulder butt roast, cut into 1-inch cubes**
- **1 tablespoon canola oil**
- **2¾ cups cubed peeled butternut squash**
- **1 can (14½ ounces) diced tomatoes, undrained**
- **1 cup frozen corn, thawed**
- **1 medium onion, chopped**
- **2 tablespoons cider vinegar**
- **1 bay leaf**
- **2½ cups reduced-sodium chicken broth**
- **1⅔ cups frozen shelled edamame, thawed**

1. In a large resealable plastic bag, combine ⅓ cup flour, paprika, salt and coriander. Add pork, a few pieces at a time, and shake to coat.
2. In a large skillet, brown the pork in oil in batches; drain. Transfer to a 5-qt. slow cooker. Add squash, tomatoes, corn, onion, vinegar and bay leaf. In a small bowl, combine broth and the remaining flour until smooth; stir into the slow cooker.
3. Cover and cook on low for 8-10 hours or until pork and vegetables are tender. Stir in edamame; cover and cook 30 minutes longer. Discard bay leaf.

GARLIC LOVER'S BEEF STEW

Red wine gives a mellow flavor to this stew, with its tender beef and carrots and lashings of garlic. We like to serve it over mashed potatoes, but you could also use noodles.

—**ALISSA BROWN** FORT WASHINGTON, PA

PREP: 30 MIN. • **COOK:** 8 HOURS
MAKES: 10 SERVINGS

- **1 boneless beef chuck roast (3 pounds), cut into 2-inch pieces**
- **1¼ teaspoons salt**
- **¾ teaspoon coarsely ground pepper**
- **½ cup all-purpose flour**
- **2 tablespoons olive oil**
- **12 garlic cloves, minced**
- **1 cup dry red wine, or reduced-sodium beef broth**
- **2 cans (14½ ounces each) diced tomatoes, undrained**
- **1 can (14½ ounces) reduced-sodium beef broth**
- **6 medium carrots, thinly sliced**
- **2 medium onions, chopped**
- **2 tablespoons tomato paste**
- **2 teaspoons minced fresh rosemary or ½ teaspoon dried rosemary, crushed**
- **2 teaspoons minced fresh thyme or ½ teaspoon dried thyme**
- **2 bay leaves**
- **Dash ground cloves**
- **Hot mashed potatoes**

1. Sprinkle beef with salt, pepper and flour; toss to coat.
2. In a large skillet, heat oil over medium-high heat. Brown the beef in batches. Remove with a slotted spoon. Reduce heat to medium. Add garlic; cook and stir 1 minute.
3. Add wine to the skillet; stir to loosen browned bits from pan. Transfer to a 5- or 6-qt. slow cooker. Stir in tomatoes, broth, carrots, onions, tomato paste, rosemary, thyme, bay leaves, cloves and beef.
4. Cook, covered, on low for 8-10 hours or until the beef is tender. Remove the bay leaves. Serve with mashed potatoes.

GARLIC LOVER'S BEEF STEW

CARRIE'S CINCINNATI CHILI

CARRIE'S CINCINNATI CHILI

Every time we had a gathering or company, folks would request this. My husband convinced me to enter it in a local chili contest, and I won third place! It's quick and easy. If I don't have fresh garlic, I use minced garlic in the jar.

—**CARRIE BIRDSALL** DALLAS, GA

PREP: 20 MIN. • **COOK:** 6 HOURS
MAKES: 6 SERVINGS

- **1½ pounds ground beef**
- **1 small onion, chopped**
- **1 can (29 ounces) tomato puree**
- **1 can (14½ ounces) whole tomatoes, crushed**
- **2 tablespoons brown sugar**
- **4 teaspoons chili powder**
- **1 tablespoon white vinegar**
- **1 teaspoon salt**
- **¾ teaspoon ground cinnamon**
- **½ teaspoon ground allspice**
- **½ teaspoon pepper**
- **1 garlic clove, crushed**
- **3 bay leaves**
- **Hot cooked spaghetti**
- **Shredded cheddar cheese, optional**
- **Additional chopped onion, optional**

1. In a large skillet over medium heat, cook beef and onion, crumbling meat, until beef is no longer pink and onion is tender, 6-8 minutes; drain. Transfer to a 3- or 4-qt. slow cooker. Add next 11 ingredients.

2. Cook, covered, on low 6-8 hours. Discard garlic clove and bay leaves. Serve on hot cooked spaghetti; if desired, top with shredded cheddar cheese and additional chopped onion.

To freeze: Before adding toppings, cool chili. Freeze chili in freezer containers. To use, partially thaw in refrigerator overnight. Heat through in a saucepan, stirring occasionally and adding a little water or broth if necessary. Serve as directed.

AFRICAN PEANUT SWEET POTATO STEW

When I was in college, my mom made an addicting sweet potato stew. I shared it with friends, and now all of us serve it to our own kids. They all love it, of course.

—**ALEXIS SCATCHELL** NILES, IL

PREP: 20 MIN. • **COOK:** 6 HOURS
MAKES: 8 SERVINGS (2½ QUARTS)

- **1 can (28 ounces) diced tomatoes, undrained**
- **1 cup fresh cilantro leaves**
- **½ cup chunky peanut butter**
- **3 garlic cloves, halved**
- **2 teaspoons ground cumin**
- **1 teaspoon salt**
- **½ teaspoon ground cinnamon**
- **¼ teaspoon smoked paprika**
- **3 pounds sweet potatoes (about 6 medium), peeled and cut into 1-inch pieces**
- **1 can (15 ounces) garbanzo beans or chickpeas, rinsed and drained**
- **1 cup water**
- **8 cups chopped fresh kale**
- **Chopped peanuts and additional cilantro leaves, optional**

1. Place the first eight ingredients in a food processor; process until pureed. Transfer to a 5-qt. slow cooker; stir in sweet potatoes, beans and water.

2. Cook, covered, on low for 6-8 hours or until the potatoes are tender; add kale during the last 30 minutes. If desired, top individual servings with chopped peanuts and additional cilantro.

CHIPOTLE BEEF CHILI

I love spicy food, so I think this chili really hits the spot. If you are sensitive to chili peppers, start out with one or two chipotles and go up from there.

—**STEVEN SCHEND** GRAND RAPIDS, MI

PREP: 15 MIN. • **COOK:** 6 HOURS
MAKES: 8 SERVINGS (ABOUT 2½ QUARTS)

- **2 pounds beef flank steak, cut into 1-inch pieces**
- **2 to 4 chipotle peppers in adobo sauce, chopped**
- **¼ cup chopped onion**
- **1 tablespoon chili powder**
- **2 garlic cloves, minced**
- **1 teaspoon salt**
- **½ teaspoon ground cumin**
- **3 cans (15 ounces each) tomato puree**
- **1 can (14½ ounces) beef broth**
- **¼ cup minced fresh cilantro**

In a 4- or 5-qt. slow cooker, combine the first nine ingredients. Cook, covered, on low 6-8 hours or until meat is tender. Stir in cilantro.

To freeze: Freeze cooled chili in freezer containers. To use, partially thaw in refrigerator overnight. Heat through in a saucepan, stirring occasionally and adding a little broth or water if necessary.

SLOW-COOKED STUFFED PEPPER STEW

This is my go-to pepper stew. When my garden yields green peppers, I dice and freeze them for those cold, blustery days to come.

—**DEBBIE JOHNSON** CENTERTOWN, MO

PREP: 20 MIN. • **COOK:** 4¼ HOURS
MAKES: 8 SERVINGS (3 QUARTS)

- **1½ pounds bulk Italian sausage**
- **1 large onion, chopped**
- **2 medium green peppers, chopped**
- **2 to 4 tablespoons brown sugar**
- **2 teaspoons beef base**
- **½ teaspoon salt**
- **¼ teaspoon pepper**
- **2 cans (15 ounces each) tomato sauce**
- **1 can (28 ounces) diced tomatoes, undrained**
- **2 cups tomato juice**
- **¾ cup uncooked instant rice**

1. In a large skillet over medium heat, cook sausage and onion for 8-10 minutes or until the sausage is no longer pink, breaking up the sausage into crumbles; drain.

2. In a 6-qt. slow cooker, combine the sausage mixture, green peppers, brown sugar, beef base, salt, pepper, tomato sauce, tomatoes and tomato juice. Cook, covered, on low for 4-5 hours or until the vegetables are tender.

3. Stir in rice. Cook, covered, 15-20 minutes longer or until the rice is tender.

To freeze: Freeze cooled stew in freezer containers. To use, partially thaw in refrigerator overnight. Heat through in a saucepan, stirring occasionally and adding a little water if necessary.

Note: At the grocery store, look for beef base near the broth and bouillon.

SLOW-COOKED
STUFFED PEPPER STEW

SPLIT PEA SOUP WITH HAM & JALAPENO

SPLIT PEA SOUP WITH HAM & JALAPENO

To me, this spicy pea soup is total comfort food. I cook it low and slow all day, and it fills the house with a yummy aroma. It's so good with a nice, crispy baguette.

—**CHELSEA TICHENOR** HUNTINGTON BEACH, CA

PREP: 15 MIN. • **COOK:** 6 HOURS
MAKES: 6 SERVINGS (2¼ QUARTS)

- **2 smoked ham hocks**
- **1 package (16 ounces) dried green split peas**
- **4 medium carrots, cut into ½-inch slices**
- **1 medium onion, chopped**
- **1 jalapeno pepper, seeded and minced**
- **3 garlic cloves, minced**
- **8 cups water**
- **1 teaspoon salt**
- **1 teaspoon pepper**

In a 4- or 5-qt. slow cooker, combine all ingredients. Cook, covered, on low until the meat is tender, 6-8 hours. Remove ham hocks from slow cooker; when cool enough to handle, remove meat from bones, cut ham into small pieces and return to slow cooker.

Note: Wear disposable gloves when cutting hot peppers; the oils can burn exposed skin. Avoid touching your face.

★★★★★ **READER REVIEW**

"This has become my favorite pea soup recipe."

1GOODFOODLOVER TASTEOFHOME.COM

CHICKEN CASSOULET SOUP

After my sister spent a year in France as an au pair, I created this lighter, easier version of traditional French cassoulet for her. It uses chicken instead of the usual duck.

—**BRIDGET KLUSMAN** OTSEGO, MI

PREP: 35 MIN. • **COOK:** 6 HOURS
MAKES: 7 SERVINGS (2¾ QUARTS)

- **½ pound bulk pork sausage**
- **5 cups water**
- **½ pound cubed cooked chicken**
- **1 can (16 ounces) kidney beans, rinsed and drained**
- **1 can (15 ounces) black beans, rinsed and drained**
- **1 can (15 ounces) garbanzo beans or chickpeas, rinsed and drained**
- **2 medium carrots, shredded**
- **1 medium onion, chopped**
- **¼ cup dry vermouth or chicken broth**
- **5 teaspoons chicken bouillon granules**
- **4 garlic cloves, minced**
- **½ teaspoon dried thyme**
- **¼ teaspoon fennel seed, crushed**
- **1 teaspoon dried lavender flowers, optional**
- **½ pound bacon strips, cooked and crumbled**

1. In a large skillet, cook sausage over medium heat until no longer pink; drain.
2. Transfer to a 4- or 5-qt. slow cooker. Add water, chicken, beans, carrots, onion, vermouth, bouillon, garlic, thyme, fennel and if desired, lavender. Cover and cook on low 6-8 hours or until heated through.
3. Divide among bowls; sprinkle with bacon.

Note: Look for dried lavender flowers in spice shops; be sure it's culinary lavender and not intended for use only in crafts and potpourri. If using lavender from the garden, make sure it hasn't been treated with chemicals.

SATAY-STYLE PORK STEW

Thai cuisine features flavors that are hot and sour, salty and sweet. This one-dish pork satay balances all those flavors with ginger and red pepper flakes, rice vinegar, garlic and creamy peanut butter.

—**NICOLE WERNER** ANN ARBOR, MI

PREP: 25 MIN. • **COOK:** 8 HOURS
MAKES: 6 SERVINGS

- **1 boneless pork shoulder butt roast (3 to 4 pounds), cut into 1½ inch cubes**
- **2 medium parsnips, peeled and sliced**
- **1 small sweet red pepper, thinly sliced**
- **1 cup chicken broth**
- **¼ cup reduced-sodium teriyaki sauce**
- **2 tablespoons rice vinegar**
- **1 tablespoon minced fresh gingerroot**
- **1 tablespoon honey**
- **2 garlic cloves, minced**
- **½ teaspoon crushed red pepper flakes**
- **¼ cup creamy peanut butter**
- **Hot cooked rice, optional**
- **2 green onions, chopped**
- **2 tablespoons chopped dry roasted peanuts**

In a 3-qt. slow cooker, combine the first 10 ingredients. Cover and cook on low for 8-10 hours or until the pork is tender. Skim fat; stir in peanut butter. Serve with rice if desired; top with onions and peanuts.

To freeze: Before adding toppings, freeze cooled stew in freezer containers. To use, partially thaw in refrigerator overnight. Heat through in a saucepan, stirring occasionally and adding a little broth or water if necessary.

SALMON SWEET POTATO SOUP

I created this recipe as a healthier alternative to whitefish chowder, which is a favorite in the area where I grew up. Salmon and sweet potatoes boost the nutrition, and the slow cooker makes this soup convenient. It's especially comforting on a cold fall or winter day!

—**MATTHEW HASS** FRANKLIN, WI

PREP: 20 MIN. • **COOK:** 5½ HOURS
MAKES: 8 SERVINGS (3 QUARTS)

- **1 tablespoon olive oil**
- **1 medium onion, chopped**
- **1 medium carrot, chopped**
- **1 celery rib, chopped**
- **3 garlic cloves, minced**
- **2 medium sweet potatoes, peeled and cut into ½-inch cubes**
- **1½ cups frozen corn, thawed**
- **6 cups reduced-sodium chicken broth**
- **1 teaspoon celery salt**
- **1 teaspoon dill weed**
- **½ teaspoon salt**
- **¾ teaspoon pepper**
- **1½ pounds salmon fillets, skin removed and cut into ¾-inch pieces**
- **1 can (12 ounces) fat-free evaporated milk**
- **2 tablespoons minced fresh parsley**

1. In a large skillet, heat oil over medium heat. Add onion, carrot and celery; cook and stir until tender, 4-5 minutes. Add garlic; cook 1 minute longer. Transfer to a 5-qt. slow cooker. Add the next seven ingredients. Cook, covered, on low until the sweet potatoes are tender, 5-6 hours.

2. Stir in salmon, milk and parsley. Cook, covered, until the fish just begins to flake easily with a fork, 30-40 minutes longer.

SALMON SWEET POTATO SOUP
Matthew Hass
Franklin, WI

SPICED LAMB STEW WITH APRICOTS

SPICED LAMB STEW WITH APRICOTS

During his first year of college, my son said he was a vegetarian. When he came home, I had a batch of my lamb stew simmering in the kitchen. By dinnertime, there were only a few shreds of meat left floating in the gravy—and my son confessed that he was the culprit!

—**ARLENE ERLBACH** MORTON GROVE, IL

PREP: 30 MIN. • **COOK:** 5 HOURS • **MAKES:** 5 SERVINGS

- **2 pounds lamb stew meat, cut into ¾-inch cubes**
- **3 tablespoons butter**
- **1½ cups chopped sweet onion**
- **¾ cup dried apricots**
- **½ cup orange juice**
- **½ cup chicken broth**
- **2 teaspoons paprika**
- **2 teaspoons ground allspice**
- **2 teaspoons ground cinnamon**
- **1½ teaspoons salt**
- **1 teaspoon ground cardamom**
- **Hot cooked couscous**
- **Chopped dried apricots, optional**

1. In a large skillet, brown lamb in butter in batches. With a slotted spoon, transfer to a 3-qt. slow cooker. In the same skillet, saute onion in drippings until tender. Stir in apricots, orange juice, broth and seasonings; pour over the lamb.

2. Cover and cook on high for 5-6 hours or until meat is tender. Serve with couscous. Sprinkle with chopped apricots if desired.

Note: Not a fan of lamb? The flavors meld wonderfully with pork, too. Substitute cubed pork shoulder for the lamb stew meat.

BEEF VEGETABLE SOUP

This nicely seasoned soup tastes especially good on a chilly day. It's so convenient to do the prep work in the morning and then let the soup simmer all day.

—**JEAN HUTZELL** DUBUQUE, IA

PREP: 20 MIN. • **COOK:** 9 HOURS • **MAKES:** 7 SERVINGS

- 1 pound lean ground beef (90% lean)
- 1 medium onion, chopped
- ½ teaspoon salt
- ¼ teaspoon pepper
- 3 cups water
- 3 medium potatoes, peeled and cut into ¾-inch cubes
- 1 can (14½ ounces) Italian diced tomatoes, undrained
- 1 can (11½ ounces) V8 juice
- 1 cup chopped celery
- 1 cup sliced carrots
- 2 tablespoons sugar
- 1 tablespoon dried parsley flakes
- 2 teaspoons dried basil
- 1 bay leaf

1. In a nonstick skillet, cook beef and onion over medium heat until the meat is no longer pink; drain. Stir in salt and pepper.

2. Transfer to a 5-qt. slow cooker. Add the remaining ingredients. Cover and cook on low for 9-11 hours or until the vegetables are tender. Discard bay leaf before serving.

SLOW COOKER CHICKEN & SWEET POTATO CHILI

As a college student, one of the things I miss most is my mom's cooking...and her well-stocked kitchen! This recipe is perfect because I can make it in my dorm and come back later to a fresh bowl of chili.

—**BAILEY STARKEY** MOUNT VERNON, WA

PREP: 15 MIN. • **COOK:** 5 HOURS
MAKES: 8 SERVINGS (3 QUARTS)

- 1½ pounds sweet potatoes, peeled and cut into ½-inch cubes (about 6 cups)
- 2 cans (15 ounces each) black beans, rinsed and drained
- 1 pound boneless skinless chicken thighs, cubed
- 2 cups chicken broth
- 1 jar (16 ounces) salsa
- 1 can (14½ ounces) diced tomatoes, undrained
- 1 package (10 ounces) frozen corn, thawed
- 1 medium onion, chopped
- 1 tablespoon chili powder
- 3 garlic cloves, minced
- 1 teaspoon ground coriander
- ½ teaspoon ground cinnamon
- Shredded cheddar cheese, sour cream and tortilla chips

In a greased 6-qt. slow cooker, combine the first 12 ingredients. Cook, covered, on low for 5-6 hours or until the chicken and sweet potatoes are tender. Serve with cheese, sour cream and chips.

SLOW COOKER CHICKEN & DUMPLINGS

Here's a homey dish that people just can't wait to dive into! Yes, you can have chicken and dumplings from the slow cooker. The homemade classic takes a bit of work but is certainly worth it.

—**DANIEL ANDERSON** KENOSHA, WI

PREP: 20 MIN. • **COOK:** 6 HOURS + STANDING
MAKES: 8 SERVINGS

- **6 boneless skinless chicken thighs, chopped**
- **½ teaspoon salt, divided**
- **½ teaspoon pepper, divided**
- **1 tablespoon canola oil**
- **3 celery ribs, chopped**
- **2 medium carrots, peeled and chopped**
- **1 large onion, chopped**
- **3 garlic cloves, minced**
- **2 tablespoons tomato paste**
- **⅓ cup all-purpose flour**
- **4 cups chicken broth, divided**
- **2 bay leaves**
- **1 teaspoon dried thyme**

DUMPLINGS

- **2 cups all-purpose flour**
- **3 teaspoons baking powder**
- **1 teaspoon salt**
- **¼ teaspoon pepper**
- **1 cup whole milk**
- **4 tablespoons melted butter**

1. Sprinkle chicken with ¼ teaspoon salt and ¼ teaspoon pepper. Meanwhile, in a large skillet, heat oil over medium-high heat. Add chicken; cook and stir until no longer pink, 6-8 minutes. Transfer to a 6-qt. slow cooker.
2. In the same skillet, cook celery, carrots and onion until tender, 6-8 minutes. Add garlic, tomato paste and the remaining salt and pepper; cook 1 minute. Stir in flour; cook 1 minute longer. Whisk in 2 cups chicken broth; cook and stir until thickened. Transfer to slow cooker. Stir in bay leaves, thyme and the remaining chicken broth.
3. For dumplings, whisk together flour, baking powder, salt and pepper in a large bowl. Stir in milk and butter to form a thick batter. Drop by ¼ cupfuls over the chicken mixture. Cook, covered, on low until bubbly and the dumplings are set, 6-8 hours. Discard bay leaves. Remove insert and let stand, uncovered, for 15 minutes before serving.

UPSIDE-DOWN FRITO PIE

Using ground turkey is a smart way to lighten up this hearty, family-pleasing chili.

—**MARY BERG** LAKE ELMO, MN

PREP: 15 MIN. • **COOK:** 2 HOURS
MAKES: 6 SERVINGS

- **2 pounds ground turkey or beef**
- **1 medium onion, chopped**
- **2 envelopes chili seasoning mix**
- **1 can (10 ounces) diced tomatoes and green chilies, undrained**
- **1 can (8 ounces) tomato sauce**
- **1 can (15 ounces) pinto beans, rinsed and drained**
- **1 cup shredded cheddar cheese**
- **3 cups corn chips**
- **Sour cream, minced fresh cilantro and additional chopped onion, optional**

1. In a large skillet, cook turkey and onion over medium heat for 8-10 minutes or until no longer pink, breaking into crumbles; stir in chili seasoning. Transfer to a 3- or 4-qt. slow cooker. Pour tomatoes and tomato sauce over the turkey.
2. Cook, covered, on low 2-3 hours or until heated through. Stir to combine. Top with the pinto beans. Sprinkle with cheese. Cook, covered, 5-10 minutes or until the cheese is melted. Top with corn chips. If desired, serve with sour cream, minced cilantro and additional onion.

★★★★★ **READER REVIEW**

"This was fantastic and had the whole family begging for seconds."

ANGEL182009 TASTEOFHOME.COM

UPSIDE-DOWN FRITO PIE

THAI CHICKEN NOODLE SOUP

THAI CHICKEN NOODLE SOUP

This slow cooker soup is a semi-homemade version that coaxes all the flavor from a rotisserie chicken. All the prep work for this can be done the day before so you can toss it into the slow cooker with ease.

—**BETH JACOBSON** MILWAUKEE, WI

PREP: 20 MIN. • **COOK:** 6 HOURS • **MAKES:** 8 SERVINGS

- **1 large onion, halved**
- **1 piece fresh ginger (3 to 4 inches), halved lengthwise**
- **1 tablespoon canola oil**
- **1 rotisserie chicken**
- **1 cinnamon stick (3 inches)**
- **5 whole cloves**
- **3 whole star anise**
- **1 teaspoon coriander seeds**
- **1 teaspoon fennel seed**
- **3 quarts reduced-sodium chicken broth**
- **1 package (8.8 ounces) rice noodles**
- **2 tablespoons brown sugar**
- **2 tablespoons fish sauce**
- **1 tablespoon lime juice**
- **Optional ingredients: bean sprouts, fresh basil leaves, fresh cilantro leaves, thinly sliced green onions, chili garlic sauce, fish sauce and lime wedges**

1. Preheat broiler. Place onion and ginger in a foil-lined 15x10x1-in. baking pan; drizzle with oil. Broil 3-4 in. from heat 8-10 minutes or until well browned. Meanwhile, remove chicken from bones; reserve carcass and shred meat. Place carcass, onion, ginger, spices and broth in a 6-qt. slow cooker. Cook on low 6-8 hours.

2. Cook noodles according to package instructions. Strain soup and keep warm; discard carcass, vegetables and spices. Stir in brown sugar, fish sauce and lime juice. Place noodles and chicken in soup bowls. Ladle broth into soup bowls. Add toppings of your choice.

LENTIL & PASTA STEW

Warm up with a big bowl of this stick-to-your-ribs stew. Loaded with chopped smoked sausage, hearty veggies and tender lentils, it's terrific with bread fresh from the oven.

—**GERALDINE SAUCIER** ALBUQUERQUE, NM

PREP: 25 MIN. • **COOK:** 8 HOURS • **MAKES:** 8 SERVINGS

- **½ pound smoked kielbasa or Polish sausage, chopped**
- **3 tablespoons olive oil**
- **3 tablespoons butter**
- **1 cup cubed peeled potatoes**
- **¾ cup sliced fresh carrots**
- **1 celery rib, sliced**
- **1 small onion, finely chopped**
- **5 cups beef broth**
- **1 cup dried lentils, rinsed**
- **1 cup canned diced tomatoes**
- **1 bay leaf**
- **1 teaspoon coarsely ground pepper**
- **¼ teaspoon salt**
- **1 cup uncooked ditalini or other small pasta**
- **Shredded Romano cheese**

1. Brown kielbasa in oil and butter in a large skillet. Add potatoes, carrots, celery and onion. Cook and stir for 3 minutes over medium heat. Transfer to a 4- or 5-qt. slow cooker. Stir in the broth, lentils, tomatoes, bay leaf, pepper and salt.

2. Cover and cook on low for 8-10 hours or until the lentils are tender. Cook pasta according to the package directions; drain. Stir the pasta into the slow cooker. Discard the bay leaf. Sprinkle each serving with cheese.

HOBO MEATBALL STEW

This hearty, satisfying stew hits all the right notes for a classic thick vegetable soup—with the added extra bonus of meatballs!

—**MARGERY BRYAN** MOSES LAKE, WA

PREP: 20 MIN. • **COOK:** 5 HOURS • **MAKES:** 4 SERVINGS

- **1 pound ground beef**
- **1½ teaspoons salt or salt-free seasoning blend, divided**
- **½ teaspoon pepper, divided**
- **4 medium potatoes, peeled and cut into chunks**
- **4 medium carrots, cut into chunks**
- **1 large onion, cut into chunks**
- **½ cup water**
- **½ cup ketchup**
- **1½ teaspoons cider vinegar**
- **½ teaspoon dried basil**
- **¾ cup frozen peas**

1. In a large bowl, combine the beef, 1 teaspoon salt and ¼ teaspoon pepper. Shape into 1-in. balls. In a large skillet over medium heat, brown meatballs on all sides; drain.

2. Place potatoes, carrots and onion in a 3-qt. slow cooker; top with meatballs. Combine water, ketchup, vinegar, basil, and the remaining salt and pepper; pour over the meatballs.

3. Cover and cook on high for 4¾ hours. Stir in peas; cook 15 minutes longer or until the vegetables are tender.

TEST KITCHEN TIP For meatballs to cook evenly, it's important for them to be the same size. The easiest way to do this is by using a 1-inch cookie scoop. Scoop the meat mixture and level off the top. Gently roll into a ball.

SPICY LENTIL SOUP

I've finally found a lentil soup my husband goes for. Adjust the spice level to your taste, and present this yummy soup with warm pita bread.

—**EVA BARKER** LEBANON, NH

PREP: 25 MIN. • **COOK:** 9 HOURS
MAKES: 14 SERVINGS (3½ QUARTS)

- **1½ pounds potatoes, peeled and cubed (about 5 cups)**
- **1 large onion, chopped**
- **2 large carrots, chopped**
- **2 celery ribs, chopped**
- **¼ cup olive oil**
- **4 teaspoons ground cumin**
- **2 teaspoons chili powder**
- **1 teaspoon salt**
- **1 teaspoon ground coriander**
- **1 teaspoon coarsely ground pepper**
- **½ teaspoon ground turmeric**
- **½ teaspoon cayenne pepper**
- **5 garlic cloves, minced**
- **2 cartons (32 ounces each) reduced-sodium chicken broth**
- **2 cans (15 ounces each) tomato sauce**
- **1 package (16 ounces) dried lentils, rinsed**
- **¼ cup lemon juice**

1. Place potatoes, onion, carrots and celery in a 6-qt. slow cooker. In a small skillet, heat oil over medium heat. Add seasonings; cook and stir 2 minutes. Add garlic; cook 1-2 minutes longer. Transfer to slow cooker.

2. Stir in broth, tomato sauce and lentils. Cook, covered, on low for 9-11 hours or until the lentils are tender. Stir in lemon juice.

SPICY LENTIL SOUP

SLOW-COOKED
WHITE BEAN CHILI

SLOW-COOKED WHITE BEAN CHILI

My friend and I came up with this delicious slow-cooked chicken chili together. The Alfredo sauce base makes it stand apart from other white chilis. Reduce the amount of cayenne pepper if you'd like a little less heat.

—**CINDI MITCHELL** ST. MARYS, KS

PREP: 15 MIN. • **COOK:** 3 HOURS
MAKES: 12 SERVINGS

- **3 cans (15½ ounces each) great northern beans, rinsed and drained**
- **3 cups cubed cooked chicken breast**
- **1 jar (15 ounces) Alfredo sauce**
- **2 cups chicken broth**
- **1½ cups frozen gold and white corn (about 8 ounces), thawed**
- **1 cup shredded Monterey Jack cheese**
- **1 cup shredded pepper jack cheese**
- **1 cup sour cream**
- **1 small sweet yellow pepper, chopped**
- **1 small onion, chopped**
- **1 to 2 cans (4 ounces each) chopped green chilies**
- **3 garlic cloves, minced**
- **3 teaspoons ground cumin**
- **1½ teaspoons white pepper**
- **1 to 1½ teaspoons cayenne pepper**
- **Salsa verde and chopped fresh cilantro, optional**

In a 5- or 6-qt. slow cooker, combine all ingredients except salsa and cilantro. Cook, covered, on low until vegetables are tender and flavors are blended, 3-4 hours, stirring once. If desired, top individual servings with salsa and cilantro.

GINGER CHICKEN NOODLE SOUP

This is one of my favorite soup recipes to serve in the winter time because it's easy and comforting, and it fills the entire house with a wonderful aroma. My whole family loves it!

—**BRANDY STANSBURY** EDNA, TX

PREP: 15 MIN. • **COOK:** 3½ HOURS
MAKES: 8 SERVINGS (2½ QUARTS)

- **1 pound boneless skinless chicken breasts, cubed**
- **2 medium carrots, shredded**
- **3 tablespoons sherry or reduced-sodium chicken broth**
- **2 tablespoons rice vinegar**
- **1 tablespoon reduced-sodium soy sauce**
- **2 to 3 teaspoons minced fresh gingerroot**
- **¼ teaspoon pepper**
- **6 cups reduced-sodium chicken broth**
- **1 cup water**
- **2 cups fresh snow peas, halved**
- **2 ounces uncooked angel hair pasta, broken into thirds**

1. In a 5-qt. slow cooker, combine the first seven ingredients; stir in broth and water. Cook, covered, on low 3-4 hours or until the chicken is tender.

2. Stir in snow peas and pasta. Cook, covered, on low for 30 minutes longer or until the snow peas and pasta are tender.

★★★★★ **READER REVIEW**

"This soup was really delicious! It was nice to find something a little different as far as chicken noodle soup."

CHERIE HILL TASTEOFHOME.COM

SLOW COOKER BEEF TIPS, PAGE 89

BEEFY ENTREES

Meatballs, chili, pot roast...the slow cooker is perfectly suited to simmering savory beef dishes. But go beyond the expected, too, with fajitas, steaks and even meat loaf!

LUCKY CORNED BEEF

It's not luck; it's just an amazing Irish recipe. With this in the slow cooker by sunrise, you can definitely fill the seats at the dinner table by sundown. This recipe makes two full briskets—serve them both for a big crowd, or save one for sandwiches or other recipes.

—**HEATHER PARRAZ** ROCHESTER, WA

PREP: 20 MIN. • **COOK:** 9 HOURS
MAKES: 6 SERVINGS PLUS LEFTOVERS

- **6 medium red potatoes, quartered**
- **2 medium carrots, cut into chunks**
- **1 large onion, sliced**
- **2 corned beef briskets with spice packets (3 pounds each)**
- **¼ cup packed brown sugar**
- **2 tablespoons sugar**
- **2 tablespoons coriander seeds**
- **2 tablespoons whole peppercorns**
- **4 cups water**

1. In a 6-qt. slow cooker, combine potatoes, carrots and onion. Add corned beef briskets (discard spice packets or save for another use). Sprinkle the brown sugar, sugar, coriander and peppercorns over meat. Pour water over top.
2. Cover and cook on low for 9-11 hours or until the meat and vegetables are tender.

Remove the meat and vegetables to a serving platter. Thinly slice brisket across the grain and serve with vegetables.

★★★★★ **READER REVIEW**

"This recipe reminded me of the way my mom would make corned beef! Super easy to put together and the house smelled great all day."

MAMAKNOWSBEST TASTEOFHOME.COM

SHREDDED BEEF BURRITO FILLING

Make your next office party a taco bar or burrito bar! Set out the beef in the slow cooker on warm, along with tortillas and bowls of toppings. For a variation, I make Beef & Bean Burritos by mixing a can of refried beans into 3-4 cups of cooked beef filling.

—**HOPE WASYLENKI** GAHANNA, OH

PREP: 20 MIN. • **COOK:** 7 HOURS
MAKES: 12 SERVINGS

- **5 pounds boneless beef chuck roast, cut into 4 pieces**
- **½ cup beef broth**
- **2 tablespoons canola oil**
- **1 medium onion, finely chopped**
- **2 jalapeno peppers, seeded and finely chopped**
- **2 garlic cloves, minced**
- **2 tablespoons chili powder**
- **1 tablespoon ground cumin**
- **⅛ teaspoon salt**
- **1 can (28 ounces) crushed tomatoes in puree**
- **1 jar (16 ounces) salsa verde**
- **Shredded cheddar cheese, sour cream, guacamole, salsa and fresh cilantro leaves, optional**

1. In a 6-qt. slow cooker, combine beef and broth. Cook, covered, on low until the beef is tender, 6-8 hours. Remove beef; discard juices. When the beef is cool enough to handle, shred with two forks. Return meat to slow cooker.
2. In a large skillet, heat oil over medium heat. Add onion and jalapenos; cook and stir until softened, 3-4 minutes. Add garlic and seasonings; cook 1 minute longer. Stir in crushed tomatoes and salsa; bring to a boil. Pour the mixture over the shredded beef; stir to combine. Cook, covered, on high until heated through, about 1 hour.
3. Using tongs, serve on tortillas for burritos or tacos; add toppings as desired.

To freeze: Freeze the cooled meat mixture in freezer containers. To use, partially thaw in the refrigerator overnight. Heat through in a saucepan, stirring occasionally.

SHREDDED BEEF BURRITO FILLING

SOUTHWESTERN SHREDDED BEEF SANDWICHES

SOUTHWESTERN SHREDDED BEEF SANDWICHES

I am the typical busy wife and love a recipe that goes into the slow cooker in the morning and comes out delicious and ready to go when I get home from work.
—**ALMA WINDERS** SEQUIM, WA

PREP: 20 MIN. • **COOK:** 8 HOURS • **MAKES:** 8 SERVINGS

- **1 boneless beef chuck roast (3 to 4 pounds), trimmed**
- **1 tablespoon ground cumin**
- **1 tablespoon chili powder**
- **1 tablespoon smoked paprika**
- **1 teaspoon salt**
- **1 teaspoon pepper**
- **1 medium onion, chopped**
- **1 can (14½ ounces) stewed tomatoes**
- **1 can (7 ounces) chopped green chilies**
- **1 tablespoon chopped seeded jalapeno pepper**
- **¼ cup minced fresh cilantro, optional**
- **8 kaiser rolls, split and toasted**
- **Deli coleslaw and pickled jalapeno slices, optional**
- **2 cups shredded cheddar or Monterey Jack cheese**

1. Place roast in a 5- or 6-qt. slow cooker; sprinkle with seasonings. In a small bowl, mix the onion, tomatoes, chilies and jalapeno; pour over the roast. Cook, covered, on low 8-10 hours or until the meat is tender.
2. Remove roast; cool slightly. Shred with two forks. Return meat to slow cooker; heat through. If desired, stir in cilantro. Serve on rolls with cheese and, if desired, coleslaw and pickled jalapeno.

Note: Wear disposable gloves when cutting hot peppers; the oils can burn exposed skin. Avoid touching your face.

FAST FIX

FLANK STEAK FAJITAS

Our family loves Mexican food, and this is one of our favorites. The slow cooker tenderizes the flank steak for these filling fajitas, which have just the right amount of spice.

—**TWILA BURKHOLDER** MIDDLEBURG, PA

PREP: 10 MIN. • **COOK:** 8 HOURS
MAKES: 8-10 SERVINGS

- **1½ to 2 pounds beef flank steak, cut into thin strips**
- **1 can (10 ounces) diced tomatoes and green chilies, undrained**
- **2 garlic cloves, minced**
- **1 jalapeno pepper, seeded and chopped**
- **1 tablespoon minced fresh cilantro or parsley**
- **1 teaspoon chili powder**
- **½ teaspoon ground cumin**
- **¼ teaspoon salt**
- **1 medium sweet red pepper, julienned**
- **1 medium green pepper, julienned**
- **8 to 10 flour tortillas (7 to 8 inches)**
- **Sour cream, salsa and shredded cheddar cheese, optional**

1. Place beef in a 3-qt. slow cooker. In a small bowl, combine tomatoes, garlic, jalapeno, cilantro, chili powder, cumin and salt; pour over beef. Cover and cook on low for 7-8 hours.
2. Stir in red and green peppers. Cook for 1 hour longer or until the meat and peppers are tender. Thicken juices if desired.
3. Using a slotted spoon, place about ½ cup beef mixture down the center of each tortilla; fold sides over filling. Serve with sour cream, salsa and cheese if desired.

Note: Wear disposable gloves when cutting hot peppers; the oils can burn exposed skin. Avoid touching your face.

CREAMY CELERY BEEF STROGANOFF

Cream of celery soup adds richness to a recipe that has become a family favorite. Besides the delicious flavor, I appreciate the ease of preparation.

—**KIMBERLY WALLACE** DENNISON, OH

PREP: 20 MIN. • **COOK:** 8 HOURS
MAKES: 6 SERVINGS

- **2 pounds beef stew meat, cut into 1-inch cubes**
- **1 can (10¾ ounces) condensed cream of celery soup, undiluted**
- **1 can (10¾ ounces) condensed cream of mushroom soup, undiluted**
- **1 medium onion, chopped**
- **1 jar (6 ounces) sliced mushrooms, drained**
- **1 envelope onion soup mix**
- **½ teaspoon pepper**
- **1 cup (8 ounces) sour cream**
- **Hot cooked noodles**

In a 3-qt. slow cooker, combine the first seven ingredients. Cover and cook on low for 8 hours or until the beef is tender. Stir in sour cream. Serve with noodles.

SHORT RIBS WITH SALT-SKIN POTATOES

I enjoy short ribs, which are best prepared low and slow in a flavorful sauce. I also love salt potatoes, so I combined the two with an Italian twist. My family was wowed!

—**DEVON DELANEY** WESTPORT, CT

PREP: 40 MIN. • **COOK:** 6 HOURS
MAKES: 8 SERVINGS

- **6 thick slices pancetta or thick-sliced bacon, chopped**
- **6 pounds bone-in beef short ribs**
- **1 teaspoon plus 1 cup kosher salt, divided**
- **1 teaspoon pepper**
- **1 tablespoon olive oil**
- **3 medium carrots, chopped**
- **1 medium red onion, chopped**
- **1 cup beef broth**
- **1 cup dry red wine**
- **¼ cup honey**
- **¼ cup balsamic vinegar**
- **1 tablespoon minced fresh thyme or 1 teaspoon dried thyme**
- **2 teaspoons minced fresh oregano or ¾ teaspoon dried oregano**
- **2 garlic cloves, minced**
- **2 pounds small red potatoes**
- **4 teaspoons cornstarch**
- **3 tablespoons cold water**

1. In a large skillet, cook pancetta over medium heat until crisp, stirring occasionally. Remove with a slotted spoon; drain on paper towels.
2. Meanwhile, sprinkle ribs with 1 teaspoon salt and pepper. In another large skillet, heat oil over medium high heat. In batches, brown the ribs on all sides; transfer to a 4- or 5-qt. slow cooker. To the same skillet, add carrots and onion; cook and stir over medium heat 2-4 minutes or until crisp-tender. Add broth, wine, honey and vinegar, stirring to loosen browned bits from pan. Transfer to the slow cooker; add pancetta, herbs and garlic.
3. Cook, covered, on low for 6-8 hours or until meat is tender. In the last hour of cooking, place potatoes in a 6-qt. stockpot and cover with water. Add the remaining salt. Cover and bring to a boil over medium-high heat; stir to dissolve the salt. Cook 15-30 minutes or until tender. Drain well.
4. Remove ribs to a serving platter; keep warm. Strain cooking juices into a small saucepan; skim fat. Add vegetables and pancetta to platter. Bring juices to a boil. In a small bowl, mix cornstarch and water until smooth; stir into cooking juices. Return to a boil; cook and stir 1-2 minutes or until thickened. Serve with ribs and vegetables.

CRANBERRY MEATBALLS

Whether you serve them as appetizers or the main course, these tasty meatballs are sure to be popular. Cranberry and chili sauces give them extra sweetness.

—**NINA HALL** SPOKANE, WA

PREP: 20 MIN. • **COOK:** 6 HOURS
MAKES: 6 SERVINGS

- **2 large eggs, beaten**
- **1 cup dry bread crumbs**
- **⅓ cup minced fresh parsley**
- **2 tablespoons finely chopped onion**
- **1½ pounds lean ground beef (90% lean)**
- **1 can (14 ounces) jellied cranberry sauce**
- **1 bottle (12 ounces) chili sauce**
- **⅓ cup ketchup**
- **2 tablespoons brown sugar**
- **1 tablespoon lemon juice**

1. In a large bowl, combine eggs, bread crumbs, parsley and onion. Crumble beef over the bread crumb mixture and mix well. Shape into 1½-in. balls. Place in a 3-qt.slow cooker.
2. In another bowl, combine cranberry sauce, chili sauce, ketchup, brown sugar and lemon juice. Pour over the meatballs. Cover and cook on low for 6-7 hours or until the meat is no longer pink.

SHORT RIBS WITH SALT-SKIN POTATOES

THAI COCONUT BEEF
Ashley Lecker
Green Bay, WI

THAI COCONUT BEEF

My husband and I love Thai food, but going out on weeknights can be challenging with our busy schedules. I wanted to create a Thai-inspired dinner that could double as an easy lunch the following day. The beef is fantastic in this dish, but chicken or pork would be equally delicious!

—**ASHLEY LECKER** GREEN BAY, WI

PREP: 30 MIN. • **COOK:** 7¾ HOURS
MAKES: 10 SERVINGS

- **1 boneless beef chuck roast (3 pounds), halved**
- **1 teaspoon salt**
- **1 teaspoon pepper**
- **1 large sweet red pepper, sliced**
- **1 can (13.66 ounces) coconut milk**
- **¾ cup beef stock**
- **½ cup creamy peanut butter**
- **¼ cup red curry paste**
- **2 tablespoons soy sauce**
- **2 tablespoons honey**
- **2 teaspoons minced fresh gingerroot**
- **½ pound fresh sugar snap peas, trimmed**
- **¼ cup minced fresh cilantro**
- **Hot cooked brown or white rice**
- **Optional toppings: thinly sliced green onions, chopped peanuts, hot sauce and lime wedges**

1. Sprinkle beef with salt and pepper. Place beef and pepper slices in a 5-qt. slow cooker. In a bowl, whisk coconut milk, beef stock, peanut butter, curry paste, soy sauce, honey and ginger; pour over meat. Cook, covered, on low 7-8 hours or until the meat is tender.
2. Remove beef; cool slightly. Skim fat from the reserved juices. Shred beef with two forks. Return the meat to slow cooker; stir in snap peas. Cook, covered, on low 45-60 minutes longer or until the peas are crisp-tender. Stir in cilantro. Serve with rice and, if desired, toppings of your choice.

To freeze: Place the cooled meat mixture in freezer containers. To use, partially thaw in refrigerator overnight. Microwave, covered, on high in a microwave-safe dish until heated through, gently stirring and adding a little broth or water if necessary.

SLOW COOKER BEEF TIPS

These slow-cooked beef tips remind me of a favorite childhood dish. I cook them with mushrooms and serve over brown rice, noodles or mashed potatoes.

—**AMY LENTS** GRAND FORKS, ND

PREP: 25 MIN. • **COOK:** 6¼ HOURS
MAKES: 4 SERVINGS

- **½ pound sliced baby portobello mushrooms**
- **1 small onion, halved and sliced**
- **1 beef top sirloin steak (1 pound), cubed**
- **½ teaspoon salt**
- **¼ teaspoon pepper**
- **2 teaspoons olive oil**
- **⅓ cup dry red wine or beef broth**
- **2 cups beef broth**
- **1 tablespoon Worcestershire sauce**
- **2 tablespoons cornstarch**
- **¼ cup cold water**
- **Hot cooked mashed potatoes**

1. Place mushrooms and onion in a 3-qt. slow cooker. Sprinkle beef with salt and pepper. In a large skillet, heat 1 teaspoon oil over medium-high heat; brown the beef in batches, adding additional oil as needed. Transfer beef to slow cooker.
2. Add wine to skillet, stirring to loosen browned bits from pan. Stir in broth and Worcestershire sauce; pour over the beef. Cook, covered, on low 6-8 hours or until the meat is tender.
3. In a small bowl, mix cornstarch and cold water until smooth; gradually stir into the slow cooker. Cook, covered, on high 15-30 minutes or until the gravy is thickened. Serve with mashed potatoes.

TEST KITCHEN TIP

Beef tips often come precut; they are usually from either the sirloin or the tenderloin. For recipes that require long, low slow cooking (such as a slow cooker recipe), stew meat is a more budget-friendly alternative to sirloin; the cooking method will ensure that the meat is tender.

FAST FIX

SLOW COOKER MEATBALL SANDWICHES

Our approach to meatball sandwiches is a simple one—cook the meatballs low and slow, load them into hoagie buns, and top with provolone cheese and pepperoncini.

—**STACIE NICHOLLS** SPRING CREEK, NV

PREP: 5 MIN. • **COOK:** 3 HOURS
MAKES: 8 SERVINGS

- **2 packages (12 ounces each) frozen fully cooked Italian meatballs, thawed**
- **2 jars (24 ounces each) marinara sauce**
- **8 hoagie buns, split**
- **8 slices provolone cheese**
- **Sliced pepperoncini, optional**

1. Place meatballs and sauce in a 3- or 4-qt. slow cooker. Cook, covered, on low 3-4 hours until meatballs are heated through.
2. On each bun bottom, layer meatballs, cheese and, if desired, pepperoncini; replace tops.

SPECIAL SAUERBRATEN

After simmering in the slow cooker for hours, this rump roast is fork tender and has taken on the flavors of the sauce. I serve it with mashed potatoes and corn.

—**LAURA EHLERS** LAFAYETTE, IN

PREP: 25 MIN. • **COOK:** 6 HOURS
MAKES: 6 SERVINGS

- **1 beef rump roast or bottom round roast (3 to 4 pounds), cut in half**
- **1 tablespoon olive oil**
- **1½ cups cider vinegar**
- **1 medium onion, chopped**
- **⅔ cup packed brown sugar**
- **1 envelope onion soup mix**
- **⅓ cup shredded carrot**
- **2 tablespoons beef bouillon granules**
- **1 tablespoon Worcestershire sauce**
- **1 bay leaf**
- **1 garlic clove, minced**
- **1 teaspoon salt**
- **1 teaspoon celery seed**
- **1 teaspoon ground ginger**
- **½ teaspoon mixed pickling spices**
- **¼ teaspoon ground allspice**
- **¼ teaspoon pepper**
- **¼ cup cornstarch**
- **½ cup water**

1. In a large skillet, brown meat in oil on all sides. Transfer meat and drippings to a 5-qt. slow cooker. In a large bowl, combine the vinegar, onion, sugar, soup mix, carrot, bouillon, Worcestershire sauce and seasonings; pour over roast. Cover and cook on low for 6-8 hours or until tender.
2. Remove meat to a serving platter; keep warm. Strain cooking juices, discarding the vegetables and seasonings.
3. Skim fat from the cooking juices; transfer to a large saucepan. Bring to a boil. Combine cornstarch and water until smooth; gradually stir into the pan. Bring to a boil; cook and stir for 2 minutes or until thickened. Serve with beef.

FAST FIX

SMOKY BEEF & BEANS

Here's a thick and hearty side dish that's sure to be popular. Serve it with a crisp salad and your favorite grilled fare for an awesome picnic!

—**ANITA CURTIS** CAMARILLO, CA

PREP: 10 MIN. • **COOK:** 6 HOURS
MAKES: 8 SERVINGS

- **1 pound ground beef**
- **1 cup chopped onion**
- **12 bacon strips, cooked and crumbled**
- **2 cans (16 ounces each) pork and beans**
- **1 can (16 ounces) kidney beans, rinsed and drained**
- **1 can (16 ounces) butter beans, drained**
- **1 cup ketchup**
- **¼ cup packed brown sugar**
- **3 tablespoons white vinegar**
- **1 teaspoon Liquid Smoke, optional**
- **½ teaspoon salt**
- **¼ teaspoon pepper**

In a skillet, cook the beef and onion until the meat is no longer pink; drain. Transfer to a 3-qt. slow cooker. Stir in the remaining ingredients. Cover and cook on low for 6-7 hours or until heated through.

SLOW COOKER BEEF TIPS BURGUNDY

Here's a heartwarming classic made simple in the slow cooker. Mushrooms, red wine and tender beef make an easy, elegant supper.

—**DEANNA ZEWEN** UNION GROVE, WI

PREP: 15 MIN. • **COOK:** 6¾ HOURS
MAKES: 10 SERVINGS

- **1 boneless beef chuck roast (3 pounds), trimmed and cut into 1-in. pieces**
- **2 medium onions, halved and sliced**
- **½ pound sliced fresh mushrooms**
- **4 garlic cloves, minced**
- **3 cups beef stock**
- **½ cup dry red wine or additional beef stock**
- **2 tablespoons Worcestershire sauce**
- **2 tablespoons red wine vinegar**
- **1¼ teaspoons salt**
- **1 teaspoon crushed red pepper flakes**
- **½ teaspoon pepper**
- **⅓ cup cornstarch**
- **⅓ cup cold water**
- **Hot cooked egg noodles**
- **Minced fresh parsley**

1. In a 5-qt. slow cooker, combine beef, onions, mushrooms and garlic. In a small bowl, mix the next seven ingredients; pour over beef mixture. Cook, covered, on low until the meat is tender, for 6-8 hours.

2. Skim fat from the juices. In a small bowl, mix cornstarch and water until smooth; gradually stir into the slow cooker. Cook, covered, on high until thickened, about 45 minutes. Serve with noodles; sprinkle with parsley.

To freeze: Omit parsley; freeze the cooled meat mixture, sauce and noodles in freezer containers. To use, partially thaw in refrigerator overnight. Microwave, covered, on high until heated through, stirring gently and adding a little water if necessary. Sprinkle with parsley.

STUFFED CABBAGE CASSEROLE

I love cabbage rolls but don't always have time to prepare them, so I created this easy recipe. It uses the traditional ingredients and delivers the same great taste.

—**JOANN ALEXANDER** CENTER, TX

PREP: 20 MIN. • **COOK:** 4 HOURS • **MAKES:** 6 SERVINGS

- 1 pound ground beef
- ⅓ cup chopped onion
- 4 cups chopped cabbage
- 1 medium green pepper, chopped
- 1 cup uncooked instant rice
- 1 cup water
- 1 can (6 ounces) tomato paste
- 1 can (14½ ounces) diced tomatoes, undrained
- ½ cup ketchup
- 2 tablespoons cider vinegar
- 1 to 2 tablespoons sugar, optional
- 1 tablespoon Worcestershire sauce
- 1 teaspoon salt
- ½ teaspoon pepper
- ¼ teaspoon garlic powder

1. In a large skillet, cook beef and onion over medium heat until the meat is no longer pink; drain. Transfer to a 5-qt. slow cooker; add cabbage, green pepper and rice.
2. In a large bowl, combine water and tomato paste. Stir in the remaining ingredients. Pour over beef mixture; mix well. Cover and cook on low for 4-5 hours or until rice and vegetables are tender.

★★★★★ **READER REVIEW**

"This recipe was outstanding! Reminded me of my mother's stuffed cabbage rolls I would beg her to make as a child."

SUZY425 TASTEOFHOME.COM

MEAT LOAF WITH CHILI SAUCE

I used to serve this meat loaf recipe in my cafe. Everyone asked for it. I adapted it for home with my slow cooker, where it's quite popular, too.

—**ROBERT COX** LAS CRUCES, NM

PREP: 20 MIN. • **COOK:** 3 HOURS + STANDING
MAKES: 8 SERVINGS

- 1 large onion, finely chopped
- ½ cup seasoned bread crumbs
- 1 small green pepper, chopped
- 2 large eggs, lightly beaten
- ½ cup chili sauce
- 2 tablespoons spicy brown mustard
- 3 to 4 garlic cloves, minced
- ¾ teaspoon salt
- ¼ teaspoon dried oregano
- ¼ teaspoon dried basil
- 2 pounds lean ground beef (90% lean)
- Additional chili sauce, optional

1. Cut four 20x3-in. strips of heavy-duty foil; crisscross so they resemble spokes of a wheel. Place strips on the bottom and up the sides of a 5-qt. slow cooker. Coat strips with cooking spray.
2. In a large bowl, combine the first 10 ingredients. Add beef; mix lightly but thoroughly. Shape into a 9-in. round loaf. Place loaf in center of strips in slow cooker.
3. Cook, covered, on low for 3-4 hours or until a thermometer reads at least 160°. If desired, spoon additional chili sauce over meat loaf; let stand for 10 minutes. Using the foil strips as handles, remove meat loaf to a platter.

To freeze: Cover and freeze leftover meat loaf slices in a greased 2-qt. shallow baking dish. To use, partially thaw in refrigerator overnight. Remove from refrigerator 30 minutes before baking. Preheat oven to 350°. Reheat meat slices, covered, until a thermometer inserted in center reads 165°.

MEAT LOAF WITH CHILI SAUCE

MEATBALLS IN HONEY BUFFALO SAUCE

MEATBALLS IN HONEY BUFFALO SAUCE

My family loves the sweet and spicy combination in this recipe and declared it an instant favorite just for that reason. The meatballs start sweet but finish with a little heat!

—**ANNE ORMOND** DOVER, NH

PREP: 45 MIN. • **COOK:** 2 HOURS
MAKES: ABOUT 2½ DOZEN

- 2 large eggs, lightly beaten
- 15 Ritz crackers, crushed
- ½ medium onion, finely chopped
- ¼ cup 2% milk
- 4 teaspoons brown sugar
- ½ teaspoon garlic powder
- ½ teaspoon ground chipotle pepper
- ¼ teaspoon smoked paprika
- ¼ teaspoon salt
- ⅛ teaspoon pepper
- ½ pound ground beef
- ½ pound ground pork
- ½ pound ground veal

SAUCE

- ½ cup honey
- ¼ cup Buffalo wing sauce
- ¼ cup packed brown sugar
- 2 tablespoons orange marmalade
- 2 tablespoons apricot spreadable fruit
- 2 tablespoons reduced-sodium soy sauce
- ¼ teaspoon crushed red pepper flakes
- Hot cooked rice or pasta
- Sliced celery, optional

1. Preheat oven to 400°. Combine the first 10 ingredients. Add the meat; mix lightly but thoroughly. Shape meat mixture into 1½-in. balls; bake on a greased rack in a 15x10x1-in. baking pan lined with foil until lightly browned, 12-15 minutes. Meanwhile, in a small saucepan over medium heat, whisk together the sauce ingredients until the brown sugar is dissolved.
2. Transfer meatballs to a 3-qt. slow cooker; add sauce. Cook, covered, on low until meatballs are cooked through, about 2 hours. Serve with hot cooked rice or pasta and, if desired, sliced celery.

To freeze: Freeze the cooled meatballs and sauce in freezer containers. To use, partially thaw in the refrigerator overnight. Heat through in a covered saucepan, stirring gently and adding a little water or broth if necessary. Serve as directed.

FAST FIX

ITALIAN BOW TIE SUPPER

For a family-pleasing Italian dinner, you can't go wrong with this all-in-one meal featuring bow tie pasta. Any leftovers taste just as good the next day.

—**JOY FREY** KELSO, MO

PREP: 10 MIN. • **COOK:** 7¼ HOURS
MAKES: 6 SERVINGS

- 1½ pounds ground beef
- 1 medium onion, chopped
- 1 garlic clove, minced
- 2 cans (8 ounces each) tomato sauce
- 1 can (14½ ounces) stewed tomatoes, chopped
- 1 teaspoon dried oregano
- 1 teaspoon Italian seasoning
- Salt and pepper to taste
- 1 package (16 ounces) bow tie pasta, cooked and drained
- 1 package (10 ounces) frozen chopped spinach, thawed and squeezed dry
- 1½ cups shredded part-skim mozzarella cheese
- ½ cup grated Parmesan cheese

1. In a large skillet, cook the beef and onion over medium heat until the meat is no longer pink. Add garlic; cook 1 minute longer. Drain.
2. Transfer to a 3-qt. slow cooker. Stir in tomato sauce, tomatoes and seasonings. Cover and cook on low for 7-8 hours or until bubbly.
3. Increase heat to high; stir in pasta, spinach and cheeses. Cover and cook 10 minutes longer or until heated through and the cheese is melted.

CUBED STEAKS WITH GRAVY

Here's a hearty, home-style dinner your family will love after a busy day. The slow-cooked beef is wonderful served over mashed potatoes or noodles.

—**JUDY LONG** LIMESTONE, TN

PREP: 15 MIN. • **COOK:** 8½ HOURS
MAKES: 6 SERVINGS

- ⅓ cup all-purpose flour
- 6 beef cube steaks (4 ounces each)
- 1 tablespoon canola oil
- 1 large onion, sliced and separated into rings
- 3 cups water, divided
- 1 envelope brown gravy mix
- 1 envelope mushroom gravy mix
- 1 envelope onion gravy mix
- Hot mashed potatoes or cooked noodles

1. Place flour in a large resealable plastic bag. Add the steaks, a few at a time, and shake until completely coated.
2. In a skillet, cook the steaks in oil until lightly browned on each side. Transfer to a 3-qt. slow cooker. Add onion and 2 cups water. Cover and cook on low for 8 hours or until meat is tender.
3. In a bowl, whisk together gravy mixes with the remaining water. Add to the slow cooker; cook 30 minutes longer. Serve over mashed potatoes or noodles.

MEATY SUN-DRIED TOMATO SAUCE

Marinated artichokes, celery and sweet green pepper are wonderful additions to this hearty spaghetti sauce. Don't be afraid of leftovers—this tangy sauce is even better the next day.

—**AYSHA SCHURMAN** AMMON, ID

PREP: 35 MIN. • **COOK:** 8 HOURS
MAKES: 12 SERVINGS (2¼ QUARTS)

- 1 pound bulk Italian sausage
- ½ pound ground beef
- 1 medium red onion, chopped
- 1 medium green pepper, chopped
- 2 celery ribs, chopped
- 3 garlic cloves, minced
- 3 cans (14½ ounces each) diced tomatoes
- 1 can (6 ounces) Italian tomato paste
- 1 jar (7½ ounces) marinated quartered artichoke hearts, drained and chopped
- 1 cup sun-dried tomatoes (not packed in oil), chopped
- 3 tablespoons minced fresh parsley
- 1½ teaspoons minced fresh rosemary or ½ teaspoon dried rosemary, crushed
- 1 bay leaf
- 1 teaspoon pepper
- ½ teaspoon salt

1. In a large skillet, cook the sausage, beef, onion, green pepper, celery and garlic over medium heat until the meat is no longer pink; drain. Transfer to a 4-qt. slow cooker.
2. Stir in the remaining ingredients. Cover and cook on low for 8-10 hours. Discard the bay leaf.

CINCINNATI CHILI DOGS

CINCINNATI CHILI DOGS

My in-laws are from Ohio, so we have Cincinnati chili at many of our family gatherings. I spiced up this family classic with cinnamon and cocoa powder and ladled it over hot dogs. It's perfect for game day, tailgates and potlucks.

—**JENNIFER GILBERT** BRIGHTON, MI

PREP: 20 MIN. • **COOK:** 4 HOURS
MAKES: 10 SERVINGS

- **1½ pounds ground beef**
- **2 small yellow onions, chopped and divided**
- **2 cans (15 ounces each) tomato sauce**
- **1½ teaspoons baking cocoa**
- **½ teaspoon ground cinnamon**
- **¼ teaspoon chili powder**
- **¼ teaspoon paprika**
- **¼ teaspoon garlic powder**
- **2 tablespoons Worcestershire sauce**
- **1 tablespoon cider vinegar**
- **10 hot dogs**
- **10 hot dog buns, split**
- **Shredded cheddar cheese**

1. In a large skillet over medium heat, cook and stir ground beef, crumbling meat, until no longer pink; drain.
2. In a 3-qt. slow cooker, combine the beef with one chopped onion; add the next eight ingredients. Cook, covered, on low for about 2 hours; add hot dogs. Continue cooking, covered, on low until heated through, about 2 hours longer.
3. Serve on buns; top with shredded cheese and the remaining chopped onion.

SPICE-BRAISED POT ROAST

SPICE-BRAISED POT ROAST

Just pour these ingredients over your pot roast and let the slow cooker do the work. Herbs and spices give the beef an excellent taste. I serve this roast over noodles or mashed potatoes, using the juices as a gravy.

—**LOREN MARTIN** BIG CABIN, OK

PREP: 15 MIN. • **COOK:** 7 HOURS
MAKES: 8 SERVINGS

- **1 boneless beef chuck roast (2½ pounds)**
- **1 can (14½ ounces) diced tomatoes, undrained**
- **1 medium onion, chopped**
- **¼ cup white vinegar**
- **3 tablespoons tomato puree**
- **1 tablespoon poppy seeds**
- **1 bay leaf**
- **2¼ teaspoons sugar**
- **2 teaspoons Dijon mustard**
- **2 garlic cloves, minced**
- **½ teaspoon salt**
- **½ teaspoon ground ginger**
- **½ teaspoon dried rosemary, crushed**
- **½ teaspoon lemon juice**
- **¼ teaspoon ground cumin**
- **¼ teaspoon ground turmeric**
- **¼ teaspoon crushed red pepper flakes**
- **⅛ teaspoon ground cloves**
- **Hot cooked egg noodles**

1. Place roast in a 5-qt. slow cooker. Mix all the remaining ingredients except noodles; pour over the roast. Cook, covered, on low until the meat is tender, 7-9 hours.
2. Discard the bay leaf. If desired, skim fat and thicken the cooking juices. Serve pot roast with noodles and juices.

VERY BEST BARBECUE BEEF SANDWICHES

These sweet and tangy barbecue beef sandwiches definitely live up to their name. Friends will want the recipe—they're that good.

—TASTE OF HOME **TEST KITCHEN**

PREP: 20 MIN. • **COOK:** 8 HOURS
MAKES: 12 SERVINGS

- **1 boneless beef chuck roast (3 to 4 pounds)**
- **1½ cups ketchup**
- **1 small onion, finely chopped**
- **¼ cup packed brown sugar**
- **¼ cup red wine vinegar**
- **1 tablespoon Dijon mustard**
- **1 tablespoon Worcestershire sauce**
- **2 garlic cloves, minced**
- **½ teaspoon salt**
- **¼ teaspoon celery seed**
- **¼ teaspoon paprika**
- **¼ teaspoon pepper**
- **2 tablespoons cornstarch**
- **2 tablespoons cold water**
- **12 kaiser rolls, split**
- **Dill pickle slices, optional**

1. Cut roast in half. Place in a 5-qt. slow cooker. In a small bowl, combine ketchup, onion, brown sugar, vinegar, mustard, Worcestershire sauce, garlic, salt, celery seed, paprika and pepper; pour over roast. Cover and cook on low for 8-10 hours or until the meat is tender.
2. Remove the beef. Skim fat from the cooking juices; transfer to a large saucepan. Bring to a boil. Combine cornstarch and water until smooth, then gradually stir into the juices. Return to a boil; cook and stir for 2 minutes or until thickened.
3. When beef is cool enough to handle, shred with two forks. Return meat to the slow cooker and stir in the sauce mixture; heat through. Serve on rolls with pickle slices if desired.

SLOW-COOKED TEX-MEX FLANK STEAK

This flavorful, tender beef dish has been a go-to recipe for many years; it's a lifesaver on days when I'm going to be late getting home.

—**ANNE MERRILL** CROGHAN, NY

PREP: 20 MIN. • **COOK:** 6 HOURS • **MAKES:** 4 SERVINGS

- **1 tablespoon canola oil**
- **1 beef flank steak (1½ pounds)**
- **1 large onion, sliced**
- **⅓ cup water**
- **1 can (4 ounces) chopped green chilies**
- **2 tablespoons cider vinegar**
- **2 to 3 teaspoons chili powder**
- **1 teaspoon garlic powder**
- **1 teaspoon sugar**
- **½ teaspoon salt**
- **⅛ teaspoon pepper**

1. In a large skillet, heat oil over medium-high heat; brown steak on both sides. Transfer to a 3-qt. slow cooker.
2. Add onion to same skillet; cook and stir for 1-2 minutes or until crisp-tender. Add water; cook 30 seconds, stirring to loosen browned bits from pan. Stir in the remaining ingredients; return to a boil. Pour over the steak.
3. Cook, covered, on low for 6-8 hours or until the meat is tender. Slice steak across the grain; serve with the onion mixture.

ZESTY ORANGE BEEF

I put this recipe together in the morning before I leave for work. In the evening, the aroma hits me as soon as I open the door. All I have to do is cook some rice, and dinner is served.

—**DEBORAH PUETTE** LILBURN, GA

PREP: 15 MIN. • **COOK:** 5 HOURS • **MAKES:** 5 SERVINGS

- **1 beef top sirloin steak (1½ pounds), cut into ¼-inch strips**
- **2½ cups sliced fresh shiitake mushrooms**
- **1 medium onion, cut into wedges**
- **3 dried hot chilies**
- **¼ cup packed brown sugar**
- **¼ cup orange juice**
- **¼ cup reduced-sodium soy sauce**
- **3 tablespoons cider vinegar**
- **1 tablespoon cornstarch**
- **1 tablespoon minced fresh gingerroot**
- **1 tablespoon sesame oil**
- **2 garlic cloves, minced**
- **1¾ cups fresh snow peas**
- **1 tablespoon grated orange peel**
- **Hot cooked rice**

1. Place beef in a 4-qt. slow cooker. Add the mushrooms, onion and chilies. In a small bowl, combine brown sugar, orange juice, soy sauce, vinegar, cornstarch, ginger, oil and garlic. Pour over the beef.
2. Cover and cook on high for 5-6 hours or until the meat is tender, adding snow peas during the last 30 minutes of cooking. Stir in orange peel. Serve with rice.

ZESTY ORANGE BEEF
Deborah Puette
Lilburn, GA

BARBACOA

BARBACOA

My husband adores this roast simmered in lime juice, chipotle and cumin. I serve it over rice flavored with cilantro and more zippy lime.
—**AUNDREA MCCORMICK** DENVER, CO

PREP: 45 MIN. • **COOK:** 7 HOURS • **MAKES:** 8 SERVINGS

- ¼ **cup lime juice**
- ¼ **cup cider vinegar**
- 3 **chipotle peppers in adobo sauce**
- 4 **garlic cloves, thinly sliced**
- 4 **teaspoons ground cumin**
- 3 **teaspoons dried oregano**
- 1½ **teaspoons pepper**
- ¾ **teaspoon salt**
- ½ **teaspoon ground cloves**
- 1 **cup reduced-sodium chicken broth**
- 1 **boneless beef chuck roast (3 to 4 pounds)**
- 3 **bay leaves**

RICE

- 3 **cups water**
- 2 **cups uncooked jasmine rice**
- 3 **tablespoons butter**
- 1½ **teaspoons salt**
- ½ **cup minced fresh cilantro**
- 2 **tablespoons lime juice**

1. Place the first nine ingredients in a blender; cover and process until smooth. Add broth; pulse to combine.
2. Place roast and bay leaves in a 4- or 5-qt. slow cooker; pour the sauce over top. Cook, covered, on low 7-9 hours or until the meat is tender.
3. Prepare rice about 30 minutes before serving. Rinse and drain the uncooked rice. In a large saucepan, combine water, rice, butter and salt; bring to a boil. Reduce heat; simmer, covered, for 12-15 minutes or until liquid is absorbed and the rice is tender. Remove from heat; gently stir in cilantro and lime juice.
4. Remove the roast from the slow cooker; cool slightly. Discard the bay leaves and skim fat from cooking juices. Shred the beef with two forks; return meat to slow cooker. Serve with rice.

SLOW COOKER JERKED SHORT RIBS

Sweet and spicy jerk seasonings give these saucy ribs an unforgettable taste! They're great in the summer because they don't heat up the kitchen.

—**SUSAN HEIN** BURLINGTON, WI

PREP: 15 MIN. • **COOK:** 6 HOURS
MAKES: 10 SERVINGS

- 1 tablespoon ground coriander
- 2 teaspoons ground ginger
- 2 teaspoons onion powder
- 2 teaspoons garlic powder
- 1 teaspoon salt
- 1 teaspoon pepper
- 1 teaspoon dried thyme
- ¾ teaspoon ground allspice
- ¾ teaspoon ground nutmeg
- ½ teaspoon ground cinnamon
- 10 bone-in beef short ribs (about 5 pounds)
- 1 large sweet onion, chopped
- ½ cup beef broth
- 1 jar (10 ounces) apricot preserves
- 3 tablespoons cider vinegar
- 3 garlic cloves, minced

1. Combine the first 10 ingredients, reserving 2 tablespoons. Rub the remaining seasoning mixture over ribs. Place the onion and broth in a 6-qt. slow cooker; cover with ribs. Cook, covered, on low until the ribs are tender, 6-8 hours.
2. Meanwhile, combine preserves, vinegar, garlic and reserved seasoning mixture. Serve with ribs.

FAVORITE ITALIAN BEEF SANDWICHES

I'm a paramedic/firefighter, and slow-cooked recipes like this one suit my unpredictable schedule. My husband and children and the hungry bunch at the firehouse love these robust sandwiches that have a little zip.

—**KRIS SWIHART** PERRYSBURG, OH

PREP: 20 MIN. • **COOK:** 8 HOURS
MAKES: 12 SERVINGS

- 1 jar (11½ ounces) pepperoncini
- 1 boneless beef chuck roast (3½ to 4 pounds)
- ¼ cup water
- 1¾ teaspoons dried basil
- 1½ teaspoons garlic powder
- 1½ teaspoons dried oregano
- 1¼ teaspoons salt
- ¼ teaspoon pepper
- 1 large onion, sliced and quartered
- 12 hard rolls, split

1. Drain the pepperoncini, reserving liquid. Remove and discard stems of the peppers; set the peppers aside. Cut roast into large chunks; place a third of the meat in a 5-qt. slow cooker. Add water.
2. In a small bowl, combine seasonings; sprinkle half over the beef. Layer with half of the remaining meat, then the onion and pepperoncini. Pour the pepperoncini liquid over the top. Add the remaining meat to slow cooker; sprinkle with the remaining seasonings.
3. Cover and cook on low for 8-9 hours or until the beef is tender. Shred meat with two forks. Using a slotted spoon, serve beef and peppers on rolls.

Note: Look for pepperoncini (pickled peppers) in the pickle and olive section of your grocery store.

BEEF BRISKET TACOS

BEEF BRISKET TACOS

Birthday parties back home were big gatherings of cousins, aunts, uncles, grandparents and anyone considered family. As soon as guests arrived, pans of shredded brisket, or carne deshebrada, appeared, with huge bowls of salads, frijoles, tostadas and salsas. Brisket also showed up at quinceaneras, baptisms, and bridal and baby showers. It was the dish we counted on because it could be made in the oven or a slow cooker.

—**YVETTE MARQUEZ** LITTLETON, CO

PREP: 15 MIN. + MARINATING • **COOK:** 8 HOURS
MAKES: 10 SERVINGS

- **1 bottle (12 ounces) beer or nonalcoholic beer**
- **1 cup brisket marinade sauce or liquid smoke plus 1 tablespoon salt**
- **2 bay leaves**
- **½ teaspoon salt**
- **½ teaspoon pepper**
- **1 fresh beef brisket (3 to 4 pounds), fat trimmed**
- **20 corn tortillas (6 inches), warmed**
- **Shredded cheddar cheese, media crema table cream, fresh cilantro leaves, thinly sliced green onions, avocado slices and salsa, optional**

1. In a large resealable plastic bag, combine the first five ingredients. Add brisket; seal bag and turn to coat. Refrigerate overnight.
2. Transfer brisket and marinade to a 6-qt. slow cooker. Cook, covered, on low until tender, 8-10 hours. Remove meat; discard bay leaves. Reserve juices in slow cooker. When cool enough to handle, shred meat with two forks. Return to slow cooker.
3. Using tongs, serve shredded brisket in tortillas. Add toppings as desired.

To freeze: Freeze cooled meat mixture and juices in freezer containers. To use, partially thaw in refrigerator overnight. Heat through in a saucepan, stirring occasionally.

BRAISED SHORT RIBS

I've been relying on this recipe ever since I bought my first slow cooker some 19 years ago. The fall-off-the-bone-tender ribs are so good to come home to after a busy day.

—**PEGGY EDWARDS** HEBER CITY, UT

PREP: 20 MIN. • **COOK:** 6 HOURS
MAKES: 7 SERVINGS

- **½ cup all-purpose flour**
- **1½ teaspoons salt**
- **1½ teaspoons paprika**
- **½ teaspoon ground mustard**
- **4 pounds bone-in beef short ribs**
- **2 tablespoons canola oil**
- **2 medium onions, sliced**
- **1 cup beer or beef broth**
- **1 garlic clove, minced**

GRAVY

- **2 teaspoons all-purpose flour**
- **1 tablespoon cold water**

1. In a large resealable plastic bag, combine the flour, salt, paprika and mustard. Add ribs in batches and shake to coat. In a large skillet, brown the ribs in oil; drain.
2. Place onions in a 5-qt. slow cooker; add the ribs. Top with beer and garlic. Cover and cook on low for 6-7 hours or until the meat is tender.
3. Remove ribs and onions to a serving platter; keep warm. Skim the fat from the cooking juices; transfer to a small saucepan. Bring to a boil. Combine flour and water until smooth; gradually stir into the pan. Bring to a boil; cook and stir for 2 minutes or until thickened. Serve with ribs.

GINGERED SHORT RIBS WITH GREEN RICE

I love Korean cooking and converted this recipe to give it slow cooker convenience.

—**LILY JULOW** LAWRENCEVILLE, GA

PREP: 35 MIN. • **COOK:** 8 HOURS
MAKES: 6 SERVINGS

- ½ cup reduced-sodium beef broth
- ⅓ cup sherry or additional reduced-sodium beef broth
- ¼ cup reduced-sodium soy sauce
- 3 tablespoons honey
- 1 tablespoon rice vinegar
- 1 tablespoon minced fresh gingerroot
- 3 garlic cloves, minced
- 4 medium carrots, chopped
- 2 medium onions, chopped
- 3 pounds bone-in beef short ribs
- ½ teaspoon salt
- ½ teaspoon pepper
- 3 cups uncooked instant brown rice
- 3 green onions, thinly sliced
- 3 tablespoons minced fresh cilantro
- 2 tablespoons chopped pickled jalapenos
- ¾ teaspoon grated lime peel
- 1 tablespoon cornstarch
- 1 tablespoon cold water

1. In a small bowl, whisk the first seven ingredients until blended. Place carrots and onions in a 5-qt. slow cooker. Sprinkle ribs with salt and pepper; place over the vegetables. Pour the broth mixture over top. Cook, covered, on low 8-10 hours or until the meat is tender.
2. Just before serving, prepare rice according to package directions. Stir in green onions, cilantro, jalapenos and lime peel.
3. Remove ribs to a serving plate; keep warm. Transfer cooking juices to a small saucepan; skim fat. Bring juices to a boil. Mix cornstarch and water until smooth; stir into the cooking juices. Return to a boil; cook and stir 2 minutes or until thickened. Serve with ribs and rice.

SPRING HERB ROAST

This is a wonderful roast that you can forget about while it's cooking (though the aroma is sure to remind you). It's great served with brown rice or mashed potatoes.

—**DONNA ROBERTS** MANHATTAN, KS

PREP: 20 MIN. • **COOK:** 4 HOURS + STANDING
MAKES: 8 SERVINGS

- 2 large onions, halved and sliced (about 3 cups)
- ½ pound sliced fresh mushrooms
- 1 beef rump roast or bottom round roast (3 to 4 pounds)
- 2 teaspoons salt
- ½ teaspoon pepper
- 1 tablespoon canola oil
- 1½ cups water
- 2 tablespoons tomato paste
- 3 garlic cloves, minced
- ½ teaspoon each dried basil, marjoram and thyme
- Minced fresh parsley

1. Place onions and mushrooms in a 5- or 6-qt. slow cooker. Sprinkle roast with salt and pepper. In a large skillet, heat oil over medium-high heat; brown roast on all sides. Transfer to slow cooker.
2. In a small bowl, mix water, tomato paste, garlic, basil, marjoram and thyme; pour over roast. Cook, covered, on low for 4-5 hours or until meat is tender (a thermometer should read at least 145°).
3. Remove roast from the slow cooker; tent with foil. Let stand for 15 minutes before slicing. Serve with the onion mixture; sprinkle with parsley.

TEST KITCHEN TIP

To clean mushrooms, gently remove dirt by rubbing with a mushroom brush or a damp paper towel. Do not peel mushrooms. Trim stems. For shiitake mushrooms, remove and discard stems. For enoki, trim base and separate stems.

SPRING HERB ROAST

FRESH SPINACH TAMALE PIE
Nancy Heishman
Las Vegas, NV

FRESH SPINACH TAMALE PIE

I got this recipe from my mother, who loved quick and easy meals. I made a few variations by adding spinach, bell peppers and fresh corn. The changes were well worth it—my family and friends love this dish!

—**NANCY HEISHMAN** LAS VEGAS, NV

PREP: 20 MIN. • **COOK:** 3 HOURS
MAKES: 10 SERVINGS

- 8 frozen beef tamales, thawed
- 2 cans (15 ounces each) pinto beans, rinsed and drained
- 2 cups fresh or frozen corn
- 4 green onions, chopped
- 1 can (2¼ ounces) sliced ripe olives, drained
- ½ teaspoon garlic powder
- ¾ cup chopped sweet red pepper
- ¾ cup sour cream
- 1 can (4 ounces) whole green chilies, drained and chopped
- 3 cups chopped fresh spinach
- 12 bacon strips, cooked and crumbled
- 2 cups shredded cheddar cheese
- Additional green onions, chopped

1. Place tamales in a single layer in a greased 6-qt. slow cooker. In a large bowl, combine beans, corn, onions, olives and garlic powder; spoon over tamales. In same bowl, combine pepper, sour cream and chilies; spoon over the bean mixture. Top with spinach.
2. Cook, covered, on low for 3-4 hours or until heated through. Sprinkle with bacon, cheese and additional green onions.

MOM'S SPAGHETTI SAUCE

Mom made this when we were kids, and it was always my first choice for birthday dinners. Now I do the prep work in the morning and just let it simmer all day. When I get home, all I have to do is boil the spaghetti, brown some garlic bread and dinner is on!

—**KRISTY HAWKES** SOUTH WEBER, UT

PREP: 20 MIN. • **COOK:** 4 HOURS
MAKES: 10-12 SERVINGS

- 1 pound ground beef
- 1 medium onion, chopped
- 1 medium green pepper, chopped
- 8 to 10 fresh mushrooms, sliced
- 3 celery ribs, chopped
- 1½ teaspoons minced garlic
- 2 cans (14½ ounces each) Italian stewed tomatoes
- 1 jar (26 ounces) spaghetti sauce
- ½ cup ketchup
- 2 teaspoons brown sugar
- 1 teaspoon sugar
- 1 teaspoon salt
- 1 teaspoon dried oregano
- 1 teaspoon chili powder
- 1 teaspoon prepared mustard
- Hot cooked spaghetti

1. In a large skillet, cook beef, onion, green pepper, mushrooms and celery over medium heat until the meat is no longer pink. Add garlic; cook 1 minute longer. Drain.
2. In a 3-qt. slow cooker, combine tomatoes, spaghetti sauce, ketchup, sugars, salt, oregano, chili powder and mustard. Stir in the beef mixture. Cover and cook on low for 4-5 hours or until heated through. Serve immediately with spaghetti.

To freeze: Let sauce cool before placing in a freezer container. Cover and freeze for up to 3 months. To use, thaw in the refrigerator overnight. Place in a large saucepan; heat through, stirring occasionally. Serve with spaghetti.

FAST FIX

SWEET-SOUR MEATBALLS

For a great meal on busy days, I pop ready-made meatballs in the slow cooker and come home later to the heartwarming aroma of this Asian-style specialty. Nothing is more convenient than coming home to dinner that's ready to go.

—**LISA STEPANSKI** MUNNSVILLE, NY

PREP: 10 MIN. • **COOK:** 5 HOURS
MAKES: 2 SERVINGS

- **16 frozen fully cooked homestyle meatballs (½ ounce each), thawed**
- **½ cup sugar**
- **2 tablespoons plus 2 teaspoons cornstarch**
- **⅓ cup white vinegar**
- **1 tablespoon reduced-sodium soy sauce**
- **½ medium green pepper, cut into 1-inch pieces**
- **1 can (8 ounces) pineapple chunks, undrained**
- **Hot cooked rice, optional**

1. Place meatballs in a 1½-qt. slow cooker. In a small bowl, combine sugar, cornstarch, vinegar and soy sauce; pour over meatballs. Add green pepper. Cover and cook on low for 4½ hours or until the pepper is crisp-tender.
2. Stir in pineapple; cover and cook 30 minutes longer. Serve with rice if desired.

SWEET & SAVORY PULLED BEEF DINNER

Flavorful pulled beef is great served over rice or noodles for a more formal meal, or inside hard rolls for casual party sandwiches.

—**PATTY MANOCCHI** GLENVILLE, NY

PREP: 25 MIN. • **COOK:** 6 HOURS • **MAKES:** 6 SERVINGS

- **1 teaspoon salt**
- **1 teaspoon ground mustard**
- **1 teaspoon barbecue seasoning**
- **1 teaspoon paprika**
- **1 teaspoon chili powder**
- **½ teaspoon pepper**
- **1 boneless beef chuck roast (3 pounds)**
- **3 tablespoons olive oil**
- **1 large onion, halved and sliced**
- **1 large sweet red pepper, sliced**

SAUCE

- **1 can (8 ounces) tomato sauce**
- **⅓ cup packed brown sugar**
- **3 tablespoons honey**
- **2 tablespoons Dijon mustard**
- **2 tablespoons Worcestershire sauce**
- **2 tablespoons soy sauce**
- **5 garlic cloves, minced**
- **4 teaspoons balsamic vinegar**
- **¾ teaspoon salt**
- **Cooked egg noodles**

1. Combine the first six ingredients. Cut roast in half; rub with seasonings. In a large skillet, brown beef in oil on all sides. Transfer to a 4- or 5-qt. slow cooker. Top with onion and red pepper.
2. In a small bowl, combine tomato sauce, brown sugar, honey, mustard, Worcestershire sauce, soy sauce, garlic, vinegar and salt; pour over the vegetables. Cover and cook on low for 6-8 hours or until the meat is tender.
3. Remove roast; cool slightly. Strain the cooking juices, reserving vegetables and 1¼ cups juices; skim fat from the reserved juices. Shred beef with two forks and return to slow cooker. Stir in the reserved vegetables and cooking juices; heat through. Serve with noodles.

HOT PEPPER-BEEF SANDWICHES

HOT PEPPER-BEEF SANDWICHES

If you like your shredded beef with a little kick, then this recipe is for you. For an even zestier version, add another jar of jalapenos or use hot peppers instead of the pepperoncini.

—**KRISTEN LANGMEIER** FARIBAULT, MN

PREP: 15 MIN. • **COOK:** 8 HOURS
MAKES: 12 SERVINGS

- **1 boneless beef chuck roast (4 to 5 pounds)**
- **2 medium onions, coarsely chopped**
- **1 jar (16 ounces) sliced pepperoncini, undrained**
- **1 jar (8 ounces) pickled jalapeno slices, drained**
- **1 bottle (12 ounces) beer or nonalcoholic beer**
- **1 envelope onion soup mix**
- **5 garlic cloves, minced**
- **½ teaspoon pepper**
- **12 kaiser rolls, split**
- **12 slices provolone cheese**

1. Cut roast in half; place in a 4- or 5-qt. slow cooker. Add onions, pepperoncini, jalapenos, beer, soup mix, garlic and pepper.
2. Cover and cook on low for 8-10 hours or until the meat is tender.
3. Remove the meat. Skim fat from the cooking liquid. When the meat is cool enough to handle, shred with two forks and return to slow cooker; heat through. Serve ½ cup meat mixture on each roll with a slice of cheese.

Note: Look for pepperoncini (pickled peppers) in the pickles and olives section of your grocery store.

SLOW COOKER BEEF CARNITAS

SLOW COOKER BEEF CARNITAS

I came up with this recipe while trying to figure out what I could do with a pot roast that had been in the freezer. Now I keep the rub in a plastic bag, ready and waiting in my cupboard, and I can get the roast in the slow cooker in less than 15 minutes.

—**ANN PISCITELLI** NOKOMIS, FL

PREP: 40 MIN. • **COOK:** 8 HOURS
MAKES: 16 SERVINGS (PLUS ¼ CUP LEFTOVER SPICE MIXTURE)

- **2 tablespoons kosher salt**
- **2 tablespoons brown sugar**
- **1 tablespoon ground cumin**
- **1 tablespoon smoked paprika**
- **1 tablespoon chili powder**
- **1 teaspoon garlic powder**
- **1 teaspoon ground mustard**
- **1 teaspoon dried oregano**
- **1 teaspoon cayenne pepper**
- **1 boneless beef chuck roast (3 pounds)**
- **2 large sweet onions, thinly sliced**
- **3 poblano peppers, seeded and thinly sliced**
- **2 chipotle peppers in adobo sauce, finely chopped**
- **3 tablespoons canola oil**
- **1 jar (16 ounces) salsa**
- **16 flour tortillas (8 inches), warmed**
- **3 cups crumbled queso fresco or shredded Monterey Jack cheese**
- **Optional toppings: cubed avocado, sour cream and minced fresh cilantro**

1. Mix the first nine ingredients. Cut roast in half; rub with ¼ cup spice mixture. Cover and store the remaining mixture in a cool, dry place up to 1 year. Place onions and peppers in a 4-qt. slow cooker. In a large skillet, heat oil over medium heat. Brown roast on all sides. Transfer meat and drippings to slow cooker. Top with salsa. Cook, covered, on low until meat is tender, 8-10 hours.
2. Remove roast; shred with two forks. Skim fat from the cooking juices. Return the meat to slow cooker; heat through. Using a slotted spoon, place ½ cup of the meat mixture on each tortilla. Sprinkle with cheese. Add toppings of your choice.

POT ROAST WITH ASIAN BLACK BEAN SAUCE

I enjoy stir-fry with black bean sauce. This recipe takes the flavor of that delicious sauce and joins it with fork-tender pot roast.

—**JUDY LAWSON** CHELSEA, MI

PREP: 25 MIN. • **COOK:** 6 HOURS
MAKES: 10 SERVINGS

- **1 boneless beef chuck roast (3 to 4 pounds)**
- **½ teaspoon salt**
- **½ teaspoon pepper**
- **1 tablespoon olive oil**
- **1 medium onion, cut into 1-inch pieces**
- **¾ cup Asian black bean sauce**
- **¼ cup reduced-sodium beef broth**
- **½ pound sliced fresh mushrooms**
- **8 ounces fresh snow peas, trimmed**
- **1 tablespoon cornstarch**
- **1 tablespoon cold water**
- **Hot cooked rice**
- **4 green onions, sliced**

1. Sprinkle roast with salt and pepper. In a large skillet, heat oil over medium-high heat. Brown roast 3-4 minutes on each side. Transfer to a 6-qt. slow cooker. Add onion. Whisk together black bean sauce and broth; pour over roast. Cook, covered, on low 5-6 hours.
2. Add mushrooms and snow peas; continue cooking on low until the meat is tender, about 30 minutes.
3. Remove roast and vegetables to a serving platter; keep warm. Transfer cooking juices to a small saucepan; skim fat. Bring cooking juices to a boil. In a small bowl, mix cornstarch and cold water until smooth; stir into cooking juices. Return to a boil; cook and stir 1-2 minutes or until thickened. Serve roast with hot cooked rice and sauce. Sprinkle with green onions.

SLOW-COOKED
CRANBERRY CHICKEN,
PAGE 120

POULTRY MEALS

From traditional favorites to international dishes, slow-cooked chicken and turkey fill your kitchen with irresistible aromas, welcoming you home.

CREAMY GARLIC-LEMON CHICKEN

I needed an easy way to prepare my family's favorite meal, lemon chicken, and this rich slow-cooker dish is it! I serve the chicken on a bed of rice or couscous and spoon the creamy sauce over the top.

—**NANETTE SLAUGHTER** SAMMAMISH, WA

PREP: 15 MIN. • **COOK:** 3 HOURS • **MAKES:** 6 SERVINGS

- **1 cup vegetable broth**
- **1½ teaspoons grated lemon peel**
- **3 tablespoons lemon juice**
- **2 tablespoons capers, drained**
- **3 garlic cloves, minced**
- **½ teaspoon pepper**
- **6 boneless skinless chicken breast halves (6 ounces each)**
- **2 tablespoons butter**
- **2 tablespoons all-purpose flour**
- **½ cup heavy whipping cream**
- **Hot cooked rice**

1. In a small bowl, combine the first six ingredients. Place chicken in a 5-qt. slow cooker; pour the broth mixture over chicken. Cook, covered, on low for 3-4 hours or until the chicken is tender.

2. Remove chicken from slow cooker; keep warm. In a large saucepan, melt butter over medium heat. Stir in flour until smooth; gradually whisk in cooking juices. Bring to a boil, stirring constantly; cook and stir 1-2 minutes or until thickened. Remove from heat and stir in cream. Serve chicken and rice with sauce.

SPICY SHREDDED CHICKEN

I love Mexican food but not the high calorie count that often comes with it. This easy dish is healthy, delicious and a crowd favorite! I like to serve the chicken with warm tortillas, rice, beans and salsa.

—**HEATHER WALKER** SCOTTSDALE, AZ

PREP: 40 MIN. • **COOK:** 4¼ HOURS
MAKES: 8 SERVINGS

- **2 tablespoons olive oil**
- **1 pound boneless skinless chicken thighs**
- **1 pound boneless skinless chicken breasts**
- **3 cups reduced-sodium chicken broth, divided**
- **6 green onions, chopped**
- **1 medium green pepper, chopped**
- **2 tablespoons ground cumin**
- **1 tablespoon garlic powder**
- **1 tablespoon chili powder**
- **1 tablespoon paprika**
- **1 teaspoon cayenne pepper**
- **½ teaspoon salt**
- **¼ teaspoon pepper**
- **1 plum tomato, chopped**

1. In a large skillet, heat oil over medium-high heat. Brown chicken in batches. Transfer to a 3- or 4-qt. slow cooker. Add 1 cup broth to pan. Cook, stirring to loosen browned bits from pan. Add onions and green pepper; cook and stir for 3-5 minutes or until vegetables are tender. Stir in the seasonings; cook 1-2 minutes. Add tomato and the remaining broth; pour over chicken. Cook, covered, on low for 4-5 hours or until the chicken is tender.

2. Remove the chicken from slow cooker. When cool enough to handle, shred chicken with two forks; return meat to slow cooker. Cook, covered, on low for 15-20 minutes longer or until heated through. Serve with a slotted spoon.

To freeze: Freeze the cooled chicken mixture in freezer containers. To use, partially thaw in refrigerator overnight. Heat through in a saucepan, stirring occasionally and adding a little reduced-sodium broth or water if necessary.

SPICY SHREDDED CHICKEN
Heather Walker
Scottsdale, AZ

SAUCY CHICKEN & TORTELLINI

FAST FIX

SAUCY CHICKEN & TORTELLINI

This heartwarming dish is something I threw together years ago for my oldest daughter. When she's having a rough day, I pull out the slow cooker and prepare this special recipe.

—**MARY MORGAN** DALLAS, TX

PREP: 10 MIN. • **COOK:** 6¼ HOURS
MAKES: 8 SERVINGS

- **1½ pounds boneless skinless chicken breasts, cut in 1-inch cubes**
- **½ pound sliced fresh mushrooms**
- **1 large onion, chopped**
- **1 medium sweet red pepper, cut in ½-inch pieces**
- **1 medium green pepper, cut in ½-inch pieces**
- **1 can (2¼ ounces) sliced ripe olives, drained**
- **1 jar (24 ounces) marinara sauce**
- **1 jar (15 ounces) Alfredo sauce**
- **2 packages (9 ounces each) refrigerated cheese tortellini**
- **Grated Parmesan cheese, optional**
- **Torn fresh basil, optional**

1. In a 5-qt. slow cooker, combine the first seven ingredients. Cook, covered, on low until the chicken is tender, 6-8 hours.

2. Stir in the Alfredo sauce and tortellini. Cook, covered, until the tortellini is tender, 15-20 minutes. If desired, top with Parmesan cheese and basil.

To freeze: Place chicken and vegetables in freezer containers; top with sauce. Cool and freeze. To use, partially thaw in refrigerator overnight. Microwave, covered, on high in a microwave-safe dish until heated through, stirring gently and adding a little water if necessary.

CHICKEN MOLE

If you're not familiar with mole, don't be afraid of this versatile Mexican sauce. I love sharing this recipe because it's a great one to experiment with.

—**DARLENE MORRIS** FRANKLINTON, LA

PREP: 25 MIN. • **COOK:** 6 HOURS
MAKES: 12 SERVINGS

- **12 bone-in chicken thighs (about 4½ pounds), skin removed**
- **1 teaspoon salt**

MOLE SAUCE

- **1 can (28 ounces) whole tomatoes, drained**
- **1 medium onion, chopped**
- **2 dried ancho chilies, stems and seeds removed**
- **½ cup sliced almonds, toasted**
- **¼ cup raisins**
- **3 ounces bittersweet chocolate, chopped**
- **3 tablespoons olive oil**
- **1 chipotle pepper in adobo sauce**
- **3 garlic cloves, peeled and halved**
- **¾ teaspoon ground cumin**
- **½ teaspoon ground cinnamon**
- **Fresh cilantro leaves, optional**

1. Sprinkle chicken with salt; place in a 5- or 6-qt. slow cooker. Place the tomatoes, onion, chilies, almonds, raisins, chocolate, oil, chipotle pepper, garlic, cumin and cinnamon in a food processor; cover and process until blended. Pour over chicken.

2. Cover and cook on low for 6-8 hours or until the chicken is tender; skim fat. Serve chicken with sauce, and sprinkle with cilantro if desired.

To freeze: Cool chicken in sauce. Freeze in freezer containers. To use, partially thaw in refrigerator overnight. Heat through slowly in a covered skillet or Dutch oven until a thermometer inserted in chicken reads 165°, stirring occasionally and adding a little broth or water if necessary.

CHIPOTLE PULLED CHICKEN

At our house, low-and-slow recipes have to have kid and husband appeal, plus good marks for nutrition. This chipotle chicken wins in both categories. Use leftovers for zippy barbecue pizzas or burritos.

—**TAMRA PARKER** MANLIUS, NY

PREP: 15 MIN. • **COOK:** 3 HOURS
MAKES: 12 SERVINGS

- **2 cups ketchup**
- **1 small onion, finely chopped**
- **¼ cup Worcestershire sauce**
- **3 tablespoons reduced-sodium soy sauce**
- **2 tablespoons brown sugar**
- **2 tablespoons cider vinegar**
- **3 garlic cloves, minced**
- **1 tablespoon molasses**
- **2 teaspoons dried oregano**
- **2 teaspoons minced chipotle pepper in adobo sauce plus 1 teaspoon sauce**
- **1 teaspoon ground cumin**
- **1 teaspoon smoked paprika**
- **¼ teaspoon salt**
- **¼ teaspoon crushed red pepper flakes**
- **2½ pounds boneless skinless chicken breasts**
- **12 sesame seed hamburger buns, split and toasted**

1. In a 3-qt. slow cooker, combine the first 14 ingredients; add the chicken. Cook, covered, on low for 3-4 hours or until the chicken is tender (a thermometer should read at least 165°).
2. Remove chicken from slow cooker. Shred with two forks; return meat to slow cooker. Using tongs, place the chicken mixture on bun bottoms. Replace the tops.
To freeze: Freeze cooled meat mixture and sauce in freezer containers. To use, partially thaw in the refrigerator overnight. Heat through in a saucepan, stirring occasionally.

FAST FIX

SLOW-COOKED CRANBERRY CHICKEN

I wanted to find a creative way to use my leftover cranberries from Thanksgiving dinner. This sounds like an unlikely combination, but the results are incredible!

—**LISA WORKMAN** BOONES MILL, VA

PREP: 10 MIN. • **COOK:** 5 HOURS • **MAKES:** 4 SERVINGS

- **4 bone-in chicken breast halves (10 ounces each), skin removed**
- **1½ cups fresh or frozen cranberries, chopped**
- **½ cup packed brown sugar**
- **¼ cup molasses**
- **2 tablespoons orange juice**
- **2 tablespoons cider vinegar**
- **2 teaspoons prepared mustard**
- **Hot cooked rice**

1. Place chicken in a 4-qt. slow cooker. Combine cranberries, brown sugar, molasses, orange juice, vinegar and mustard; pour over the chicken.
2. Cook, covered, on low for 4-5 hours or until the chicken is tender. Remove meat from bone or shred if desired. Serve with cranberry mixture and rice.

SAUCY THAI CHICKEN PIZZAS

SAUCY THAI CHICKEN PIZZAS

I cook up this sweet and salty chicken as a topping for a Thai-style pizza—but it's also delicious served over rice.

—**GIGI MILLER** STOUGHTON, WI

PREP: 4¼ HOURS • **BAKE:** 10 MIN.
MAKES: 2 PIZZAS (6 SLICES EACH)

- 3 **pounds boneless skinless chicken thighs**
- ¾ **cup sugar**
- ¾ **cup reduced-sodium soy sauce**
- ⅓ **cup cider vinegar**
- 1 **garlic clove, minced**
- ¾ **teaspoon ground ginger**
- ¼ **teaspoon pepper**
- 1 **cup Thai peanut sauce**
- 2 **prebaked 12-inch pizza crusts**
- 2 **cups coleslaw mix**
- 2 **cups shredded part-skim mozzarella cheese**
- 4 **green onions, thinly sliced**
- ½ **cup chopped salted peanuts**
- ¼ **cup minced fresh cilantro**

1. Place chicken in a 4- or 5-qt. slow cooker. In a small bowl, mix sugar, soy sauce, vinegar, garlic, ginger and pepper; pour over the chicken. Cook, covered, on low 4-5 hours or until the chicken is tender.

2. Preheat oven to 450°. Remove chicken from slow cooker; discard the cooking juices. Shred chicken with two forks; transfer to large bowl. Add peanut sauce; toss to coat.

3. Place crusts on two ungreased 12-in. pizza pans or baking sheets. Spoon chicken mixture over crusts; top with coleslaw mix and cheese. Bake for 10-12 minutes or until the cheese is melted. Sprinkle with green onions, peanuts and cilantro.

AUTUMN APPLE CHICKEN

AUTUMN APPLE CHICKEN

I'd just been apple picking and wanted to bake something new with the bounty. Slow-cooking chicken with apples and barbecue sauce filled my whole house with the most delicious smell. We couldn't wait to eat.

—**CAITLYN HAUSER** BROOKLINE, NH

PREP: 20 MIN. • **COOK:** 3½ HOURS
MAKES: 4 SERVINGS

- **1 tablespoon canola oil**
- **4 bone-in chicken thighs (about 1½ pounds), skin removed**
- **¼ teaspoon salt**
- **¼ teaspoon pepper**
- **2 medium Fuji or Gala apples, coarsely chopped**
- **1 medium onion, chopped**
- **1 garlic clove, minced**
- **⅓ cup barbecue sauce**
- **¼ cup apple cider or juice**
- **1 tablespoon honey**

1. In a large skillet, heat oil over medium heat. Brown chicken thighs on both sides; sprinkle with salt and pepper. Transfer to a 3-qt. slow cooker; top with apples.
2. Add onion to the same skillet; cook and stir over medium heat for 2-3 minutes or until tender. Add garlic; cook 1 minute longer. Stir in barbecue sauce, apple cider and honey; increase heat to medium-high. Cook 1 minute, stirring to loosen browned bits from pan. Pour over chicken and apples. Cook, covered, on low for 3½ to 4½ hours or until the chicken is tender.
To freeze: Freeze cooled chicken mixture in freezer containers. To use, partially thaw in refrigerator overnight. Heat through in a covered saucepan, stirring occasionally.

CHICKEN CURRY FOR 2

I love to try new recipes, and I have cookbooks and recipes from all over the world. When I find a well-received recipe, I make a copy and put it in a protective sleeve in a binder. I now have quite a few huge binders!

—**SHARON DELANEY-CHRONIS** SOUTH MILWAUKEE, WI

PREP: 20 MIN. • **COOK:** 3 HOURS
MAKES: 2 SERVINGS

- **1 small onion, sliced**
- **1 tablespoon plus ⅓ cup water, divided**
- **½ pound boneless skinless chicken breasts, cubed**
- **1 small apple, peeled and chopped**
- **¼ cup raisins**
- **1 garlic clove, minced**
- **1 teaspoon curry powder**
- **¼ teaspoon ground ginger**
- **⅛ teaspoon salt**
- **1½ teaspoons all-purpose flour**
- **1 teaspoon chicken bouillon granules**
- **½ cup sour cream**
- **¾ teaspoon cornstarch**
- **1 tablespoon thinly sliced green onion**
- **Hot cooked rice**

1. Place onion and 1 tablespoon water in a microwave-safe bowl. Cover and microwave on high for 1 to 1½ minutes or until crisp-tender.
2. In a 1½-qt. slow cooker, combine chicken, apple, raisins, garlic, curry, ginger, salt and onion. Combine flour, bouillon and remaining water; pour over chicken mixture. Cover and cook on low for 3 to 3½ hours or until the chicken juices run clear.
3. Bring sour cream to room temperature. Remove chicken mixture to a bowl; keep warm. Transfer juices to a small saucepan. Combine the sour cream and cornstarch until smooth; add to juices. Cook and stir over medium heat until thickened. Pour over the chicken mixture; toss to coat. Sprinkle with green onion and serve with rice.

EASY CHICKEN TAMALE PIE

All you need are some simple ingredients from the pantry to put this together. I love the fact I can go fishing while it cooks!

—**PETER HALFERTY** CORPUS CHRISTI, TX

PREP: 20 MIN. • **COOK:** 7 HOURS • **MAKES:** 8 SERVINGS

- **1 pound ground chicken**
- **1 teaspoon ground cumin**
- **1 teaspoon chili powder**
- **½ teaspoon salt**
- **¼ teaspoon pepper**
- **1 can (15 ounces) black beans, rinsed and drained**
- **1 can (14½ ounces) diced tomatoes, undrained**
- **1 can (11 ounces) whole kernel corn, drained**
- **1 can (10 ounces) enchilada sauce**
- **2 green onions, chopped**
- **¼ cup minced fresh cilantro**
- **1 package (8½ ounces) corn bread/muffin mix**
- **2 large eggs, lightly beaten**
- **1 cup shredded Mexican cheese blend**
- **Optional toppings: sour cream, salsa and minced fresh cilantro**

1. In a large skillet, cook chicken over medium heat for 6-8 minutes or until no longer pink, breaking into crumbles. Stir in seasonings.

2. Transfer to a 4-qt. slow cooker. Stir in beans, tomatoes, corn, enchilada sauce, green onions and cilantro. Cook, covered, on low for 6-8 hours or until heated through.

3. In a small bowl, combine muffin mix and eggs; spoon over chicken mixture. Cook, covered, on low 1-1½ hours longer or until a toothpick inserted in corn bread layer comes out clean.

4. Sprinkle with cheese; let stand, covered, 5 minutes. If desired, serve with toppings.

APPLE BALSAMIC CHICKEN

I just love the sweet and tart flavor that balsamic vinegar gives to this dish. It's easy to prepare and after cooking in the slow cooker, the chicken thighs are tender and flavorful.

—**JULI SNAER** ENID, OK

PREP: 15 MIN. • **COOK:** 4 HOURS
MAKES: 4 SERVINGS

- **4 bone-in chicken thighs (about 1½ pounds), skin removed**
- **½ cup chicken broth**
- **¼ cup apple cider or juice**
- **¼ cup balsamic vinegar**
- **2 tablespoons lemon juice**
- **½ teaspoon salt**
- **½ teaspoon garlic powder**
- **½ teaspoon dried thyme**
- **½ teaspoon paprika**
- **½ teaspoon pepper**
- **2 tablespoons butter**
- **2 tablespoons all-purpose flour**

1. Place chicken in a 1½-qt. slow cooker. In a small bowl, combine the broth, cider, vinegar, lemon juice and seasonings; pour over chicken. Cover and cook on low for 4-5 hours or until chicken is tender.

2. Remove chicken; keep warm. Skim fat from cooking liquid. In a small saucepan, melt butter; stir in flour until smooth. Gradually add the cooking liquid. Bring to a boil; cook and stir 2-3 minutes or until thickened. Serve with chicken.

MEATY SLOW-COOKED JAMBALAYA

MEATY SLOW-COOKED JAMBALAYA

This recipe makes a big batch of delicious, meaty gumbo. Stash some away in the freezer for days you don't feel like cooking.

—**DIANE SMITH** PINE MOUNTAIN, GA

PREP: 25 MIN. • **COOK:** 7¼ HOURS
MAKES: 12 SERVINGS (3½ QUARTS)

- **1 can (28 ounces) diced tomatoes, undrained**
- **1 cup reduced-sodium chicken broth**
- **1 large green pepper, chopped**
- **1 medium onion, chopped**
- **2 celery ribs, sliced**
- **½ cup white wine or additional reduced-sodium chicken broth**
- **4 garlic cloves, minced**
- **2 teaspoons Cajun seasoning**
- **2 teaspoons dried parsley flakes**
- **1 teaspoon dried basil**
- **1 teaspoon dried oregano**
- **¾ teaspoon salt**
- **½ to 1 teaspoon cayenne pepper**
- **2 pounds boneless skinless chicken thighs, cut into 1-inch pieces**
- **1 package (12 ounces) fully cooked andouille or other spicy chicken sausage links**
- **2 pounds uncooked medium shrimp, peeled and deveined**
- **8 cups hot cooked brown rice**

1. In a large bowl, combine the first 13 ingredients. Place the chicken and sausage in a 6-qt. slow cooker. Pour tomato mixture over top. Cook, covered, on low for 7-9 hours or until the chicken is tender.

2. Stir in shrimp. Cook, covered, 15-20 minutes longer or until the shrimp turn pink. Serve with rice.

SAUCY INDIAN-STYLE CHICKEN & VEGETABLES

SAUCY INDIAN-STYLE CHICKEN & VEGETABLES

This easy Indian dish will be loved by all. Feel free to add more or less tikka masala sauce according to your taste.

—**ERICA POLLY** SUN PRAIRIE, WI

PREP: 15 MIN. • **COOK:** 4 HOURS • **MAKES:** 8 SERVINGS

- **2 medium sweet potatoes, peeled and cut into 1½-inch pieces**
- **2 tablespoons water**
- **2 medium sweet red peppers, cut into 1-inch pieces**
- **3 cups fresh cauliflowerets**
- **2 pounds boneless skinless chicken thighs, cubed**
- **2 jars (15 ounces each) tikka masala curry sauce**
- **¾ teaspoon salt**
- **Minced fresh cilantro, optional**
- **Naan flatbreads, warmed**

1. Microwave sweet potatoes and water, covered, on high just until the potatoes begin to soften, 3-4 minutes.

2. In a 5- or 6-qt. slow cooker, combine potatoes, peppers, cauliflowerts and chicken; add sauce and salt. Cook, covered, on low until meat is tender, 4-5 hours. If desired, top with cilantro; serve with warmed naan.

To freeze: Omit cilantro and naan; freeze cooled chicken and vegetable mixture in freezer containers. To use, partially thaw in refrigerator overnight. Microwave, covered, on high in a microwave-safe dish until heated through, stirring gently and adding a little water if necessary. If desired, sprinkle with cilantro. Serve with warmed naan.

HARVEST TIME CHICKEN WITH COUSCOUS

Even on busy days, I can start this chicken in a slow cooker and still get to work on time. When I come home, I add spinach salad and crescent rolls.

—**HEIDI RUDOLPH** OREGON, IL

PREP: 30 MIN. • **COOK:** 3 HOURS • **MAKES:** 6 SERVINGS

- **2 medium sweet potatoes (about 1¼ pounds), peeled and cut into ½-inch pieces**
- **1 medium sweet red pepper, coarsely chopped**
- **1½ pounds boneless skinless chicken breasts**
- **1 can (14½ ounces) stewed tomatoes, undrained**
- **½ cup peach or mango salsa**
- **¼ cup golden raisins**
- **½ teaspoon salt**
- **¼ teaspoon ground cumin**
- **¼ teaspoon ground cinnamon**
- **¼ teaspoon pepper**

COUSCOUS

- **1 cup water**
- **½ teaspoon salt**
- **1 cup uncooked whole wheat couscous**

1. In a 4-qt. slow cooker, layer sweet potatoes, red pepper and chicken breasts. In a small bowl, mix tomatoes, salsa, raisins and seasonings; pour over the chicken. Cook, covered, on low 3-4 hours or until the sweet potatoes and chicken are tender.

2. About 10 minutes before serving, prepare couscous. In a small saucepan, bring water and salt to a boil. Stir in the couscous. Remove from heat; let stand, covered, 5 minutes or until the water is absorbed. Fluff with a fork.

3. Remove the chicken from the slow cooker; coarsely shred it with two forks. Return the chicken to the slow cooker, stirring gently to combine. Serve with couscous.

To freeze: Place cooled chicken mixture in freezer containers. To use, partially thaw in refrigerator overnight. Microwave, covered, on high in a microwave-safe dish until heated through, stirring gently and adding a little broth or water if necessary.

FAST FIX

SLOW COOKER MUSHROOM CHICKEN & PEAS

Some amazingly fresh mushrooms I found at our local farmers market inspired this recipe. When you start with the best ingredients, you can't go wrong.

—**JENN TIDWELL** FAIR OAKS, CA

PREP: 10 MIN. • **COOK:** 3 HOURS 10 MIN.
MAKES: 4 SERVINGS

- **4 boneless skinless chicken breast halves (6 ounces each)**
- **1 envelope onion mushroom soup mix**
- **1 cup water**
- **½ pound sliced baby portobello mushrooms**
- **1 medium onion, chopped**
- **4 garlic cloves, minced**
- **2 cups frozen peas, thawed**

1. Place chicken in a 3-qt. slow cooker. Sprinkle with soup mix, pressing to help seasonings adhere. Add water, mushrooms, onion and garlic.
2. Cook, covered, on low 3-4 hours or until chicken is tender (a thermometer inserted in the chicken should read at least 165°). Stir in peas; cook, covered, 10 minutes longer or until heated through.

PINEAPPLE CURRY CHICKEN

Curry has a moderate to strong delivery, so add it early in the cooking process for good balance with pineapple, coconut and ginger.

—**ROBIN HAAS** CRANSTON, RI

PREP: 25 MIN. • **COOK:** 6 HOURS • **MAKES:** 6 SERVINGS

- **2 cans (8 ounces each) unsweetened pineapple chunks, undrained**
- **6 bone-in chicken breast halves, skin removed (12 ounces each)**
- **1 can (15 ounces) garbanzo beans, rinsed and drained**
- **1 large onion, cut into 1-inch pieces**
- **1 cup julienned carrots**
- **1 medium sweet red pepper, cut into strips**
- **½ cup light coconut milk**
- **2 tablespoons cornstarch**
- **2 tablespoons sugar**
- **3 teaspoons curry powder**
- **2 garlic cloves, minced**
- **2 teaspoons minced fresh gingerroot**
- **1 teaspoon salt**
- **1 teaspoon pepper**
- **1 teaspoon lime juice**
- **½ teaspoon crushed red pepper flakes**
- **Hot cooked rice**
- **⅓ cup minced fresh basil**
- **Toasted sweetened shredded coconut, optional**

1. Drain pineapple, reserving ¾ cup juice. Place the chicken, beans, vegetables and pineapple in a 6-qt. slow cooker. In a small bowl, combine coconut milk and cornstarch until smooth. Stir in the sugar, curry powder, garlic, ginger, salt, pepper, lime juice, pepper flakes and reserved juice; pour over chicken.
2. Cover and cook on low for 6-8 hours or until chicken is tender. Serve with rice; sprinkle with basil and, if desired, coconut.

CHICKEN-CRANBERRY HOT DISH

CHICKEN-CRANBERRY HOT DISH

In my family, we never eat chicken without cranberry sauce! This chicken is fall-off-the-bone tender; the sauce is divine with mashed potatoes.

—**LORRAINE CALAND** SHUNIAH, ON

PREP: 30 MIN. • **COOK:** 4 HOURS
MAKES: 4 SERVINGS (2 CUPS SAUCE)

- **2 tablespoons canola oil**
- **1 broiler/fryer chicken (4 pounds), cut up**
- **½ teaspoon salt**
- **¼ teaspoon pepper**
- **1 medium onion, chopped**
- **1 celery rib, chopped**
- **1 cup whole-berry cranberry sauce**
- **½ cup chili sauce**
- **2 tablespoons brown sugar**
- **1 tablespoon grated lemon peel**
- **1 tablespoon balsamic vinegar**
- **1 tablespoon A.1. steak sauce**
- **1 tablespoon Dijon mustard**

1. In a large skillet, heat oil over medium-high heat. Brown chicken on both sides in batches; sprinkle with salt and pepper. Transfer to a 4-qt. slow cooker.
2. Add onion and celery to the skillet; saute over medium-high heat until tender, 3-4 minutes. Stir in remaining ingredients. Pour over chicken.
3. Cook, covered, on low until the chicken is tender, 4-5 hours. Skim fat from the cooking juices; serve with chicken.

TARRAGON CHICKEN

TARRAGON CHICKEN

I tried this one night when I had friends coming for dinner and was amazed at how deliciously fresh-tasting it was. Even my picky husband liked it! Serve it with crusty French bread to soak up the delicious sauce.

—**SHANELLE LEE** EPHRATA, PA

PREP: 30 MIN. • **COOK:** 6 HOURS
MAKES: 6 SERVINGS

- 1 pound fresh baby carrots
- ½ pound medium fresh mushrooms, halved
- 1 small onion, chopped
- 6 bone-in chicken thighs (about 2¼ pounds), skin removed
- 1 cup chicken broth
- 1 teaspoon dried tarragon
- ½ teaspoon salt
- ¼ teaspoon pepper
- 2 tablespoons cornstarch
- ½ cup heavy whipping cream

1. In a 5-qt. slow cooker, combine carrots, mushrooms and onion. Top with chicken. In a small bowl, combine broth, tarragon, salt and pepper; pour over the chicken. Cook, covered, on low until the chicken is tender, 6-8 hours. Remove chicken; when cool enough to handle, shred with two forks. Transfer chicken and vegetables to a serving platter; keep warm.
2. Pour the cooking juices into a small saucepan. Skim fat. In a small bowl, mix cornstarch with ½ cup cooking juices until smooth. Whisk into pan. Bring to a boil; cook and stir for 1-2 minutes or until thickened. Add cream; heat through. Serve with chicken and vegetables.

MEXICAN TURKEY MEAT LOAF

Here's a zesty, flavorful meat loaf you can really sink your teeth into! Great with black beans, rice, green salad with lime vinaigrette, or any of your favorite Tex-Mex sides

—**KRISTEN MILLER** GLENDALE, WI

PREP: 25 MIN. • **COOK:** 3 HOURS + STANDING
MAKES: 1 LOAF (6 SERVINGS)

- 2 slices white bread, torn into small pieces
- ⅓ cup 2% milk
- 1 pound lean ground turkey
- ½ pound fresh chorizo
- 1 medium sweet red pepper, finely chopped
- 1 small onion, finely chopped
- 1 jalapeno pepper, seeded and finely chopped
- 2 large eggs, lightly beaten
- 2 tablespoons minced fresh cilantro
- 2 garlic cloves, minced
- 2 teaspoons chili powder
- 1 teaspoon salt
- 1 teaspoon ground cumin
- ½ teaspoon dried oregano
- ½ teaspoon pepper
- ¼ teaspoon cayenne pepper
- ⅔ cup salsa, divided
- Additional minced fresh cilantro
- Hot cooked Spanish rice

1. Combine bread and milk in a large bowl; let stand until liquid is absorbed. Add the next 14 ingredients and ⅓ cup salsa; mix lightly but thoroughly.
2. On an 18x7-in. piece of heavy-duty foil, shape meat mixture into a 10x6-in. oval loaf. Lifting with foil, transfer to a 6-qt. oval slow cooker. Press ends of the foil up the sides of the slow cooker.
3. Cook, covered, on low until a thermometer reads 165°, 3-4 hours. Lifting with foil, drain fat into the slow cooker before removing meat loaf to a platter; top with the remaining salsa and sprinkle with cilantro. Let stand 10 minutes before slicing. Serve with rice.

SLOW-SIMMERED MEAT RAGU

After a day spent simmering in the slow cooker, this ragu is not your typical spaghetti sauce. It's so hearty, it's almost like a stew.

—**LAURIE LACLAIR** NORTH RICHLAND HILLS, TX

PREP: 30 MIN. • **COOK:** 6 HOURS
MAKES: 10 SERVINGS

- 1 jar (24 ounces) tomato basil pasta sauce
- 1 can (14½ ounces) Italian diced tomatoes, undrained
- 2 jars (6 ounces each) sliced mushrooms, drained
- 1 can (8 ounces) tomato sauce
- 1 jar (3½ ounces) prepared pesto
- 1½ pounds chicken tenderloins
- 1 medium sweet red pepper, chopped
- ½ cup chopped pepperoni
- ½ cup pitted ripe olives, halved
- 1 teaspoon dried oregano
- ½ teaspoon hot pepper sauce
- 1 pound Italian sausage links, cut into 1-inch pieces
- 1 medium onion, chopped
- Hot cooked angel hair pasta

1. In a 5- or 6-qt. slow cooker, combine the first 11 ingredients. Heat a large skillet over medium heat. Add sausage and onion; cook and stir until the sausage is no longer pink and the onion is tender. Drain. Add to the slow cooker.

2. Cook, covered, on low 6-8 hours or until the chicken is tender. Serve with pasta.

To freeze: Omit pasta. Freeze cooled sauce in freezer containers. To use, partially thaw in refrigerator overnight. Cook pasta according to package directions. Place meat mixture in a large saucepan; heat through, stirring occasionally and adding a little water if necessary.

TUSCAN-STYLE CHICKEN

I found an Italian-style chicken recipe in a magazine and tweaked it to my family's tastes. I have taken it to potlucks and served it at dinner parties. I serve this with crusty bread and spinach salad with lemon vinaigrette.

—**MARY WATKINS** LITTLE ELM, TX

PREP: 25 MIN. • **COOK:** 6 HOURS • **MAKES:** 4 SERVINGS

- 2 cans (14½ ounces each) Italian stewed tomatoes, undrained
- 10 small red potatoes (about 1 pound), quartered
- 1 medium onion, chopped
- 1 can (6 ounces) tomato paste
- 2 fresh rosemary sprigs
- 4 garlic cloves, minced
- 1 teaspoon olive oil
- ½ teaspoon dried basil
- 1 teaspoon Italian seasoning, divided
- 1 broiler/fryer chicken (3 to 4 pounds), cut up and skin removed
- ½ teaspoon salt
- ½ teaspoon pepper
- 1 jar (5¾ ounces) pimiento-stuffed olives, drained

1. In a 5-qt. slow cooker, combine the first eight ingredients. Stir in ½ teaspoon Italian seasoning. Place the chicken on top. Sprinkle with salt, pepper and the remaining Italian seasoning. Top with olives.

2. Cover and cook on low for 6-7 hours or until the chicken is tender. Discard the rosemary sprigs before serving.

TUSCAN-STYLE CHICKEN

CHICKEN & MUSHROOM ALFREDO

Everyone in my family loves when I make this dinner...even my kids! You can add vegetables you have on hand to make it heartier, such as corn, peas, or diced red bell pepper.

—**MONICA WERNER** ONTARIO, CA

PREP:20 MIN. • **COOK:** 4 HOURS • **MAKES:** 4 SERVINGS

- **4 bone-in chicken breast halves (12 to 14 ounces each), skin removed**
- **2 tablespoons canola oil**
- **1 can (10¾ ounces) condensed cream of chicken soup, undiluted**
- **1 can (10¾ ounces) condensed cream of mushroom soup, undiluted**
- **1 cup chicken broth**
- **1 small onion, chopped**
- **1 jar (6 ounces) sliced mushrooms, drained**
- **¼ teaspoon garlic salt**
- **¼ teaspoon pepper**
- **8 ounces fettuccine**
- **1 package (8 ounces) cream cheese, softened and cubed**
- **Shredded Parmesan cheese, optional**

1. In a large skillet, brown chicken in oil in batches. Transfer to a 4- or 5-qt. slow cooker. In a large bowl, combine the soups, broth, onion, mushrooms, garlic salt and pepper; pour over meat. Cover and cook on low for 4-5 hours or until chicken is tender.
2. Cook fettuccine according to the package directions; drain. Remove chicken from slow cooker and keep warm. Turn slow cooker off and stir in cream cheese until melted. Serve chicken and sauce with fettucine. Top with Parmesan cheese if desired.

FAST FIX

SPICY LIME CHICKEN

I've been turning this spicy lime chicken into tacos for years, but it was my son who put it on cooked rice with all his favorite taco toppings. A new family favorite was created out of leftovers!

—**CHRISTINE HAIR** ODESSA, FL

PREP: 10 MIN. • **COOK:** 3 HOURS • **MAKES:** 6 SERVINGS

- **1½ pounds boneless skinless chicken breast halves (about 4)**
- **2 cups chicken broth**
- **3 tablespoons lime juice**
- **1 tablespoon chili powder**
- **1 teaspoon grated lime peel**

1. Place chicken in a 3-qt. slow cooker. Combine broth, lime juice and chili powder; pour over chicken. Cook, covered, on low until the chicken is tender, about 3 hours.
2. Remove the chicken. When cool enough to handle, shred meat with two forks; return to the slow cooker. Stir in lime peel.

SLOW COOKER GARLIC CLOVE CHICKEN

Dinner guests and cooks alike will rave about this chicken recipe. Your guests will be delighted with the tasty poultry, and you'll appreciate the stress-free slow cooker preparation.

—**RUTH RIGONI** HURLEY, WI

PREP: 45 MIN. • **COOK:** 3½ HOURS
MAKES: 6 SERVINGS

- **40 garlic cloves, peeled**
- **4 celery ribs, sliced**
- **1 broiler/fryer chicken (3 to 4 pounds), cut up and skin removed**
- **½ teaspoon salt**
- **¼ teaspoon pepper**
- **1 tablespoon olive oil**
- **¼ cup white wine or reduced-sodium chicken broth**
- **3 tablespoons lemon juice**
- **2 tablespoons dry vermouth**
- **2 tablespoons grated lemon peel**
- **2 tablespoons minced fresh parsley**
- **2 teaspoons dried basil**
- **1 teaspoon dried oregano**
- **Dash crushed red pepper flakes**

1. Place garlic and celery in a 5-qt. slow cooker. Sprinkle chicken with salt and pepper. In a large nonstick skillet, brown chicken in oil in batches; transfer to slow cooker.
2. In a small bowl, combine the remaining ingredients. Pour over the chicken. Cover and cook on low for 3½ to 4 hours or until the chicken juices run clear.

PEACHY CHICKEN WITH SWEET POTATOES

When my mother was pregnant with me, one of the only things she could eat was home-canned peaches. To this day, I love, love recipes with peaches.

—**SANDRA BONOW** LEWISTON, MN

PREP: 25 MIN. • **COOK:** 6 HOURS • **MAKES:** 4 SERVINGS

- **2 medium sweet potatoes, peeled and cubed**
- **1 medium onion, chopped**
- **8 boneless skinless chicken thighs (about 2 pounds)**
- **1 teaspoon paprika**
- **1 teaspoon dried thyme**
- **½ teaspoon salt**
- **⅛ teaspoon cayenne pepper**
- **1 cup peach preserves**
- **2 tablespoons cornstarch**
- **½ cup cold water**

1. In a 4- or 5-qt. slow cooker, combine sweet potatoes and onion. Sprinkle chicken with paprika, thyme, salt and cayenne; arrange over the sweet potatoes. Top with preserves. Cover and cook on low for 6-8 hours or until the chicken and potatoes are tender.
2. Remove the chicken and vegetables to a serving platter; keep warm. Skim fat from cooking juices; transfer to a small saucepan. Bring liquid to a boil. Combine cornstarch and water until smooth. Gradually stir into the pan. Bring to a boil; cook and stir for 2 minutes or until thickened. Serve with chicken and vegetables.

GULF COAST JAMBALAYA RICE

GULF COAST JAMBALAYA RICE

As the stew of the South, jambalaya is a definite staple. For ages, home cooks have been making their own versions of the traditional recipe. This slow-cooked rendition is my personal favorite.

—**JUDY BATSON** TAMPA, FL

PREP: 20 MIN. • **COOK:** 3¼ HOURS
MAKES: 8 SERVINGS

- **1 pound boneless skinless chicken breasts, cut into 1-inch cubes**
- **1 pound smoked kielbasa, cut into ¼-inch slices**
- **2 cups chicken stock**
- **1 large green pepper, chopped**
- **1 cup chopped sweet onion**
- **2 celery ribs, chopped**
- **2 garlic cloves, minced**
- **2 teaspoons Creole seasoning**
- **1 teaspoon seafood seasoning**
- **1 teaspoon pepper**
- **1 pound uncooked medium shrimp, peeled and deveined**
- **2 cups uncooked instant rice**

1. Place the first 10 ingredients in a 5-qt. slow cooker. Cook, covered, on low for 3-4 hours or until the chicken is tender.

2. Stir in shrimp and rice. Cook, covered, for 15-20 minutes longer or until shrimp turn pink and the rice is tender.

Note: The following spice blend may be substituted for 1 teaspoon Creole seasoning: ¼ teaspoon each salt, garlic powder and paprika; and a pinch each of dried thyme, ground cumin and cayenne pepper.

ITALIAN TURKEY MEATBALLS

What's not to love about moist and tender homemade Italian meatballs? Because they're made with lean turkey, they're lower in saturated fat, too!

—**MARY BERG** LAKE ELMO, MN

PREP: 45 MIN. • **COOK:** 4 HOURS
MAKES: 12 SERVINGS

- **3 slices white bread, torn into small pieces**
- **½ cup fat-free milk**
- **2 pounds lean ground turkey**
- **¼ cup grated Parmesan cheese**
- **¼ cup minced fresh parsley**
- **2 large eggs, lightly beaten**
- **3 garlic cloves, minced**
- **4 teaspoons Italian seasoning, divided**
- **1 teaspoon salt, divided**
- **1 teaspoon pepper, divided**
- **2 medium onions, chopped**
- **1 medium green pepper, chopped**
- **4 garlic cloves, minced**
- **2 cans (28 ounces each) crushed tomatoes in puree**
- **2 cans (6 ounces each) tomato paste**
- **1 tablespoon sugar**
- **2 bay leaves**
- **Hot cooked pasta**
- **Additional minced fresh parsley and grated Parmesan cheese, optional**

1. Preheat broiler. Combine bread and milk in a large bowl; let stand until liquid is absorbed. Add the next five ingredients, 2 teaspoons Italian seasoning, ½ teaspoon salt and ½ teaspoon pepper; mix lightly but thoroughly. Shape into 1½-in. balls; place on a greased rack of a broiler pan. Broil 5-6 in. from heat until lightly browned, 4-5 minutes.

2. In a 6-qt. slow cooker, mix the next six ingredients and the remaining Italian seasoning, salt and pepper. Add bay leaves and meatballs; gently stir into sauce.

3. Cook, covered, on low until the meatballs are cooked through, 4-5 hours. Discard bay leaves. Serve with pasta; if desired, sprinkle with additional parsley and Parmesan cheese.

To freeze: Omit additional parsley and Parmesan cheese; freeze the cooled meatball mixture in freezer containers. To use, partially thaw in the refrigerator overnight. Microwave, covered, on high in a microwave-safe dish until heated through, stirring gently and adding a little water if necessary. If desired, sprinkle with additional parsley and Parmesan cheese.

SAUCY BBQ CHICKEN THIGHS

Barbecued chicken gets a makeover in this recipe. The combination of ingredients makes for a mellow, not-too-sweet flavor that's more grown-up than the original. It's great over rice, pasta or potatoes.
—**SHARON FRITZ** MORRISTOWN, TN

PREP: 15 MIN. • **COOK:** 5 HOURS • **MAKES:** 6 SERVINGS

- **6 boneless skinless chicken thighs (about 1½ pounds)**
- **½ teaspoon poultry seasoning**
- **1 medium onion, chopped**
- **1 can (14½ ounces) diced tomatoes, undrained**
- **1 can (8 ounces) tomato sauce**
- **½ cup barbecue sauce**
- **¼ cup orange juice**
- **1 teaspoon garlic powder**
- **¾ teaspoon dried oregano**
- **½ teaspoon hot pepper sauce**
- **¼ teaspoon pepper**
- **Hot cooked brown rice, optional**

1. Place chicken in a 3-qt. slow cooker; sprinkle with poultry seasoning. Top with onion and tomatoes. In a small bowl, mix tomato sauce, barbecue sauce, orange juice and seasonings; pour over top.

2. Cook, covered, on low 5-6 hours or until the chicken is tender. If desired, serve with rice.

To freeze: Place the cooked chicken mixture in freezer containers. Cool and freeze. To use, partially thaw in refrigerator overnight. Microwave, covered, on high in a microwave-safe dish until heated through, gently stirring and adding a little water if necessary.

SLOW-COOKED TURKEY WITH HERBED STUFFING

I'm all for turkey dinner, especially around the holidays. A whole turkey won't fit in my slow cooker, so thank goodness for turkey breast. I cook it with my grandma's easy stuffing recipe for a great meal that doesn't require hard work.
—**CAMILLE BECKSTRAND** LAYTON, UT

PREP: 20 MIN. • **COOK:** 3 HOURS + STANDING
MAKES: 8 SERVINGS

- **2 boneless skinless turkey breast halves (1 pound each) or 2 pounds turkey breast tenderloins**
- **1 jar (12 ounces) turkey gravy, divided**
- **1 can (10½ ounces) reduced-fat reduced-sodium condensed cream of mushroom soup, undiluted**
- **½ teaspoon salt**
- **½ teaspoon poultry seasoning**
- **¼ teaspoon pepper**
- **1 medium Granny Smith apple, finely chopped**
- **2 celery ribs, thinly sliced**
- **1 small onion, finely chopped**
- **1 cup sliced fresh mushrooms, optional**
- **6 cups seasoned stuffing cubes**

1. Place turkey in a 5- or 6-qt. slow cooker. Whisk ¼ cup gravy, condensed soup and seasonings. Cover and refrigerate the remaining gravy. Stir apple, celery, onion and, if desired, mushrooms into the gravy mixture. Stir in stuffing cubes; spoon over turkey. Cook, covered, on low until a thermometer reads 170° and the meat is tender, 3-4 hours.

2. Remove turkey from slow cooker; tent with foil. Let stand 10 minutes before slicing. Warm the remaining gravy. Serve with turkey and stuffing.

SLOW-COOKED TURKEY WITH HERBED STUFFING
Camille Beckstrand
Layton, UT

SHREDDED CHICKEN GYROS

SHREDDED CHICKEN GYROS

Our family has no links to Greece of any kind, but we always have such a great time at Salt Lake City's annual Greek Festival. One of my favorite parts is all the awesome food. This meal is a good way to mix up our menu, and my kids are big fans.

—**CAMILLE BECKSTRAND** LAYTON, UT

PREP: 20 MIN. • **COOK:** 3 HOURS
MAKES: 8 SERVINGS

- **2 medium onions, chopped**
- **6 garlic cloves, minced**
- **1 teaspoon lemon-pepper seasoning**
- **1 teaspoon dried oregano**
- **½ teaspoon ground allspice**
- **½ cup water**
- **½ cup lemon juice**
- **¼ cup red wine vinegar**
- **2 tablespoons olive oil**
- **2 pounds boneless skinless chicken breasts**
- **8 whole pita breads**
- **Toppings: tzatziki sauce, torn romaine and sliced tomato, cucumber and onion**

1. In a 3-qt. slow cooker, combine the first nine ingredients; add chicken. Cook, covered, on low 3-4 hours or until chicken is tender (a thermometer should read at least 165°).

2. Remove chicken from slow cooker. Shred with two forks; return to slow cooker. Using tongs, place the chicken mixture on pita breads. Serve with toppings.

MOIST ITALIAN TURKEY BREAST

This recipe produces some of the juiciest turkey I have ever eaten. High in lean protein, it's a smart entree for a special occasion.

—**JESSICA KUNZ** SPRINGFIELD, IL

PREP: 25 MIN. • **COOK:** 5 HOURS + STANDING
MAKES: 12 SERVINGS

- **1 pound medium carrots, cut into 2-inch pieces**
- **2 medium onions, cut into wedges**
- **3 celery ribs, cut into 2-inch pieces**
- **1 can (14½ ounces) chicken broth**
- **1 bone-in turkey breast (6 to 7 pounds), thawed and skin removed**
- **2 tablespoons olive oil**
- **1½ teaspoons seasoned salt**
- **1 teaspoon Italian seasoning**
- **½ teaspoon pepper**

1. Place vegetables and broth in a 6- or 7-qt. slow cooker; top with turkey breast. Brush turkey with oil; sprinkle with seasonings.

2. Cook, covered, on low until the turkey is tender and a thermometer reads at least 170°, 5-6 hours. Remove turkey from cooker; let stand, covered, 15 minutes before carving. Serve with vegetables. If desired, strain cooking juices and thicken for gravy.

TOMATO BALSAMIC CHICKEN

I came up with this saucy chicken during a particularly busy holiday season. As new parents, my husband and I both appreciate having a go-to dinner that's easy, homemade and delicious.

—**ANNE COLVIN** CHICAGO, IL

PREP: 25 MIN. • **COOK:** 6 HOURS • **MAKES:** 6 SERVINGS

- **2 medium carrots, chopped**
- **½ cup thinly sliced shallots**
- **2 pounds bone-in chicken thighs, skin removed**
- **1 tablespoon all-purpose flour**
- **½ cup reduced-sodium chicken broth**
- **1 can (14½ ounces) petite diced tomatoes, undrained**
- **¼ cup balsamic vinegar**
- **1 tablespoon olive oil**
- **2 garlic cloves, minced**
- **1 bay leaf**
- **½ teaspoon Italian seasoning**
- **½ teaspoon salt**
- **¼ teaspoon pepper**
- **Hot cooked orzo**

1. Place carrots and shallots in a 3- or 4-qt. slow cooker; top with chicken. In a bowl, whisk flour and broth until smooth; stir in tomatoes, vinegar, oil, garlic and seasonings. Pour over chicken. Cook, covered, on low until chicken and carrots are tender, 6-8 hours.

2. Remove chicken; cool slightly. Discard bay leaf and, if desired, skim fat from the carrot mixture.

3. Remove chicken from bones; shred slightly with two forks. Return to slow cooker and heat through. Serve with orzo.

To freeze: Freeze the cooled chicken mixture in freezer containers. To use, partially thaw in refrigerator overnight. Heat through in a saucepan, stirring occasionally.

ALFREDO CHICKEN & BISCUITS

For a cute potpie presentation, dish this creamy chicken up in ramekins and top each with a biscuit. I sometimes serve it over hot linguine, too.

—**FAITH CROMWELL** SAN FRANCISCO, CA

PREP: 40 MIN. • **COOK:** 3 HOURS
MAKES: 10 SERVINGS

- **2 jars (16 ounces each) Alfredo sauce**
- **2 cans (15¼ ounces each) whole kernel corn, drained**
- **2 cups frozen peas, thawed**
- **2 jars (4½ ounces each) sliced mushrooms, drained**
- **1 medium onion, chopped**
- **1 cup water**
- **1 teaspoon garlic salt**
- **½ teaspoon pepper**
- **2 tablespoons canola oil**
- **8 boneless skinless chicken breast halves (6 ounces each)**
- **1 tube (12 ounces) refrigerated buttermilk biscuits**
- **3 tablespoons grated Parmesan cheese**

1. In a large bowl, combine the first eight ingredients. Pour half into a 6-qt. slow cooker.
2. In a large skillet, heat oil over medium-high heat. Brown chicken in batches on both sides. Transfer to slow cooker.
3. Pour remaining Alfredo mixture over chicken. Cook, covered, on low 3-4 hours or until chicken is tender (a thermometer inserted in chicken should read at least 165°).
4. Arrange the biscuits on an ungreased baking sheet; sprinkle with cheese. Bake according to package directions.
5. Remove chicken from slow cooker. Shred with two forks; return to slow cooker. Serve chicken mixture in ramekins or shallow bowls topped with a biscuit.

GARLIC CHICKEN & BROCCOLI

This simple riff on Chinese chicken proves you can savor the take-out taste you crave while still eating right.

—**CONNIE KRUPP** RACINE, WI

PREP: 15 MIN. • **COOK:** 3 HOURS
MAKES: 8 SERVINGS

- **2 pounds boneless skinless chicken breasts, cut into 1-in. pieces**
- **4 cups fresh broccoli florets**
- **4 medium carrots, julienned**
- **1 can (8 ounces) sliced water chestnuts, drained**
- **6 garlic cloves, minced**
- **3 cups reduced-sodium chicken broth**
- **¼ cup reduced-sodium soy sauce**
- **2 tablespoons brown sugar**
- **2 tablespoons sesame oil**
- **2 tablespoons rice vinegar**
- **½ teaspoon salt**
- **½ teaspoon pepper**
- **⅓ cup cornstarch**
- **⅓ cup water**
- **Hot cooked rice**

1. In a 4- or 5-qt. slow cooker, combine chicken, broccoli, carrots, water chestnuts and garlic. In a large bowl, mix the next seven ingredients; pour over the chicken mixture. Cook, covered, on low until the chicken and broccoli are tender, 3-4 hours.
2. Remove chicken and vegetables; keep warm. Strain the cooking juices into a small saucepan; skim fat. Bring juices to a boil. In a small bowl, mix cornstarch and water until smooth; stir into the cooking juices. Return to a boil; cook and stir for 1-2 minutes or until thickened. Serve with chicken, vegetables and hot cooked rice.
To freeze: Place chicken and vegetables in freezer containers; top with sauce. Cool and freeze. To use, partially thaw in refrigerator overnight. Microwave, covered, on high in a microwave-safe dish until heated through, stirring gently and adding a little broth or water if necessary.

GARLIC CHICKEN
& BROCCOLI

POLYNESIAN PULLED CHICKEN
Rebecca Taylor
Manteca, CA

POLYNESIAN PULLED CHICKEN

I adapted a pork recipe to create pulled chicken with coconut and pineapple for a Polynesian twist.

—**REBECCA TAYLOR** MANTECA, CA

PREP: 15 MIN. • **COOK:** 3¼ HOURS
MAKES: 6 SERVINGS

- **2 pounds boneless skinless chicken breasts**
- **1 cup barbecue sauce**
- **1 cup crushed pineapple, undrained**
- **1 medium onion, chopped**
- **¾ cup frozen pepper strips, thawed**
- **¼ cup sweetened shredded coconut**
- **1 tablespoon minced garlic**
- **1 tablespoon reduced-sodium soy sauce**
- **1 teaspoon salt**
- **1 tablespoon cornstarch**
- **¼ cup water**
- **6 hoagie buns, split**
- **Minced fresh cilantro, optional**

1. In a 3- or 4-qt. slow cooker, combine the first nine ingredients. Cook, covered, on low 3-4 hours or until a thermometer reads 165°. Remove chicken; cool slightly.
2. Meanwhile, in a small bowl, mix cornstarch and water until smooth; gradually stir into cooking juices. Cook, covered, on high 15-20 minutes or until sauce is thickened. Shred chicken with two forks. Return to slow cooker; heat through.
3. Serve with buns and, if desired, sprinkle with cilantro.
To freeze: Freeze cooled meat mixture in freezer containers. To use, partially thaw in refrigerator overnight. Heat through in a saucepan, stirring occasionally and adding a little broth or water if necessary. Serve on buns. If desired, sprinkle with cilantro.

CURRIED CHICKEN CACCIATORE

With a family, full-time course load at college and a part-time job, I've found that the slow cooker is my best friend when it comes to getting hot and homemade meals like this one on the table.

—**LAURA GIER** RENSSELAER, NY

PREP: 30 MIN. • **COOK:** 6¼ HOURS
MAKES: 4 SERVINGS

- **1 broiler/fryer chicken (3 to 4 pounds), cut up and skin removed**
- **2 small zucchini, halved and sliced**
- **½ pound sliced fresh mushrooms**
- **1 small green pepper, chopped**
- **1 small onion, chopped**
- **1 jar (24 ounces) spaghetti sauce**
- **1 can (14½ ounces) diced tomatoes, undrained**
- **⅔ cup dry red wine**
- **⅓ cup chicken broth**
- **1 tablespoon minced fresh parsley**
- **2 garlic cloves, minced**
- **1½ teaspoons dried thyme**
- **1½ teaspoons curry powder**
- **½ teaspoon pepper**
- **2 tablespoons cornstarch**
- **2 tablespoons cold water**
- **Hot cooked rice**

1. Place chicken and vegetables in a 5-qt. slow cooker. In a large bowl, mix spaghetti sauce, tomatoes, wine, broth, parsley, garlic and seasonings; pour over chicken. Cook, covered, on low 6-8 hours or until the chicken is tender.
2. In a small bowl, mix cornstarch and water until smooth; gradually stir into the stew. Cook, covered, on high for 15 minutes or until sauce is thickened. Serve with rice.

CASABLANCA CHUTNEY CHICKEN

If you enjoy Indian food, you'll love this dish. An array of spices and dried fruit slowly simmer with boneless chicken thighs for an aromatic and satisfying meal. To make it complete, serve over jasmine or basmati rice.

—**ROXANNE CHAN** ALBANY, CA

PREP: 25 MIN. • **COOK:** 7 HOURS • **MAKES:** 4 SERVINGS

- **1 pound boneless skinless chicken thighs, cut into ¾-inch pieces**
- **1 can (14½ ounces) chicken broth**
- **⅓ cup finely chopped onion**
- **⅓ cup chopped sweet red pepper**
- **⅓ cup chopped carrot**
- **⅓ cup chopped dried apricots**
- **⅓ cup chopped dried figs**
- **⅓ cup golden raisins**
- **2 tablespoons orange marmalade**
- **1 tablespoon mustard seed**
- **2 garlic cloves, minced**
- **½ teaspoon curry powder**
- **¼ teaspoon crushed red pepper flakes**
- **¼ teaspoon ground cumin**
- **¼ teaspoon ground cinnamon**
- **¼ teaspoon ground cloves**
- **2 tablespoons minced fresh parsley**
- **2 tablespoons minced fresh mint**
- **1 tablespoon lemon juice**
- **4 tablespoons chopped pistachios**

1. In a 3-qt. slow cooker, combine the first 16 ingredients. Cover and cook on low for 7-8 hours or until the chicken is tender.

2. Stir in parsley, mint and lemon juice; heat through. Sprinkle each serving with pistachios.

CHICKEN IN COCONUT PEANUT SAUCE

My youngest son had been out of the country for several years teaching English. When he returned to the United States, I made this home-cooked meal for him that combined Asian and American cuisine. He loved it!

—**SHEILA SUHAN** SCOTTDALE, PA

PREP: 15 MIN. • **COOK:** 5 HOURS • **MAKES:** 6 SERVINGS

- **½ cup coconut milk**
- **½ cup creamy peanut butter**
- **1 can (28 ounces) crushed tomatoes**
- **1 medium onion, finely chopped**
- **2 to 3 jalapeno peppers, seeded and finely chopped**
- **2 tablespoons brown sugar**
- **3 garlic cloves, minced**
- **2 teaspoons ground cumin**
- **1 teaspoon salt**
- **1 teaspoon pepper**
- **12 boneless skinless chicken thighs (about 3 pounds)**
- **Hot cooked rice**
- **Minced fresh cilantro**

In a 5-qt. slow cooker, whisk coconut milk and peanut butter until smooth. Stir in tomatoes, onion, peppers, brown sugar, garlic and seasonings. Add chicken; cook, covered, on low for 5-6 hours or until the chicken is tender. Stir before serving. Serve with rice; sprinkle with cilantro.

Note: Wear disposable gloves when cutting hot peppers; the oils can burn exposed skin. Avoid touching your face.

CHICKEN IN COCONUT PEANUT SAUCE

EASY SLOW-COOKED PORK TENDERLOIN, PAGE 152

PORK, HAM & MORE

Let your slow cooker tease out the flavors of pork in all its delicious forms—chops, ribs, loin, ham and, of course, pulled pork! And if you love sausage and lamb, there's plenty here for you, too!

CHERRY BALSAMIC PORK LOIN

After having a wonderful cherry Brie topping from a local market, I just knew I had to create one for pork. If you're really crazy about cherries, add even more to the slow cooker.

—**SUSAN STETZEL** GAINESVILLE, NY

PREP: 20 MIN. • **COOK:** 3 HOURS + STANDING
MAKES: 8 SERVINGS (1⅓ CUPS SAUCE)

- **1 boneless pork loin roast (3 to 4 pounds)**
- **1 teaspoon salt**
- **½ teaspoon pepper**
- **1 tablespoon canola oil**
- **¾ cup cherry preserves**
- **½ cup dried cherries**
- **⅓ cup balsamic vinegar**
- **¼ cup packed brown sugar**

1. Sprinkle roast with salt and pepper. In a large skillet, heat oil over medium-high heat. Brown roast on all sides.

2. Transfer to a 6-qt. slow cooker. In a small bowl, mix preserves, cherries, vinegar and brown sugar until blended; pour over the roast. Cook, covered, on low 3-4 hours or until tender (a thermometer inserted in the pork should read at least 145°).

3. Remove the roast from slow cooker; tent with foil. Let stand for 15 minutes before slicing. Skim fat from the cooking juices. Serve pork with sauce.

SAUCY RANCH PORK & POTATOES

A while back, my sister Elyse shared a tasty ranch pork roast recipe. I tweaked it so I could use what was already in my pantry, and this dish was born.

—**KENDRA ADAMSON** LAYTON, UT

PREP: 20 MIN. • **COOK:** 4 HOURS • **MAKES:** 6 SERVINGS

- **2 pounds red potatoes (about 6 medium), cut into ¾-inch cubes**
- **¼ cup water**
- **6 boneless pork loin chops (6 ounces each)**
- **2 cans (10¾ ounces each) condensed cream of chicken soup, undiluted**
- **1 cup 2% milk**
- **1 envelope ranch salad dressing mix**
- **Minced fresh parsley, optional**

1. Place potatoes and water in a large microwave-safe dish. Microwave, covered, on high 3-5 minutes or until the potatoes are almost tender; drain.

2. Transfer the potatoes and pork chops to a 4- or 5-qt. slow cooker. In a bowl, mix condensed soup, milk and salad dressing mix; pour over pork chops. Cook, covered, on low for 4-5 hours or until pork and potatoes are tender (a thermometer inserted in the pork should read at least 145°). If desired, sprinkle with parsley.

TEST KITCHEN TIP

Liquids given up by the ingredients in a slow cooker will remain in the pot instead of evaporating. That's why many recipes call for condensed soup instead of liquid broth or stock. When adapting a a traditional recipe for your slow cooker, reduce the liquid by a third.

SAUCY RANCH PORK & POTATOES
Kendra Adamson
Layton, UT

CHINESE-STYLE RIBS

When I was working two jobs, slow cooking was my way of life. Sometimes I had more than one slow cooker going at a time to help me feed my family delicious home-cooked meals. These ribs are quick, easy and have a delicious Asian flavor.

—**PAULA MARCHESI** LENHARTSVILLE, PA

PREP: 20 MIN. • **COOK:** 6 HOURS
MAKES: 6 SERVINGS

- **3 pounds boneless country-style pork ribs**
- **6 green onions, cut into 1-inch pieces**
- **1 can (8 ounces) sliced water chestnuts, drained**
- **¾ cup hoisin sauce**
- **3 tablespoons soy sauce**
- **2 tablespoons sherry or chicken stock**
- **5 garlic cloves, minced**
- **1 tablespoon minced fresh gingerroot**
- **1 tablespoon light corn syrup**
- **1 tablespoon orange marmalade**
- **1 teaspoon pumpkin pie spice**
- **½ teaspoon crushed red pepper flakes**
- **2 tablespoons cornstarch**
- **2 tablespoons water**
- **Hot cooked rice**
- **Additional sliced green onions, optional**

1. Place pork, green onions and water chestnuts in a 5-qt slow cooker. Mix hoisin sauce, soy sauce, sherry, garlic, gingerroot, corn syrup, marmalade, pie spice and pepper flakes in a bowl. Pour over the pork. Cook, covered, on low until meat is tender, 6-8 hours.

2. Remove to a serving platter; keep warm. Skim fat from the cooking juices; transfer to a small saucepan. Bring to a boil. Mix cornstarch and water until smooth. Gradually stir into saucepan. Return to a boil; cook and stir until thickened, about 2 minutes. Serve with ribs, rice and, if desired, additional green onions.

FAST FIX

EASY SLOW-COOKED PORK TENDERLOIN

I find that simple dinners are the comfort foods that my family of seven really desires. Simple, good ingredients are the key to my success in the kitchen. Just three ingredients poured over the pork and voila! The most mouth-watering pork you have ever tasted.

—**GRACE NELTNER** LAKESIDE PARK, KY

PREP: 5 MIN. • **COOK:** 1¾ HOURS + STANDING
MAKES: 6 SERVINGS

- **¼ cup olive oil**
- **2 tablespoons soy sauce**
- **1 tablespoon Montreal steak seasoning**
- **2 pork tenderloins (1 pound each)**
- **Mashed potatoes or cooked wild rice**

In a 5-qt. slow cooker, mix oil, soy sauce and steak seasoning. Add pork; turn to coat. Cook, covered, on low until a thermometer inserted in the pork reads 145°, 1¾ to 2¼ hours. Let stand 10 minutes before slicing. Serve with mashed potatoes.

ITALIAN SAUSAGE DINNER

My family loves this dish. It's easy to prepare before I go to work, and it makes the house smell so good by the end of the day.

—**KATHY KASPROWICZ** ARLINGTON HEIGHTS, IL

PREP: 20 MIN. • **COOK:** 6 HOURS • **MAKES:** 5 SERVINGS

- **1 pound small red potatoes**
- **2 large zucchini, cut into 1-inch slices**
- **2 large green peppers, cut into 1½-inch pieces**
- **1 large onion, cut into wedges**
- **¼ teaspoon salt**
- **¼ teaspoon pepper**
- **1 pound Italian sausage links, cut into 1½-inch pieces**
- **1 tablespoon olive oil**
- **½ cup white wine or chicken broth**
- **1 tablespoon Italian seasoning**

Place the first six ingredients in a 6-qt. slow cooker. In a large skillet, brown sausages in oil. Reduce heat. Add wine and Italian seasoning, stirring to loosen browned bits from pan. Transfer to slow cooker. Cover and cook on low for 6-8 hours or until the potatoes are tender.

CURRIED LAMB & POTATOES

Loads of rich flavors and spices make this a warming, inviting meal. It's a great way to impress at a family get-together.

—**SUBRINA GOOSCH** MONROE, NC

PREP: 30 MIN. + MARINATING • **COOK:** 4 HOURS
MAKES: 6 SERVINGS

- **6 garlic cloves, minced, divided**
- **3 tablespoons curry powder, divided**
- **2 tablespoons minced fresh gingerroot, divided**
- **2 teaspoons garam masala, divided**
- **1 teaspoon chili powder**
- **1 teaspoon paprika**
- **1 teaspoon dried thyme**
- **1 teaspoon ground coriander, divided**
- **1½ teaspoons salt, divided**
- **1 teaspoon pepper, divided**
- **¼ teaspoon ground cumin**
- **1 tablespoon olive oil**
- **2 pounds lamb shoulder blade chops**
- **4 medium red potatoes, cut into ½-inch pieces**
- **1 can (15 ounces) diced tomatoes, undrained**
- **1 cup chicken broth**
- **1 small onion, chopped**
- **Hot cooked brown rice and minced fresh cilantro, optional**

1. In a large resealable plastic bag, combine 3 garlic cloves, 1 tablespoon curry powder, 1 tablespoon ginger, 1 teaspoon garam masala, chili powder, paprika and thyme, ½ teaspoon coriander, ½ teaspoon salt, ½ teaspoon pepper, cumin and olive oil. Add lamb chops; seal bag and turn to coat. Refrigerate 8 hours or overnight.

2. Place potatoes in a 3- or 4-qt. slow cooker. Transfer lamb to slow cooker.

3. Place tomatoes, broth, onion, and remaining garlic and seasonings in a blender; cover and process until blended. Pour over the lamb and potatoes. Cook, covered, on low 4-5 hours or until the meat is tender. When cool enough to handle, remove meat from bones; discard bones. Shred meat with two forks. Strain cooking juices, reserving potatoes; skim fat. Return lamb, cooking juices and the reserved potatoes to slow cooker; heat through. If desired, serve with rice and cilantro.

SLOW COOKER MEMPHIS-STYLE RIBS
Matthew Hass
Franklin, WI

SLOW COOKER MEMPHIS-STYLE RIBS

After my dad and I had dinner at the legendary Rendezvous Restaurant, I was inspired to create a slow-cooked version of tasty dry-rub Memphis ribs. Smoked paprika in the rub mimics the flavor the ribs would get from grilling over hot coals.

—**MATTHEW HASS** FRANKLIN, WI

PREP: 15 MIN. • **COOK:** 5 HOURS • **MAKES:** 6 SERVINGS

- **½ cup white vinegar**
- **½ cup water**
- **2 racks pork baby back ribs (about 5 pounds)**
- **3 tablespoons smoked paprika**
- **2 tablespoons brown sugar**
- **2 teaspoons salt**
- **2 teaspoons coarsely ground pepper**
- **1 teaspoon garlic powder**
- **1 teaspoon onion powder**
- **1 teaspoon ground cumin**
- **1 teaspoon ground mustard**
- **1 teaspoon dried thyme**
- **1 teaspoon dried oregano**
- **1 teaspoon celery salt**
- **¾ teaspoon cayenne pepper**

1. Combine vinegar and water; brush over ribs. Pour the remaining vinegar mixture into a 6-qt. slow cooker. Mix together the remaining ingredients, reserving half. Sprinkle the ribs with the remaining seasoning blend. Cut into serving-size pieces; transfer to slow cooker.

2. Cook, covered, on low until tender, 5-6 hours. Remove ribs; skim fat from cooking juices. Using a clean brush, brush ribs generously with cooking juices; sprinkle with the reserved seasoning. Serve ribs with the remaining juices.

GREEN CHILI CHOPS WITH SWEET POTATOES

It takes only a few minutes to combine all the ingredients in a slow cooker, and you'll have a filling, healthy dinner waiting for you at the end of the day. We like to serve this delicious pork dish with fresh-baked garlic bread.

—**MARINA ASHWORTH** DENVER, CO

PREP: 20 MIN. • **COOK:** 6 HOURS • **MAKES:** 4 SERVINGS

- **3 medium sweet potatoes, peeled and cut into ½-inch slices**
- **1 large onion, chopped**
- **1 large green pepper, coarsely chopped**
- **1½ cups frozen corn**
- **½ teaspoon salt**
- **¼ teaspoon pepper**
- **4 boneless pork loin chops (6 ounces each)**
- **1 can (10 ounces) mild green enchilada sauce**
- **½ cup sour cream**
- **2 tablespoons reduced-sodium teriyaki sauce**

1. In a 6-qt. slow cooker, combine sweet potatoes, onion, green pepper, corn, salt and pepper. Top with pork chops. Mix enchilada sauce, sour cream and teriyaki sauce; pour over the meat.

2. Cook, covered, on low 6-8 hours or until the meat is tender.

CRANBERRY-GINGER PORK RIBS

This festive and spicy main dish is wonderful served for weeknight family meals or for entertaining.
—**JUDY ARMSTRONG** PRAIRIEVILLE, LA

PREP: 20 MIN. • **COOK:** 5 HOURS • **MAKES:** 8 SERVINGS

- **1 can (14 ounces) whole-berry cranberry sauce**
- **2 habanero peppers, seeded and minced**
- **4½ teaspoons minced grated gingerroot**
- **3 garlic cloves, minced**
- **2½ pounds boneless country-style pork ribs**
- **½ teaspoon salt**
- **½ teaspoon cayenne pepper**
- **½ teaspoon pepper**
- **2 tablespoons olive oil**
- **Hot cooked rice**

1. In a small bowl, combine cranberry sauce, habanero peppers, ginger and garlic. Sprinkle ribs with salt and peppers. In a large skillet, brown the ribs in oil on all sides; drain.
2. Transfer ribs to a 3-qt. slow cooker; pour the cranberry mixture over ribs. Cover and cook on low for 5-6 hours or until the meat is tender. Skim fat from the cooking juices. Serve with pork and rice.
Note: Wear disposable gloves when cutting hot peppers; the oils can burn exposed skin. Avoid touching your face.

FAMILY-FAVORITE SPAGHETTI SAUCE

My friend Mary shared this wonderful recipe for spaghetti sauce that's become an annual tradition at our campers potluck.
—**HELEN ROWE** SPRING LAKE, MI

PREP: 30 MIN. • **COOK:** 6 HOURS
MAKES: 9 SERVINGS (2¼ QUARTS)

- **1 pound bulk Italian sausage**
- **½ pound ground beef**
- **1 large onion, chopped**
- **1 celery rib, chopped**
- **3 garlic cloves, minced**
- **1 tablespoon olive oil**
- **1 can (28 ounces) diced tomatoes**
- **1 can (10¾ ounces) condensed tomato soup, undiluted**
- **1 can (8 ounces) mushroom stems and pieces, drained**
- **1 can (8 ounces) tomato sauce**
- **1 can (6 ounces) tomato paste**
- **1 tablespoon sugar**
- **½ teaspoon pepper**
- **½ teaspoon dried basil**
- **¼ teaspoon dried oregano**
- **Hot cooked spaghetti**

1. In a large skillet, cook the sausage, beef, onion, celery and garlic in oil over medium heat until the meat is no longer pink; drain. In a 4-qt. slow cooker, combine the diced tomatoes, tomato soup, mushrooms, tomato sauce, tomato paste, sugar and seasonings. Stir in the sausage mixture.
2. Cover and cook on low for 6-8 hours or until the flavors are blended. Serve with spaghetti.

SLOW-COOKED
REUBEN BRATS

SLOW-COOKED REUBEN BRATS

Sauerkraut gives these beer-simmered brats a big flavor boost, but it's the special chili sauce and melted cheese that put them over the top. Also try the chili sauce on top of your favorite burger; you won't be sorry.

—**ALANA SIMMONS** JOHNSTOWN, PA

PREP: 30 MIN. • **COOK:** 7¼ HOURS
MAKES: 10 SERVINGS

- **10 uncooked bratwurst links**
- **3 bottles (12 ounces each) light beer or nonalcoholic beer**
- **1 large sweet onion, sliced**
- **1 can (14 ounces) sauerkraut, rinsed and well drained**
- **¾ cup mayonnaise**
- **¼ cup chili sauce**
- **2 tablespoons ketchup**
- **1 tablespoon finely chopped onion**
- **2 teaspoons sweet pickle relish**
- **1 garlic clove, minced**
- **⅛ teaspoon pepper**
- **10 hoagie buns, split**
- **10 slices Swiss cheese**

1. In a large skillet, brown bratwurst in batches; drain. In a 5-qt. slow cooker, combine beer, sliced onion and sauerkraut; add the bratwurst. Cook, covered, on low 7-9 hours or until the sausages are cooked through.

2. Preheat oven to 350°. In a small bowl, mix mayonnaise, chili sauce, ketchup, chopped onion, relish, garlic and pepper until blended. Spread over cut sides of buns; top with cheese, bratwurst and the sauerkraut mixture. Place on an ungreased baking sheet. Bake for 8-10 minutes or until the cheese is melted.

LOW & SLOW PORK VERDE

LOW & SLOW PORK VERDE

My family loves this versatile pork dish. We like to have it over a serving of cheesy grits, but it also goes well with rice or potatoes. Leftovers make an excellent starter for white chili.

—**VAL RUBLE** AVA, MO

PREP: 15 MIN. • **COOK:** 5 HOURS
MAKES: 8 SERVINGS

- 1 boneless pork shoulder butt roast (3½ to 4 pounds)
- 1 large onion, chopped
- 1 jar (16 ounces) salsa verde
- 2 cans (4 ounces each) chopped green chilies
- 2 teaspoons ground cumin
- 1 teaspoon dried oregano
- 1 teaspoon salt
- 1 teaspoon pepper
- ¼ teaspoon crushed red pepper flakes
- ⅛ teaspoon ground cinnamon
- ¼ cup minced fresh cilantro
- Hot cooked grits
- Sour cream, optional

1. Place pork and onion in a 4-qt. slow cooker. In a small bowl, combine salsa, chilies, cumin, oregano, salt, pepper, pepper flakes and cinnamon; pour over meat. Cook, covered, on low 5-6 hours or until the meat is tender.

2. Remove roast; cool slightly. Skim fat from the cooking juices. Shred pork with two forks. Return meat to slow cooker; heat through. Stir in cilantro. Serve with grits and, if desired, sour cream.

To freeze: Freeze cooled meat mixture in freezer containers. To use, partially thaw in refrigerator overnight. Microwave, covered, on high in a microwave-safe dish until heated through, gently stirring and adding a little broth if necessary.

GLAZED LAMB SHANKS

Ideal on a night in for two, these slow-cooked shanks are packed with complex flavors. The Guinness and honey provide balance, while the garlic adds zing.

—**ELIZABETH MITCHELL** COCHRANVILLE, PA

PREP: 30 MIN. + MARINATING • **COOK:** 6 HOURS
MAKES: 4 SERVINGS

- 4 lamb shanks (about 20 ounces each)
- 4 garlic cloves, thinly sliced
- 1 cup lemon juice
- 4 tablespoons olive oil, divided
- 1 tablespoon each minced fresh thyme, rosemary and parsley
- 1 teaspoon salt
- ½ teaspoon pepper

SAUCE

- 1 cup Guinness (dark beer)
- ¼ cup honey
- 3 fresh thyme sprigs
- 2 bay leaves
- 1 tablespoon Dijon mustard
- 2 garlic cloves, minced
- ½ teaspoon salt
- ¼ teaspoon pepper
- ⅛ teaspoon crushed red pepper flakes
- 2 pounds Yukon Gold potatoes, peeled and cut into chunks

1. Cut slits into each lamb shank; insert garlic slices. In a large resealable plastic bag, combine the lemon juice, 2 tablespoons oil, thyme, rosemary, parsley, salt and pepper. Add the lamb; seal bag and turn to coat. Refrigerate overnight.

2. Drain and discard the marinade. In a large skillet, brown lamb in the remaining oil on all sides in batches. Place in a 5- or 6-qt. slow cooker.

3. In the same skillet, combine beer, honey, thyme, bay leaves, Dijon, garlic, salt, pepper and pepper flakes. Bring to a boil, stirring constantly. Pour over the meat. Cover and cook on low for 6-8 hours or until meat and potatoes are tender; add potatoes during the last 2 hours of cooking.

4. Remove lamb and potatoes. Strain sauce and discard bay leaves. If desired, thicken sauce. Serve with lamb and potatoes.

FAST FIX

CHALUPAS

This is such a refreshing change of pace from traditional chili. It's also fun to serve to guests—everyone who has tasted it has asked for the recipe!

—**GINNY BECKER** TORRINGTON, WY

PREP: 10 MIN. + STANDING • **COOK:** 8¼ HOURS
MAKES: 6-8 SERVINGS

- **1 cup dried pinto beans**
- **3½ cups water**
- **¼ cup chopped onion**
- **1 can (4 ounces) chopped green chilies**
- **1 garlic clove, minced**
- **1 tablespoon chili powder**
- **1½ teaspoons salt**
- **1½ teaspoons ground cumin**
- **½ teaspoon dried oregano**
- **1 boneless pork shoulder butt roast (1½ pounds)**
- **1 package (10½ ounces) corn chips**
- **¼ cup sliced green onions**
- **Shredded lettuce**
- **Shredded cheddar cheese**
- **Chopped fresh tomatoes**
- **Salsa**

1. Place beans and enough water to cover in a 3-qt. saucepan. Bring to a boil; boil for 2 minutes. Remove from the heat; let stand for 1 hour. Drain beans and discard the liquid.
2. In a 3-qt. slow cooker, combine the 3½ cups water, onion, chilies, garlic, chili powder, salt, cumin and oregano. Add roast and beans. Cover and cook on high for 2 hours. Reduce heat to low and cook for 6 hours longer or until the pork is very tender.
3. Remove roast and shred with a fork. Drain the beans, reserving the cooking liquid in a saucepan. Combine beans and meat; set aside. Skim and discard fat from cooking liquid; bring to a boil. Boil, uncovered, for 15-20 minutes or until reduced to 1½ cups. Add meat and bean mixture; heat through.
4. To serve, spoon meat mixture over corn chips; top with green onions, lettuce, cheese, tomatoes and salsa.

BUTTERMILK-MUSHROOM PORK CHOPS

I went through several variations before creating the pork chops my family considers perfect! I wanted something rich, delicious and tasty that was still relatively healthy. This makes a delicious Sunday dinner—you can pop it in the slow cooker in the morning and let it cook while you are at church! Serve it with salad or grilled asparagus.

—**KRISTIN STONE** LITTLE ELM, TX

PREP: 25 MIN. • **COOK:** 3½ HOURS
MAKES: 6 SERVINGS

- **¼ cup all-purpose flour**
- **1 teaspoon salt, divided**
- **½ teaspoon pepper**
- **2 tablespoons canola oil**
- **6 boneless pork loin chops (6 to 8 ounces each)**
- **1 tablespoon butter**
- **1 pound medium fresh mushrooms, quartered**
- **½ cup white wine or chicken broth**
- **1 tablespoon minced fresh basil**
- **1 can (10¾ ounces) condensed cream of mushroom soup, undiluted**
- **1 cup buttermilk**
- **Hot cooked egg noodles**
- **Additional basil**

1. In a shallow bowl, mix flour, ½ teaspoon salt and pepper. Add pork chops, one at a time, and toss to coat; shake off excess.
2. In a large skillet, heat oil over medium-high heat; brown pork chops in batches. Transfer the meat and drippings to a 4-qt. slow cooker.
3. In the same skillet, heat butter over medium heat. Add mushrooms; cook and stir until tender, 6-8 minutes. Add wine, stirring to loosen browned bits from pan. Pour the mushroom mixture over pork chops; sprinkle with basil.
4. Cook, covered, on low until the meat is tender, 3-4 hours. Whisk together soup, buttermilk and the remaining salt; pour over pork chops. Cook, covered, 30 minutes longer. Stir before serving. Serve with noodles; sprinkle with additional basil.
Note: Warmed buttermilk will appear curdled.

BUTTERMILK-MUSHROOM
PORK CHOPS

EASY CITRUS HAM

EASY CITRUS HAM

I created this recipe many years ago with items I already had on hand. The succulent ham has a mild citrus flavor. It was so popular at a church social that I knew I had a winner!

—**SHEILA CHRISTENSEN** SAN MARCOS, CA

PREP: 15 MIN. • **COOK:** 4 HOURS + STANDING
MAKES: 10-12 SERVINGS

- **1 boneless fully cooked ham (3 to 4 pounds)**
- **½ cup packed dark brown sugar**
- **1 can (12 ounces) lemon-lime soda, divided**
- **1 medium navel orange, thinly sliced**
- **1 medium lemon, thinly sliced**
- **1 medium lime, thinly sliced**
- **1 tablespoon chopped crystallized ginger**

1. Cut ham in half; place in a 5-qt. slow cooker. In a small bowl, combine brown sugar and ¼ cup soda; rub over the ham. Top with orange, lemon and lime slices. Add candied ginger and the remaining soda to the slow cooker.

2. Cover and cook on low for 4-5 hours or until a meat thermometer reads 140°, basting occasionally with cooking juices. Let stand for 10 minutes before slicing.

SUPREME PIZZA-STYLE PASTA

I guarantee that if this pizza mac is on the menu, everybody will be at the table come dinnertime! Use any of your favorite pizza toppings. I have used Canadian bacon and pinneapple, and my family really loved that. The combinations are limited only by your imagination.

—**KELLY SILVERS** EDMOND, OK

PREP: 20 MIN. • **COOK:** 3 HOURS
MAKES: 8 SERVINGS

- **1 pound bulk Italian sausage**
- **1 package (16 ounces) elbow macaroni**
- **2 jars (14 ounces each) pasta sauce**
- **½ cup water**
- **1 package (8 ounces) sliced pepperoni**
- **3 cups shredded part-skim mozzarella cheese, divided**
- **1 medium green pepper, chopped**
- **1 small onion, chopped**
- **1 can (6½ ounces) sliced ripe olives, drained**
- **1 can (6 ounces) sliced mushrooms, drained**
- **⅓ cup grated Parmesan cheese**
- **Additional pasta sauce, optional**

1. Fold two 18-in.-long pieces of foil into two 18x4-in. strips. Line the perimeter of a 5-qt. slow cooker with foil strips; spray with cooking spray.
2. In a 6-qt. stockpot, cook sausage over medium heat until no longer pink, breaking into crumbles. Add pasta; cook and stir 3-4 minutes or until edges become translucent. Stir in pasta sauce, water, pepperoni, and half of each of the following: mozzarella cheese, pepper, onion, olives and mushrooms. Transfer the pasta mixture to slow cooker. Top with the remaining mozzarella cheese; sprinkle with the remaining vegetables.
3. Cook, covered, on low for 3-4 hours or until pasta is tender. Just before serving, sprinkle with Parmesan cheese. If desired, serve with additional pasta sauce.

CHEESY TATER TOT DINNER

I created this slow cooker meal to pay homage to my favorite style of pizza, Hawaiian with bacon and pineapple. The Tater Tots in this recipe make it family-friendly.

—**LISA RENSHAW** KANSAS CITY, MO

PREP: 15 MIN. • **COOK:** 4 HOURS + STANDING
MAKES: 8 SERVINGS

- **1 package (32 ounces) frozen Tater Tots, thawed**
- **8 ounces Canadian bacon, chopped**
- **1 cup frozen pepper strips, thawed and chopped**
- **1 medium onion, finely chopped**
- **1 can (8 ounces) pineapple tidbits, drained**
- **2 large eggs**
- **3 cans (5 ounces each) evaporated milk**
- **1 can (15 ounces) pizza sauce**
- **1 cup shredded provolone cheese**
- **½ cup grated Parmesan cheese, optional**

1. Place half the Tater Tots in a greased 5-qt. slow cooker. Layer with Canadian bacon, peppers, onion and pineapple. Top with the remaining Tater Tots. In a large bowl, whisk eggs, milk and pizza sauce; pour over top. Sprinkle with provolone cheese.
2. Cook, covered, on low 4-5 hours or until heated through. If desired, sprinkle with Parmesan cheese; let stand, covered, 20 minutes.

RED BEANS & SAUSAGE

I'm from Louisiana, so red beans are my go-to comfort food. Putting on a big pot for our Sunday dinner goes back generations in my family. Dig in with some hot buttered corn bread.

—**LISA SUMMERS** LAS VEGAS, NV

PREP: 30 MIN. • **COOK:** 8 HOURS
MAKES: 8 SERVINGS (2¾ QUARTS)

- **1 pound dried red beans**
- **1 tablespoon olive oil**
- **1 pound fully cooked andouille sausage links, cut into ¼-inch slices**
- **1 large onion, chopped**
- **1 medium green pepper, chopped**
- **2 celery ribs, finely chopped**
- **3 teaspoons garlic powder**
- **3 teaspoons Creole seasoning**
- **2 teaspoons smoked paprika**
- **2 teaspoons dried thyme**
- **1½ teaspoons pepper**
- **6 cups chicken broth**
- **Hot cooked rice**

1. Rinse and sort beans; soak according to the package directions.
2. In a large skillet, heat oil over medium-high heat. Brown sausage. Remove with a slotted spoon. Add onion, green pepper and celery to the skillet; cook and stir 5-6 minutes or until crisp-tender.
3. In a 5- or 6-qt. slow cooker, combine beans, sausage, vegetables and seasonings. Stir in broth. Cook, covered, on low 8-10 hours or until beans are tender.
4. Remove 2 cups of the bean mixture to a bowl. Mash gently with a potato masher. Return to slow cooker; heat through. Serve with rice.
Note: The following spice blend may be used in place of 3 teaspoons Creole seasoning: ¾ teaspoon each salt, garlic powder and paprika; and ⅛ teaspoon each dried thyme, ground cumin and cayenne pepper.

SICILIAN MEAT SAUCE

People have told me this is better than the gravy their Sicilian grandmothers used to make. But don't tell the older generation that!

—**EMORY DOTY** JASPER, GA

PREP: 30 MIN. • **COOK:** 6 HOURS
MAKES: 12 SERVINGS

- **3 tablespoons olive oil, divided**
- **3 pounds bone-in country-style pork ribs**
- **1 medium onion, chopped**
- **3 to 5 garlic cloves, minced**
- **2 cans (28 ounces each) crushed or diced tomatoes, drained**
- **1 can (14½ ounces) Italian diced tomatoes, drained**
- **3 bay leaves**
- **2 tablespoons chopped fresh parsley**
- **2 tablespoons chopped capers, drained**
- **½ teaspoon dried basil**
- **½ teaspoon dried rosemary, crushed**
- **½ teaspoon dried thyme**
- **½ teaspoon crushed red pepper flakes**
- **½ teaspoon salt**
- **½ teaspoon sugar**
- **1 cup beef broth**
- **½ cup dry red wine or additional beef broth**
- **Hot cooked pasta**
- **Grated Parmesan cheese, optional**

1. In a Dutch oven, heat 2 tablespoons olive oil over medium-high heat. Brown pork ribs in batches; transfer to a 6-qt. slow cooker.
2. Add the remaining oil to the Dutch oven; saute onion for 2 minutes. Add garlic; cook 1 minute more. Add the next 11 ingredients. Pour in broth and red wine; bring to a light boil. Transfer to slow cooker. Cook, covered, until the pork is tender, about 6 hours.
3. Discard bay leaves. Remove meat from the slow cooker; shred or pull apart, discarding bones. Return meat to sauce. Serve over pasta; if desired, sprinkle with Parmesan cheese.

SICILIAN MEAT SAUCE

CHAR SIU PORK

CHAR SIU PORK

I based this juicy pork on the delicious Asian influences here in Hawaii. It's tasty as is, in a bun or over rice. Use leftovers with fried rice, ramen and salads.

—**KAREN NAIHE** KAMUELA, HI

PREP: 25 MIN. + MARINATING • **COOK:** 5½ HOURS
MAKES: 8 SERVINGS

- ½ cup honey
- ½ cup hoisin sauce
- ¼ cup soy sauce
- ¼ cup ketchup
- 4 garlic cloves, minced
- 4 teaspoons minced fresh gingerroot
- 1 teaspoon Chinese five-spice powder
- 1 boneless pork shoulder butt roast (3 to 4 pounds)
- ½ cup chicken broth
- Fresh cilantro leaves

1. Combine the first seven ingredients; pour into a large resealable plastic bag. Add pork; turn to coat. Refrigerate overnight.
2. Transfer pork and marinade to a 4-qt. slow cooker. Cook, covered, for 5-6 hours on low. Remove pork; when cool enough to handle, shred meat using two forks. Skim fat from cooking juices; stir in chicken broth. Return pork to slow cooker, and heat through. Top with fresh cilantro.

TEST KITCHEN TIP
The five spices in traditional Chinese five-spice powder are star anise, Szechuan peppercorns, fennel seeds, cassia (a more bitter relative of cinnamon) and whole cloves.

CUBAN PULLED PORK SANDWICHES

I lived in Florida for a while and loved the pulled pork they would make, so I went about making it for myself! The flavorful meat makes amazing Cuban sandwiches, but you can also use it in traditional pulled pork sandwiches or even tacos.

—**LACIE GRIFFIN** AUSTIN, TX

PREP: 30 MIN. • **COOK:** 8 HOURS
MAKES: 16 SERVINGS

- 1 cup orange juice
- ½ cup lime juice
- 12 garlic cloves, minced
- 2 tablespoons spiced rum, optional
- 2 tablespoons ground coriander
- 2 teaspoons salt
- 2 teaspoons white pepper
- 2 teaspoons pepper
- 1 teaspoon cayenne pepper
- 5 to 6 pounds boneless pork shoulder roast, cut into four pieces
- 1 tablespoon olive oil

SANDWICHES

- 2 loaves (1 pound each) French bread
- Yellow mustard, optional
- 16 dill pickle slices
- 1½ pounds thinly sliced deli ham
- 1½ pounds Swiss cheese, sliced

1. In a 6- or 7-qt. slow cooker, combine the first nine ingredients. Add pork; cook, covered, on low until tender, 8-10 hours. Remove roast; shred with two forks. In a large skillet, heat oil over medium-high heat. Cook the pork in batches until lightly browned and crisp in spots.
2. Cut each loaf of bread in half lengthwise. If desired, spread mustard over cut sides of bread. Layer bottom halves of bread with pickles, pork, ham and cheese. Replace tops. Cut each loaf into eight slices.

FAST FIX

SAUSAGE SPANISH RICE

My husband and I both work the midnight shift, so I'm always on the lookout for slow cooker recipes. This one couldn't be easier. We often enjoy it as a main course because it's so hearty, but it's also good as a side dish.

—**MICHELLE MCKAY** GARDEN CITY, MI

PREP: 10 MIN. • **COOK:** 5 HOURS
MAKES: 6 SERVINGS

- 1 pound smoked kielbasa or Polish sausage, sliced
- 2 cans (14½ ounces each) diced tomatoes, undrained
- 2 cups water
- 1½ cups uncooked converted rice
- 1 cup salsa
- 1 medium onion
- ½ cup chopped green pepper
- ½ cup chopped sweet red pepper
- 1 can (4 ounces) chopped green chilies
- 1 envelope taco seasoning

In a 3- or 4-qt. slow cooker, combine all ingredients. Cover and cook on low for 5-6 hours or until the rice is tender.

PULLED BBQ PORK

After years of vacationing on the North Carolina coast, I was hooked on their pork barbecue. The version I developed is a regular favorite at potluck dinners.

—**JOSEPH SARNOSKI** WEST CHESTER, PA

PREP: 15 MIN. • **COOK:** 10 HOURS
MAKES: 8 SERVINGS

- 2 medium onions, finely chopped
- 1 tablespoon canola oil
- 6 garlic cloves, minced
- 1 teaspoon crushed red pepper flakes
- 1 teaspoon pepper
- 1 can (14½ ounces) diced tomatoes, undrained
- ¼ cup packed brown sugar
- ¼ cup cider vinegar
- 2 tablespoons hot pepper sauce
- 1 tablespoon Worcestershire sauce
- 1 teaspoon ground cumin
- 1 boneless pork shoulder butt roast (3 to 4 pounds)
- 8 kaiser rolls, split

1. In a large skillet, saute onions in oil until tender. Add the garlic, pepper flakes and pepper; cook 1 minute longer. Stir in the tomatoes, brown sugar, vinegar, hot pepper sauce, Worcestershire and cumin. Cook over medium heat until heated through and the sugar is dissolved.

2. Cut roast in half. Place in a 5-qt. slow cooker; pour the sauce over the top. Cover and cook on low for 10-12 hours or until meat is tender. Remove roast; cool slightly. Skim fat from the cooking juices. Shred roast with two forks and return meat to the slow cooker. Heat through. With a slotted spoon, place ¾ cup meat mixture on each roll.

COUNTRY RIBS DINNER

FAST FIX

COUNTRY RIBS DINNER

This is my favorite recipe for the classic ribs dinner. It's always a treat for my family when we have this.
—**ROSE INGALL** MANISTEE, MI

PREP: 10 MIN. • **COOK:** 6¼ HOURS
MAKES: 4 SERVINGS

- **2 pounds boneless country-style pork ribs**
- **½ teaspoon salt**
- **¼ teaspoon pepper**
- **8 small red potatoes (about 1 pound), halved**
- **4 medium carrots, cut into 1-inch pieces**
- **3 celery ribs, cut into ½-inch pieces**
- **1 medium onion, coarsely chopped**
- **¾ cup water**
- **1 garlic clove, crushed**
- **1 can (10¾ ounces) condensed cream of mushroom soup, undiluted**

1. Sprinkle the ribs with salt and pepper; transfer to a 4-qt. slow cooker. Add the potatoes, carrots, celery, onion, water and garlic. Cook, covered, on low until the meat and vegetables are tender, 6-8 hours.

2. Remove the meat and vegetables; skim fat from the cooking juices. Whisk soup into the cooking juices; return meat and vegetables to the slow cooker. Cook, covered, until heated through, 15-30 minutes longer.

SPICY SAUSAGE FETTUCCINE

SPICY SAUSAGE FETTUCCINE

One time, I accidentally bought hot Italian sausage instead of mild, but didn't want to waste it. I tossed it in the slow cooker with mushrooms, tomatoes and wine, which helped to mellow out the heat. Now I buy the hot stuff on purpose!

—**JUDY BATSON** TAMPA, FL

PREP: 25 MIN. • **COOK:** 6 HOURS
MAKES: 8 SERVINGS

- **2 teaspoons canola oil**
- **8 hot Italian sausage links**
- **½ pound sliced fresh mushrooms**
- **1 small sweet onion, chopped**
- **2 garlic cloves, minced**
- **1 can (14½ ounces) diced tomatoes with mild green chilies, undrained**
- **½ cup beef stock**
- **½ cup dry white wine or additional stock**
- **1 package (12 ounces) fettuccine or tagliatelle**
- **Grated Parmesan cheese, optional**

1. In a large skillet, heat oil over medium heat; brown sausages on all sides. Transfer to a 3-qt. slow cooker, reserving drippings in pan.
2. In the same skillet, saute mushrooms and onion in the drippings over medium heat until tender, 4-5 minutes. Stir in garlic; cook and stir 1 minute. Stir in tomatoes, stock and wine; pour over the sausages. Cook, covered, on low for 6-8 hours (a thermometer inserted in sausages should read at least 160°).
3. To serve, cook fettuccine according to package directions; drain. Remove the sausages from slow cooker; cut into thick slices.
4. Skim fat from the mushroom mixture. Add fettuccine and sausage; toss to combine. Serve in bowls. If desired, top with cheese.

ITALIAN PORK CHOPS

Tomato sauce seasoned with oregano, basil and garlic gives Italian flavor to tender chops. This is one of the few ways I will eat pork chops.

—**VICKIE LOWE** LITITZ, PA

PREP: 20 MIN. • **COOK:** 6-8 HOURS
MAKES: 4 SERVINGS

- **4 bone-in pork loin chops (1 inch thick)**
- **½ pound fresh mushrooms, sliced**
- **1 medium onion, chopped**
- **1 garlic clove, minced**
- **2 cans (8 ounces each) tomato sauce**
- **1 tablespoon lemon juice**
- **½ teaspoon salt**
- **½ teaspoon each dried oregano, basil and parsley flakes**
- **¼ cup cornstarch**
- **¼ cup cold water**
- **Green pepper rings, optional**

1. In a nonstick skillet, brown pork chops on both sides. In a 3-qt. slow cooker, combine the mushrooms, onion and garlic. Top with pork chops.
2. Combine the tomato sauce, lemon juice, salt, oregano, basil and parsley. Pour over pork. Cover and cook on low for 6-8 hours or until the meat is tender. Remove pork and keep warm. Transfer the mushroom mixture to a saucepan.
3. In a small bowl, combine the cornstarch and water until smooth; add to the saucepan. Bring to a boil; cook and stir for 2 minutes or until thickened. Serve over the pork chops.
4. Garnish with green pepper rings if desired.

CAJUN-STYLE BEANS & SAUSAGE

Beans and rice make a perfect meal—well-balanced, an excellent source of protein, and easy to prepare. The sausage adds full flavor to the recipe, and traditional pork sausage lovers won't even notice that turkey sausage is used in this dish.

—**ROBIN HAAS** CRANSTON, RI

PREP: 25 MIN. • **COOK:** 6 HOURS
MAKES: 8 SERVINGS

- **1 package (12 ounces) fully cooked spicy chicken sausage links, halved lengthwise and cut into ½-inch slices**
- **2 cans (16 ounces each) red beans, rinsed and drained**
- **2 cans (14½ ounces each) diced tomatoes, undrained**
- **3 medium carrots, chopped**
- **1 large onion, chopped**
- **1 large green pepper, chopped**
- **½ cup chopped roasted sweet red peppers**
- **3 garlic cloves, minced**
- **1 teaspoon Cajun seasoning**
- **1 teaspoon dried oregano**
- **½ teaspoon dried thyme**
- **½ teaspoon pepper**
- **5⅓ cups cooked brown rice**

1. In a large nonstick skillet coated with cooking spray, brown sausage. Transfer to a 5-qt. slow cooker. Stir in beans, tomatoes, vegetables, garlic and seasonings.
2. Cook, covered, on low for 6-8 hours or until the vegetables are tender. Serve with rice.

ASIAN BBQ PORK BUNS

Here's a quick way to get a delicious and comforting dinner on the table on busy evenings. Sometimes I add a little reduced-sodium soy sauce to the barbecue sauce. If your family loves Asian food like mine does, they will fall for these pork buns.

—**TERESA RALSTON** NEW ALBANY, OH

PREP: 25 MIN. • **COOK:** 6 HOURS
MAKES: 8 SERVINGS

- **1 boneless pork shoulder butt roast (3 pounds)**
- **1¾ teaspoons salt, divided**
- **1¼ teaspoons coarsely ground pepper, divided**
- **1 tablespoon canola oil**
- **½ cup water**
- **1 bottle (12 ounces) regular chili sauce**
- **½ cup hoisin sauce**
- **3 tablespoons rice vinegar**
- **1 tablespoon minced fresh gingerroot**
- **4 cups coleslaw mix**
- **¼ cup Asian toasted sesame salad dressing**
- **8 split sesame seed hamburger buns, toasted**

1. Sprinkle pork roast with 1½ teaspoons salt and 1 teaspoon pepper. In a large skillet, heat oil over medium-high heat. Add pork; brown on all sides. Transfer pork and drippings to a greased 4-qt. slow cooker. Add water; cook, covered, on low until the pork is tender, 5-6 hours. Remove the pork; discard the cooking juices.
2. When the pork is cool enough to handle, shred with two forks. Return meat to slow cooker. Stir together chili sauce, hoisin sauce, vinegar and ginger. Pour over the pork; toss to coat. Cook until heated through, about 1 hour.
3. Meanwhile, toss coleslaw mix with dressing and the remaining salt and pepper. Serve the shredded pork topped with coleslaw on toasted buns.

ASIAN BBQ PORK BUNS
Teresa Ralston
Albany, OH

FAST FIX

SLOW COOKER KALUA PORK & CABBAGE

My slow cooker pork has four ingredients and takes less than 10 minutes to prep. The result tastes like the Kalua pork made in Hawaii that's slow roasted all day in an underground oven.

—**RHOLINELLE DETORRES** SAN JOSE, CA

PREP: 10 MIN. • **COOK:** 9 HOURS
MAKES: 12 SERVINGS

- **7 bacon strips, divided**
- **1 boneless pork shoulder butt roast (3 to 4 pounds), well trimmed**
- **1 tablespoon coarse sea salt**
- **1 medium head cabbage (about 2 pounds), coarsely chopped**

1. Line the bottom of a 6-qt. slow cooker with four bacon strips. Sprinkle all sides of the roast with salt; place in slow cooker. Arrange the remaining bacon over top of the roast.
2. Cook, covered, on low for 8-10 hours or until the pork is tender. Spread the cabbage around the roast. Cook, covered, 1 to 1¼ hours longer or until cabbage is tender.
3. Remove the pork to a serving bowl; shred with two forks. Using a slotted spoon, add the cabbage to the pork and toss to combine. If desired, skim fat from some of the cooking juices; stir juices into the pork mixture or serve on the side.

BIG EASY JAMBALAYA

Friends and family often request my jambalaya for gatherings. And I don't mind, since it's so easy to make.

—**ELIZABETH RENTERIA** VANCOUVER, WA

PREP: 25 MIN. • **COOK:** 5½ HOURS
MAKES: 8 SERVINGS

- **4½ cups chicken stock**
- **1 pound boneless skinless chicken thighs, cut into 1-inch pieces**
- **1 can (15½ ounces) black-eyed peas, rinsed and drained**
- **1 can (14½ ounces) fire-roasted diced tomatoes, undrained**
- **14 ounces smoked kielbasa, sliced**
- **2 fully cooked andouille sausage links, chopped**
- **3 celery ribs, chopped**
- **2 poblano peppers, seeded and chopped**
- **1 medium onion, chopped**
- **4 garlic cloves, minced**
- **1 tablespoon dried oregano**
- **2 teaspoons dried parsley flakes**
- **2 teaspoons dried thyme**
- **2 teaspoons Worcestershire sauce**
- **1 teaspoon salt**
- **1 teaspoon pepper**
- **¼ teaspoon cayenne pepper**
- **2 cups uncooked converted rice**

1. In a 5-qt. slow cooker, combine all ingredients except rice. Cover and cook on low for 5-6 hours or until the chicken is tender.
2. Stir in rice. Cook on high for 30 minutes longer or until the rice is tender.

BRAT SAUERKRAUT SUPPER

This stick-to-your-ribs German dish is sure to satisfy even the biggest appetites at your house. Sliced apple and apple juice lend mellowing sweetness to the tangy sauerkraut, flavorful bratwurst, red potatoes and bacon.

—**ANN CHRISTENSEN** MESA, AZ

PREP: 15 MIN. • **COOK:** 4 HOURS • **MAKES:** 6 SERVINGS

- **1 jar (32 ounces) sauerkraut, rinsed and well drained**
- **2 medium red potatoes, peeled, halved and cut into thin slices**
- **1 medium tart apple, peeled and cut into thick slices**
- **1 small onion, chopped**
- **½ cup apple juice**
- **¼ cup water**
- **2 tablespoons brown sugar**
- **1 teaspoon chicken bouillon granules**
- **1 teaspoon caraway seeds**
- **1 garlic clove, minced**
- **1 bay leaf**
- **1 pound fully cooked bratwurst links**
- **6 bacon strips, cooked and crumbled**

In a 5-qt. slow cooker, combine first 11 ingredients. Top with bratwurst. Cover and cook on high for 4-5 hours or until potatoes are tender. Discard the bay leaf. Sprinkle with bacon.

FAST FIX

SUNDAY POT ROAST

With the help of a slow cooker, you can prepare a down-home dinner any day of the week, not just on Sundays. The roast turns out tender and savory every time.

—**BRANDY SCHAEFER** GLEN CARBON, IL

PREP: 10 MIN. + CHILLING • **COOK:** 8 HOURS
MAKES: 14 SERVINGS

- **1 teaspoon dried oregano**
- **½ teaspoon onion salt**
- **½ teaspoon caraway seeds**
- **½ teaspoon pepper**
- **¼ teaspoon garlic salt**
- **1 boneless pork loin roast (3½ to 4 pounds), trimmed**
- **6 medium carrots, peeled and cut into 1½-inch pieces**
- **3 large potatoes, peeled and quartered**
- **3 small onions, quartered**
- **1½ cups beef broth**
- **⅓ cup all-purpose flour**
- **⅓ cup cold water**
- **¼ teaspoon browning sauce, optional**

1. Combine the first five ingredients; rub over the roast. Wrap in plastic; refrigerate overnight.
2. Place carrots, potatoes and onions in a 6-qt. slow cooker; add broth. Unwrap the roast; place in the slow cooker. Cook, covered, on low until the meat and vegetables are tender, 8-10 hours.
3. Transfer the roast and vegetables to a serving platter; tent with foil. Pour the cooking juices into a small saucepan. Mix flour and water until smooth; stir into the pan. Bring to a boil; cook and stir until thickened, about 2 minutes. If desired, add browning sauce. Serve the roast with gravy and vegetables.

PORK TACOS WITH MANGO SALSA
Amber Massey
Argyle, TX

PORK TACOS WITH MANGO SALSA

For tacos, you can't beat the tender filling made in a slow cooker. These are by far the best pork tacos we've had—and we've tried plenty! Make the mango salsa from scratch if you have time. Yum.

—**AMBER MASSEY** ARGYLE, TX

PREP: 25 MIN. • **COOK:** 6 HOURS
MAKES: 12 SERVINGS

- 2 tablespoons lime juice
- 2 tablespoons white vinegar
- 3 tablespoons chili powder
- 2 teaspoons ground cumin
- 1½ teaspoons salt
- ½ teaspoon pepper
- 3 cups cubed fresh pineapple
- 1 small red onion, coarsely chopped
- 2 chipotle peppers in adobo sauce
- 1 bottle (12 ounces) dark Mexican beer
- 3 pounds pork tenderloin, cut into 1-inch cubes
- ¼ cup chopped fresh cilantro
- 1 jar (16 ounces) mango salsa
- Corn tortillas (6 inches), warmed

OPTIONAL TOPPINGS

- Cubed fresh pineapple
- Cubed avocado
- Queso fresco

1. Puree the first nine ingredients in a blender; stir in beer. In a 5- or 6-qt. slow cooker, combine the pork and pineapple mixture. Cook, covered, on low until the pork is very tender, 6-8 hours. Stir to break up the pork.

2. Stir cilantro into salsa. Using a slotted spoon, serve the pork mixture in tortillas; add salsa and toppings as desired.

To freeze: Freeze the cooled meat mixture and cooking juices in freezer containers. To use, partially thaw in refrigerator overnight. Heat through in a saucepan, stirring occasionally.

WHISKEY BARBECUE PORK

The ingredient list for my saucy pork may seem long, but most of these items are things you'll already have in your kitchen. Plus, once the sauce is mixed up, the slow cooker does the rest. Liquid smoke gives the barbecue its authentic taste!

—**REBECCA HORVATH** JOHNSON CITY, TN

PREP: 15 MIN. • **COOK:** 6 HOURS
MAKES: 8 SERVINGS

- ½ to ¾ cup packed brown sugar
- 1 can (6 ounces) tomato paste
- ⅓ cup barbecue sauce
- ¼ cup whiskey
- 2 tablespoons liquid smoke
- 2 tablespoons Worcestershire sauce
- 3 garlic cloves, minced
- ½ teaspoon chili powder
- ½ teaspoon salt
- ½ teaspoon pepper
- ½ teaspoon hot pepper sauce
- ¼ teaspoon ground cumin
- 1 boneless pork shoulder butt roast (3 to 4 pounds)
- 1 medium onion, quartered
- 8 hamburger buns, split

1. In a small bowl, mix the first 12 ingredients. Place pork roast and onion in a 5-qt. slow cooker. Add the sauce mixture. Cook, covered, on low for 6-8 hours or until the pork is tender.

2. Remove roast and onion. Cool pork slightly; discard onion. Meanwhile, skim fat from the sauce. If desired, transfer sauce to a small saucepan, bring to a boil and cook to thicken slightly.

3. Shred pork with two forks. Return meat and sauce to the slow cooker; heat through. Serve on buns.

SLOW COOKER ITALIAN SLOPPY JOES

These tasty sloppy joes are perfect for a gathering. If you're taking them to an afternoon event, simplify your morning by cooking the beef mixture and stirring in other ingredients the night before. Cool the meat sauce in shallow bowls in the fridge, then cover and refrigerate them overnight. The next day, transfer the meat mixture to the slow cooker to heat through and keep it warm for the party.

—**HOPE WASYLENKI** GAHANNA, OH

PREP: 30 MIN. • **COOK:** 4 HOURS
MAKES: 36 SERVINGS

- **2 pounds lean ground beef (90% lean)**
- **2 pounds bulk Italian sausage**
- **2 medium green peppers, chopped**
- **1 large onion, chopped**
- **4 cups spaghetti sauce**
- **1 can (28 ounces) diced tomatoes, undrained**
- **½ pound sliced fresh mushrooms**
- **1 can (6 ounces) tomato paste**
- **2 garlic cloves, minced**
- **2 bay leaves**
- **36 hamburger buns, split**

1. Cook the beef, sausage, peppers and onion in a Dutch oven over medium heat until the meat is no longer pink; drain. Transfer to a 6-qt. slow cooker. Stir in the spaghetti sauce, tomatoes, mushrooms, tomato paste, garlic and bay leaves.
2. Cover and cook on high for 4-5 hours or until flavors are blended. Discard bay leaves. Serve on buns, ½ cup of filling on each.
To freeze: Freeze the cooled meat mixture in freezer containers. To use, partially thaw in the refrigerator overnight. Heat through in a saucepan, stirring occasionally and adding a little broth or water if necessary.

APRICOT PORK ROAST WITH VEGETABLES

After Sunday evening service, I like to serve a pork roast that slow-cooks with flavorful jam and veggies. The amazing aroma draws everyone to the table.

—**LISA JAMES** VANCOUVER, WA

PREP: 20 MIN. • **COOK:** 3½ HOURS + STANDING
MAKES: 10 SERVINGS

- **1½ pounds potatoes (about 3 medium), peeled and cut into wedges**
- **3 tablespoons water**
- **7 medium carrots, sliced**
- **1 large onion, quartered**
- **1 can (14½ ounces) beef broth**
- **1 teaspoon salt**
- **1 teaspoon garlic powder**
- **1 teaspoon dried thyme**
- **1 teaspoon rubbed sage**
- **½ teaspoon pepper**
- **1 boneless pork loin roast (3 to 4 pounds)**
- **1 jar (12 ounces) apricot preserves, divided**

1. In a large microwave-safe bowl, combine potatoes and 3 tablespoons water. Microwave, covered, on high for 10-12 minutes or until just tender. Drain and transfer to a 6-qt. slow cooker. Add carrots, onion and beef broth. In a small bowl, mix salt, garlic, thyme, sage and pepper; sprinkle half over vegetables.
2. Rub remaining seasoning mixture over roast; place the meat over vegetables. Spread half of the preserves over roast. Cook, covered, on low 3½ to 4½ hours or until meat is tender (a thermometer inserted in pork should read at least 145°).
3. Remove roast from slow cooker; tent with foil. Let stand 15 minutes. Serve with vegetables and remaining preserves.

APRICOT PORK ROAST WITH VEGETABLES

HERB STUFFED CHOPS

HERB STUFFED CHOPS

Guests will think you stayed home all day when you serve these tender stuffed chops. I often share this recipe with newlyweds because I know it will become a favorite.

—**DIANA SEEGER** NEW SPRINGFIELD, OH

PREP: 25 MIN. • **COOK:** 8 HOURS
MAKES: 6 SERVINGS

- **¾ cup chopped onion**
- **¼ cup chopped celery**
- **2 tablespoons butter**
- **2 cups day-old bread cubes**
- **½ cup minced fresh parsley**
- **⅓ cup evaporated milk**
- **1 teaspoon fennel seed, crushed**
- **1½ teaspoons salt, divided**
- **½ teaspoon pepper, divided**
- **6 bone-in pork rib or loin chops (8 ounces each)**
- **1 tablespoon canola oil**
- **¾ cup white wine or chicken broth**

1. In a small skillet, saute onion and celery in butter until tender. Add the bread cubes, parsley, milk, fennel, ¼ teaspoon salt and ⅛ teaspoon pepper; toss to coat.

2. Cut a pocket in each chop by slicing from the fat side almost to the bone. Spoon about ¼ cup stuffing into each pocket. Combine the remaining salt and pepper; rub over chops.

3. In a large skillet, brown chops in oil; transfer to a 3-qt. slow cooker. Pour wine over top. Cover and cook on low for 8-9 hours or until a meat thermometer inserted in the pork reads 160°.

HAM WITH CHERRY SAUCE

I often make my cherry ham for church breakfasts. It's such a favorite that I've even served it at Easter dinners and at a friend's wedding brunch.

—**CAROL LEE JONES** TAYLORS, SC

PREP: 20 MIN. • **COOK:** 4 HOURS
MAKES: 10-12 SERVINGS

- **1 boneless fully cooked ham (3 to 4 pounds)**
- **½ cup apple jelly**
- **2 teaspoons prepared mustard**
- **⅔ cup ginger ale, divided**
- **1 can (21 ounces) cherry pie filling**
- **2 tablespoons cornstarch**

1. Score the surface of ham, making diamond shapes ½ in. deep. In a small bowl, combine jelly, mustard and 1 tablespoon ginger ale; rub over the scored surface of ham. Cut ham in half; place in a 5-qt. slow cooker. Cover and cook on low for 4-5 hours or until a thermometer reads 140°, basting with cooking juices near the end of cooking time.

2. For sauce, place pie filling in a saucepan. Combine cornstarch and the remaining ginger ale; stir into pie filling until blended. Bring to a boil; cook and stir for 2 minutes or until thickened. Serve over ham.

TEXAS PORK BURRITOS

I've taken a fancy to green enchilada sauce lately and have paired it with many foods. One of my trials produced these burritos. The sauce lights up the taste of the pork mixture.

—**SALLY SIBTHORPE** SHELBY TOWNSHIP, MI

PREP: 40 MIN. • **COOK:** 6½ HOURS
MAKES: 10 SERVINGS

- **1 boneless pork shoulder butt roast (3 to 4 pounds), cubed**
- **1 teaspoon salt**
- **½ teaspoon pepper**
- **2 tablespoons canola oil**
- **2 cans (10 ounces each) green enchilada sauce**
- **1 large onion, thinly sliced**
- **2 medium carrots, thinly sliced**
- **2 cans (2¼ ounces each) sliced ripe olives, drained**
- **½ cup chicken broth**
- **2 tablespoons ground cumin**
- **3 garlic cloves, minced**
- **2 teaspoons dried oregano**
- **2 tablespoons all-purpose flour**
- **1 cup (8 ounces) sour cream**
- **½ cup minced fresh cilantro**
- **10 flour tortillas (8 inches), warmed**
- **2 cups shredded Mexican cheese blend**

1. Sprinkle pork with salt and pepper. In a large skillet, brown the meat in oil in batches. Transfer to a 3-qt. slow cooker. Combine the enchilada sauce, onion, carrots, olives, broth, cumin, garlic and oregano; pour over the meat. Cover and cook on low for 6-8 hours or until the meat is tender.

2. Combine flour and sour cream; stir into the meat mixture. Cover and cook on high for 30 minutes or until thickened. Stir in cilantro.

3. Spoon ⅔ cup of the pork mixture onto each tortilla; top with about 3 tablespoons cheese. Roll up tightly.

SLOW-COOKED PULLED PORK WITH MOJITO SAUCE

Infused with Cuban flavor, this twist on slow-cooked pulled pork is knock-your-socks-off good, whether you serve it up with rice and beans on the side or press it into a classic Cuban sandwich.

—**KRISTINA WILEY** JUPITER, FL

PREP: 25 MIN. + MARINATING • **COOK:** 8 HOURS
MAKES: 12 SERVINGS (1½ CUPS SAUCE)

- **2 large onions, quartered**
- **12 garlic cloves**
- **1 bottle (18 ounces) Cuban-style mojo sauce and marinade**
- **½ cup lime juice**
- **½ teaspoon salt**
- **¼ teaspoon pepper**
- **1 bone-in pork shoulder butt roast (5 to 5¼ pounds)**

MOJITO SAUCE

- **¾ cup canola oil**
- **1 medium onion, finely chopped**
- **6 garlic cloves, finely chopped**
- **⅓ cup lime juice**
- **½ teaspoon salt**
- **¼ teaspoon pepper**
- **Additional chopped onion and lime wedges, optional**

1. Place onions and garlic in a food processor; process until finely chopped. Add mojo marinade, lime juice, salt and pepper; process until blended. Pour half of the marinade into a large resealable plastic bag. Cut roast into quarters; add to bag. Seal bag and turn to coat. Refrigerate 8 hours or overnight. Transfer remaining marinade to a small bowl; refrigerate, covered, while marinating meat.
2. Drain pork, discarding marinade in bag. Place pork in a 5-qt. slow cooker coated with cooking spray. Top with the reserved marinade. Cook, covered, on low 8-10 hours or until meat is tender.
3. For sauce, in a small saucepan, heat oil over medium heat 2½ to 3 minutes or until a thermometer reads 200°. Carefully add onion; cook 2 minutes, stirring occasionally. Stir in garlic; remove from heat. Stir in lime juice, salt and pepper.
4. Remove the pork from the slow cooker; cool slightly. Skim fat from the cooking juices. Remove meat from bone; discard bone. Shred pork with two forks. Return meat and cooking juices to the slow cooker; heat through.
5. Transfer pork to a platter; serve with warm mojito sauce, stirring just before serving. If desired, sprinkle the pork with chopped onion and serve with lime wedges.

FAST FIX

BBQ COUNTRY-STYLE RIBS

Quick to prep for the slow cooker, this dinner goes great with a salad and fresh side. My family practically cheers whenever I make it!

—**CHERYL MANN** WINSIDE, NE

PREP: 10 MIN. • **COOK:** 6 HOURS • **MAKES:** 6 SERVINGS

- **3 pounds boneless country-style pork ribs**
- **½ teaspoon salt**
- **½ teaspoon pepper**
- **1 large onion, cut into ½-inch rings**
- **1 bottle (18 ounces) hickory smoke-flavored barbecue sauce**
- **⅓ cup maple syrup**
- **¼ cup spicy brown mustard**
- **Thinly sliced green onions, optional**

1. Sprinkle ribs with salt and pepper. Place onion in a 6-qt. slow cooker. Top with ribs. In a large bowl, combine the barbecue sauce, maple syrup and mustard; pour over the ribs. Cook, covered, on low for 6-8 hours or until the meat is tender.
2. Transfer meat to a serving platter; keep warm. Pour cooking liquid into a large saucepan; bring to a boil. Reduce heat; simmer, uncovered, 10 minutes or until the sauce is thickened. Serve with pork. If desired, sprinkle with onions.

BBQ COUNTRY-STYLE RIBS

BACON & SAUSAGE STUFFING, PAGE 192

SIDE DISHES

Why not use your slow cooker to make the side dishes? It'll free up oven space, keep the kitchen cool and make your dishes perfectly portable for potlucks and gatherings.

CELEBRATION BRUSSELS SPROUTS
Lauren Knoelke
Milwaukee, WI

CELEBRATION BRUSSELS SPROUTS

This recipe hits all the flavor points and makes a fantastic holiday side. Plus, you've got to love a dish that requires minimal effort and doesn't take up oven space. If you need a vegetarian option, omit the bacon.

—**LAUREN KNOELKE** MILWAUKEE, WI

PREP: 20 MIN. • **COOK:** 2 HOURS
MAKES: 10 SERVINGS

- **2 pounds fresh Brussels sprouts, sliced**
- **2 large apples (Fuji or Braeburn), chopped**
- **⅓ cup dried cranberries**
- **8 bacon strips, cooked and crumbled, divided**
- **⅓ cup cider vinegar**
- **¼ cup maple syrup**
- **2 tablespoons olive oil**
- **1 teaspoon salt**
- **½ teaspoon fresh ground pepper**
- **¾ cup chopped hazelnuts or pecans, toasted**

1. In a large bowl, combine the Brussels sprouts, apples, cranberries and ¼ cup bacon. In a small bowl, whisk the vinegar, syrup, oil, salt and pepper; pour over the Brussels sprouts mixture, tossing to coat. Transfer to a 5-qt. slow cooker. Cook, covered, on low until the sprouts reach desired tenderness, 2-4 hours, stirring once.
2. To serve, sprinkle with hazelnuts and the remaining bacon.

CHEESE-STUFFED SWEET ONIONS

Large onion shells are stuffed with a tasty blend of cheeses and cooked in vegetable broth. Experiment to find the blend you like: Try swapping mascarpone or cream cheese for the goat cheese, or Gorgonzola for the blue cheese. It's all delicious!

—**SONYA LABBE** WEST HOLLYWOOD, CA

PREP: 25 MIN. • **COOK:** 4 HOURS
MAKES: 8 SERVINGS

- **4 large Vidalia or other sweet onions**
- **¾ cup crumbled goat cheese**
- **¾ cup crumbled blue cheese**

- **1 teaspoon minced fresh thyme**
- **2 cups vegetable stock**
- **1 tablespoon olive oil**
- **¼ teaspoon salt**
- **⅛ teaspoon pepper**
- **¼ cup grated Romano or Parmesan cheese**
- **Fresh thyme leaves**

1. Peel onions. Cut a ½-in. slice off top of each onion; remove centers with a melon baller, leaving ½-in. shells. Chop the removed onion, reserving 3 cups (save the remaining onion for another use). Mix together the goat and blue cheeses, minced thyme and reserved onion; spoon into the onions.
2. Place the onions and stock in a 6-qt. slow cooker; drizzle with oil. Sprinkle with salt, pepper and Romano cheese. Cook, covered, on low until the onions are tender, 4-5 hours. Cut in half to serve and sprinkle with thyme leaves.

SAUSAGE-HERB DRESSING

I make this dressing every Thanksgiving. To carve out time for last-minute essentials, I prep the sausage part of this recipe a day or two ahead, then finish the dressing in my slow cooker on the big day.

—**JUDY BATSON** TAMPA, FL

PREP: 20 MIN. • **COOK:** 2 HOURS
MAKES: 10 SERVINGS

- **1 pound bulk sage pork sausage**
- **1 medium sweet onion, chopped (about 2 cups)**
- **2 celery ribs, chopped**
- **¼ cup brewed coffee**
- **½ teaspoon poultry seasoning**
- **½ teaspoon dried oregano**
- **½ teaspoon rubbed sage**
- **½ teaspoon dried thyme**
- **½ teaspoon pepper**
- **1½ cups chicken or turkey broth**
- **1 package (12 ounces) seasoned stuffing cubes (8 cups)**
- **Chopped fresh parsley**

1. In a 6-qt. stockpot, cook and crumble sausage with onion and celery over medium heat until no longer pink, 5-7 minutes; drain. Stir in coffee and seasonings; cook 3 minutes, stirring occasionally.
2. Add broth; bring to a boil. Remove from heat. Add stuffing cubes; mix lightly. Transfer to a greased 4- or 5-qt. slow cooker.
3. Cook, covered, on low until heated through and edges are lightly browned, 2-2½ hours, stirring once. Sprinkle with parsley.

SLOW-SIMMERED KIDNEY BEANS

My husband always puts us down for a side dish whenever we're invited to a potluck. Canned beans cut down on prep time yet get plenty of zip from bacon, apple, red pepper and onion. I like how the slow cooker blends the flavors and I don't have to stand over the stove!

—**SHEILA VAIL** LONG BEACH, CA

PREP: 15 MIN. • **COOK:** 6 HOURS
MAKES: 16 SERVINGS

- **6 bacon strips, diced**
- **½ pound smoked Polish sausage or kielbasa, sliced**
- **4 cans (16 ounces each) kidney beans, rinsed and drained**
- **1 can (28 ounces) diced tomatoes, drained**
- **2 medium sweet red peppers, chopped**
- **1 large onion, chopped**
- **1 cup ketchup**
- **½ cup packed brown sugar**
- **¼ cup honey**
- **¼ cup molasses**
- **1 tablespoon Worcestershire sauce**
- **1 teaspoon salt**
- **1 teaspoon ground mustard**
- **2 medium unpeeled red apples, cubed**

1. In a large skillet, cook the bacon until crisp. Remove with a slotted spoon to paper towels. Add the sausage to drippings; cook and stir for 5 minutes. Drain and set aside.
2. In a 6-qt. slow cooker, combine the beans, tomatoes, red peppers, onion, ketchup, brown sugar, honey, molasses, Worcestershire sauce, salt and mustard. Stir in the bacon and sausage. Cover and cook on low for 4-6 hours. Stir in apples. Cover and cook 2 hours longer or until bubbly.

SLOW-SIMMERED KIDNEY BEANS

BUTTERNUT COCONUT CURRY

I love my slow cooker because it makes it so easy to fix dinner! This flavorful curry was first created for a potluck and since then, the recipe has been requested often.

—**JESSIE APFE** BERKELEY, CA

PREP: 35 MIN. • **COOK:** 4 HOURS
MAKES: 9 SERVINGS

- **1 cup chopped carrots**
- **1 small onion, chopped**
- **1 tablespoon olive oil**
- **1½ teaspoons brown sugar**
- **1½ teaspoons curry powder**
- **1 garlic clove, minced**
- **½ teaspoon ground cinnamon**
- **¼ teaspoon ground ginger**
- **⅛ teaspoon salt**
- **1 medium butternut squash (about 2½ pounds), cut into 1-inch cubes**
- **2½ cups vegetable broth**
- **¾ cup coconut milk**
- **½ cup uncooked basmati or jasmine rice**

1. In a large skillet, saute carrots and onion in oil until onion is tender. Add the brown sugar, curry, garlic, cinnamon, ginger and salt. Cook and stir 2 minutes longer.

2. In a 3- or 4-qt. slow cooker, combine the butternut squash, broth, coconut milk, rice and the carrot mixture. Cover and cook on low until rice is tender, 4-5 hours.

MAPLE-ALMOND BUTTERNUT SQUASH

A heartwarming side dish, especially on chilly days, my squash is a cinch to prepare for any weeknight. It's impressive enough for company, too.

—**JUDY LAWSON** CHELSEA, MI

PREP: 20 MIN. • **COOK:** 5¼ HOURS
MAKES: 10 SERVINGS

- **½ cup maple syrup**
- **½ cup butter, melted**
- **4 garlic cloves, minced**
- **1 teaspoon salt**
- **½ teaspoon pepper**
- **1 medium butternut squash (about 4 pounds), peeled and cut into 2-inch pieces**
- **½ cup heavy whipping cream**
- **¼ cup sliced almonds**
- **¼ cup shredded Parmesan cheese**

1. Mix first five ingredients. Place squash in a 4-qt. slow cooker; toss with syrup mixture. Cook, covered, until squash is tender, 5-6 hours.

2. Stir in the cream; cook, covered, on low until heated through, 15-30 minutes. Top with almonds and cheese.

★★★★★ **READER REVIEW**

"Five stars isn't really enough for this recipe! A frequent comment was, 'I don't like squash, but that is fabulous.'"

CAOIMHEANDME TASTEOFHOME.COM

FAST FIX

SLOW-COOKED LEMONY SPRING VEGGIES

These spuds do a slow simmer with carrots and onion for a comforting side that bucks up any entree. Finish with a sprinkle of chives.

—*TASTE OF HOME* TEST KITCHEN

PREP: 10 MIN. • **COOK:** 4¼ HOURS
MAKES: 8 SERVINGS

- **4 medium carrots, halved lengthwise and cut into 1-inch pieces**
- **1 large sweet onion, coarsely chopped**
- **1½ pounds baby red potatoes, quartered**
- **3 tablespoons butter, melted**
- **¾ teaspoon salt**
- **¼ teaspoon pepper**
- **1 cup frozen peas, thawed**
- **1 teaspoon grated lemon peel**
- **¼ cup minced fresh chives**

1. Place carrots and onion in a 4-qt. slow cooker; top with potatoes. Drizzle with melted butter; sprinkle with salt and pepper. Cook, covered, on low until vegetables are tender, 4-5 hours.
2. Add peas to slow cooker. Cook, covered, on high until heated through, 10-15 minutes. Stir in lemon peel. Sprinkle with chives.

GARLIC GREEN BEANS WITH GORGONZOLA

I updated this green bean holiday side dish by adding a touch of white wine, fresh thyme and green onions. It's delicious and easy to make, and my family loves it!

—**NANCY HEISHMAN** LAS VEGAS, NV

PREP: 20 MIN. • **COOK:** 3 HOURS
MAKES: 10 SERVINGS

- **2 pounds fresh green beans, trimmed and halved**
- **1 can (8 ounces) sliced water chestnuts, drained**
- **4 green onions, chopped**
- **5 bacon strips, cooked and crumbled, divided**
- **⅓ cup white wine or chicken broth**
- **2 tablespoons minced fresh thyme or 2 teaspoons dried thyme**
- **4 garlic cloves, minced**
- **1½ teaspoons seasoned salt**
- **1 cup (8 ounces) sour cream**
- **¾ cup crumbled Gorgonzola cheese**

1. Place green beans, water chestnuts, green onions and ¼ cup cooked bacon in a 4-qt. slow cooker. In a small bowl, mix wine, thyme, garlic and seasoned salt; pour over top. Cook, covered, on low until beans are crisp-tender, 3-4 hours. Drain liquid from beans.
2. Just before serving, stir in sour cream; sprinkle with cheese and the remaining bacon.

TEST KITCHEN TIP
To trim fresh green beans quickly, simply line up the ends of the beans; then, using a chef's knife, slice several at a time.

HEAVENLY APPLESAUCE

Every year my husband and I take our two daughters to an orchard to pick fresh apples so we can make this luscious applesauce for family and neighbors.
—**JENNIFER PURCELL** VERMILION, OH

PREP: 25 MIN. • **COOK:** 6 HOURS
MAKES: 8 SERVINGS

- **5 pounds apples, peeled and sliced (about 13 cups)**
- **¾ cup packed light brown sugar**
- **⅔ cup unsweetened apple juice**
- **2 teaspoons ground cinnamon**
- **1 teaspoon pumpkin pie spice**
- **1 tablespoon vanilla extract**

1. In a 5- or 6-qt. slow cooker, combine the first five ingredients. Cook, covered, on low until the apples are soft, 6-8 hours.
2. Add vanilla; stir to break up apples. Serve warm or refrigerate and serve cold.
To freeze: Freeze cooled applesauce in freezer containers. To use, thaw in refrigerator overnight.

BACON & SAUSAGE STUFFING

This recipe was inspired by my mother's stuffing recipe. It smells like heaven while you're making it, and people can never seem to get enough.
—**STEPHAN-SCOTT RUGH** PORTLAND, OR

PREP: 25 MIN. • **COOK:** 4 HOURS + STANDING
MAKES: 20 SERVINGS

- **1 pound bulk pork sausage**
- **1 pound thick-sliced bacon strips, chopped**
- **½ cup butter, cubed**
- **1 large onion, chopped**
- **3 celery ribs, sliced**
- **10½ cups unseasoned stuffing cubes**
- **1 cup sliced fresh mushrooms**
- **1 cup chopped fresh parsley**
- **4 teaspoons dried sage leaves**
- **4 teaspoons dried thyme**
- **6 large eggs**
- **2 cans (10¾ ounces each) condensed cream of chicken soup, undiluted**
- **1¼ cups chicken stock**

1. In a large skillet, cook sausage over medium heat until no longer pink, 6-8 minutes, breaking into crumbles. Remove with a slotted spoon; drain on paper towels. Discard the drippings.
2. Add bacon to the pan; cook over medium heat until crisp. Remove to paper towels to drain. Discard the drippings and wipe out the pan. In the same pan, heat butter over medium-high heat. Add onion and celery; cook and stir until tender, 6-8 minutes. Remove from heat.
3. In a large bowl, combine stuffing cubes, sausage, bacon, onion mixture, mushrooms, parsley, sage and thyme. In a small bowl, whisk eggs, soup and stock; pour over stuffing mixture and toss to coat.
4. Transfer to a greased 6-qt. slow cooker. Cook, covered, on low until a thermometer reads 160°, 4-5 hours. Remove the lid; let stand 15 minutes before serving.

SLOW-COOKED BOSTON BEANS

FAST FIX

SLOW-COOKED BOSTON BEANS

These slow-cooked beans have a little more zip than usual Boston baked beans, and rum is my secret ingredient. My grandfather would add extra black pepper to his serving, so I now add extra pepper to the entire recipe.

—**ANN SHEEHY** LAWRENCE, MA

PREP: 10 MIN. + SOAKING • **COOK:** 9 HOURS
MAKES: 8 SERVINGS

- **1 pound dried navy beans**
- **¼ pound sliced salt pork belly or bacon strips, chopped**
- **1½ cups water**
- **1 medium onion, chopped**
- **½ cup molasses**
- **⅓ cup packed brown sugar**
- **⅓ cup rum or unsweetened apple juice**
- **2 teaspoons ground mustard**
- **½ teaspoon salt**
- **½ teaspoon pepper**

1. Sort beans and rinse in cold water. Place beans in a large bowl; add water to cover by 2 in. Let stand, covered, overnight.

2. Drain and rinse beans, discarding the liquid. Transfer beans to a greased 3-qt. slow cooker; add the salt pork. In a small bowl, combine the remaining ingredients. Stir into slow cooker.

3. Cook, covered, on low until the beans are tender, 9-11 hours.

To freeze: Let beans cool, then freeze in freezer containers. To use, partially thaw in refrigerator overnight. Heat through in a saucepan, stirring occasionally and adding a little water or broth if necessary.

GARLIC-DILL SODA BREAD

GARLIC-DILL SODA BREAD

It's amazing that bread can be made in a slow cooker, which is why this recipe is so awesome—who knew it could be so simple? Let the inviting aroma of dill and cheese fill your kitchen.

—**MELISSA HANSEN** MILWAUKEE, WI

PREP: 15 MIN. • **COOK:** 1½ HOURS
MAKES: 1 LOAF (12 WEDGES)

- **4 cups all-purpose flour**
- **2 tablespoons dried parsley flakes**
- **1 tablespoon dried minced onion**
- **2 teaspoons garlic powder**
- **1½ teaspoons dill weed**
- **1 teaspoon salt**
- **1 teaspoon baking soda**
- **1 teaspoon ground mustard**
- **1¾ cups buttermilk**
- **1 cup shredded sharp cheddar cheese**

1. In a large bowl, whisk the first eight ingredients. Add buttermilk and cheese; stir just until moistened. Turn onto a lightly floured surface; knead gently 6-8 times or just until the dough comes together. Shape into a 6-in. round loaf. Using a sharp knife, score surface with 1-in. deep cuts in a crisscross pattern. Place in a greased 5-qt. slow cooker.
2. Cook, covered, on high until a thermometer reads 190°-200°, 1½-2 hours.
3. Preheat broiler. Remove the bread; place on a baking sheet. Broil 6-8 in. from heat until golden brown, 2-3 minutes. Remove to a wire rack to cool completely.

SLOW COOKER TZIMMES

Tzimmes is a sweet Jewish dish consisting of a variety of fruits and vegetables, and it may or may not include meat. Traditionally (as it is here), it's tossed with honey and cinnamon and slowly cooked to blend the flavors.

—**LISA RENSHAW** KANSAS CITY, MO

PREP: 20 MIN. • **COOK:** 5 HOURS
MAKES: 12 SERVINGS

- **½ medium butternut squash, peeled and cubed**
- **2 medium sweet potatoes, peeled and cubed**
- **6 medium carrots, sliced**
- **2 medium tart apples, peeled and sliced**
- **1 cup chopped sweet onion**
- **1 cup chopped dried apricots**
- **1 cup golden raisins**
- **½ cup orange juice**
- **¼ cup honey**
- **2 tablespoons finely chopped crystallized ginger**
- **3 teaspoons ground cinnamon**
- **3 teaspoons pumpkin pie spice**
- **2 teaspoons grated orange peel**
- **1 teaspoon salt**
- **Vanilla yogurt, optional**

1. Place the first seven ingredients in a 5- or 6-qt. slow cooker. Combine the orange juice, honey, ginger, cinnamon, pie spice, orange peel and salt; pour over top and mix well.
2. Cover and cook on low until the vegetables are tender, 5-6 hours. Dollop each serving with yogurt if desired.

SLOW-COOKED RATATOUILLE

I get my son to eat eggplant by cooking low and slow on this classic French veggie dish. A side of rice and some garlic cheese bread also help.

—**DIANE GOEDDE** RED LODGE, MT

PREP: 25 MIN. + STANDING • **COOK:** 5 HOURS
MAKES: 10 SERVINGS

- **1 medium eggplant, peeled and cut into 1-inch cubes**
- **1 tablespoon plus 1 teaspoon salt, divided**
- **2 medium onions, halved and thinly sliced**
- **4 medium tomatoes, chopped**
- **3 medium zucchini, cut into ¾-inch slices**
- **2 celery ribs, chopped**
- **3 tablespoons olive oil**
- **2 teaspoons dried basil or 2 tablespoons minced fresh basil**
- **4 garlic cloves, minced**
- **½ teaspoon pepper**
- **1 can (6 ounces) tomato paste**
- **1 can (2¼ ounces) sliced ripe olives, drained**
- **⅓ cup coarsely chopped fresh basil**

1. Place the eggplant in a colander over a plate; sprinkle with 1 tablespoon salt and toss. Let stand for 45 minutes. Rinse and drain well; blot dry with paper towels.
2. Place eggplant and the remaining vegetables in a 5- or 6-qt. slow cooker. Add oil, dried basil, garlic, pepper and the remaining salt; toss to combine.
3. Cook, covered, on low until onions are tender, 5-6 hours. Stir in tomato paste, olives and fresh basil; heat through.
To freeze: Freeze cooled ratatouille in freezer containers. To use, partially thaw in refrigerator overnight. Microwave, covered, on high in a microwave-safe dish until heated through, stirring gently.

SWEET ONION CREAMED CORN

A friend from church gave me this easy and delicious recipe over 40 years ago. I still make it regularly, and when I cook it, I recall fond memories of her.

—**NANCY HEISHMAN** LAS VEGAS, NV

PREP: 25 MIN. • **COOK:** 3 HOURS
MAKES: 8 SERVINGS

- **5 bacon strips, chopped**
- **1 large sweet onion, chopped**
- **1 medium sweet red pepper, chopped**
- **5 cups frozen corn (about 24 ounces), thawed**
- **2 cups cubed fully cooked ham**
- **½ cup half-and-half cream**
- **1 tablespoon brown sugar**
- **1 tablespoon dried parsley flakes**
- **1 teaspoon smoked paprika**
- **½ teaspoon salt**
- **½ teaspoon pepper**
- **1 package (8 ounces) cream cheese, cubed and softened**

1. In a large skillet, cook bacon over medium heat until crisp, stirring occasionally. Remove with a slotted spoon; drain on paper towels.
2. Cook and stir onion and sweet red pepper in the bacon drippings over medium-high heat until tender, 5-6 minutes.
3. In a greased 4-qt. slow cooker, combine corn, ham, cream, brown sugar, parsley, paprika, salt, pepper, bacon and the onion mixture. Cook, covered, on low until heated through, 3-4 hours. Stir in cream cheese; cook, covered, 10 minutes longer. Stir before serving.

SWEET ONION CREAMED CORN
Nancy Heishman
Las Vegas, NV

FAST FIX

SLOW-COOKED VEGETABLES

I like to simmer an assortment of garden-fresh vegetables for this satisfying side dish. My sister-in-law shared the recipe with me, and it's become a favorite at potlucks.

—**KATHY WESTENDORF** WESTGATE, IA

PREP: 10 MIN. • **COOK:** 7 HOURS
MAKES: 8 SERVINGS

- **4 celery ribs, cut into 1-inch pieces**
- **4 small carrots, cut into 1-inch pieces**
- **2 medium tomatoes, cut into chunks**
- **2 medium onions, thinly sliced**
- **2 cups cut fresh green beans (1-inch pieces)**
- **1 medium green pepper, cut into 1-inch pieces**
- **¼ cup butter, melted**
- **3 tablespoons quick-cooking tapioca**
- **1 tablespoon sugar**
- **1 teaspoon salt**
- **⅛ teaspoon pepper**

1. Place the vegetables in a 3-qt. slow cooker. In a small bowl, combine butter, tapioca, sugar, salt and pepper; pour over the vegetables and stir well.
2. Cover and cook on low until the vegetables are tender, 7-8 hours. Serve with a slotted spoon.

FAST FIX

SLOW-COOKED GREEN BEANS

I spent hours looking up sides for a cooking demo to present to a group of women from my church. These easy green beans became my star attraction.

—**ALICE WHITE** WILLOW SPRING, NC

PREP: 10 MIN. • **COOK:** 2 HOURS
MAKES: 12 SERVINGS

- **16 cups frozen french-style green beans (about 48 ounces), thawed**
- **½ cup butter, melted**
- **½ cup packed brown sugar**
- **1½ teaspoons garlic salt**
- **¾ teaspoon reduced-sodium soy sauce**

Place beans in a 5-qt. slow cooker. Mix remaining ingredients; pour over beans and toss to coat. Cook, covered, on low until heated through, 2-3 hours. Serve with a slotted spoon.

CRANBERRY-APPLE RED CABBAGE

When I was looking for something new, I started playing with flavors and came up with this very tasty dish. My German grandmother would be impressed, I think! The colorful side dish is just right with pork.

—**ANN SHEEHY** LAWRENCE, MA

PREP: 15 MIN. • **COOK:** 3 HOURS
MAKES: 8 SERVINGS

- **1 medium head red cabbage, coarsely chopped (8 cups)**
- **1 can (14 ounces) whole-berry cranberry sauce**
- **2 medium Granny Smith apples, peeled and coarsely chopped**
- **1 large white onion, chopped**
- **½ cup cider vinegar**
- **¼ cup sweet vermouth or white wine, optional**
- **1 teaspoon kosher salt**
- **¾ teaspoon caraway seeds**
- **½ teaspoon coarsely ground pepper**

Combine all the ingredients; transfer to a 5-qt. slow cooker. Cook, covered, on low until the cabbage is tender, 3-4 hours. Serve with a slotted spoon.

SWEET & SPICY BEANS

FAST FIX

SWEET & SPICY BEANS

My husband and I love this sweet and savory bean dish. It can be used as a side or as a dip. When you fill up a corn scoop chip, the party starts in your mouth!

—**SONDRA POPE** MOORESVILLE, NC

PREP: 10 MIN. • **COOK:** 5 HOURS
MAKES: 12 SERVINGS

- **1 can (16 ounces) kidney beans, rinsed and drained**
- **1 can (15¼ ounces) whole kernel corn, drained**
- **1 can (15 ounces) garbanzo beans or chickpeas, rinsed and drained**
- **1 can (15 ounces) black beans, rinsed and drained**
- **1 can (15 ounces) chili with beans**
- **1 cup barbecue sauce**
- **1 cup salsa**
- **⅓ cup packed brown sugar**
- **¼ teaspoon hot pepper sauce**
- **Chopped green onions, optional**

In a 4- or 5-qt. slow cooker, combine the first nine ingredients. Cover and cook on low for 5-6 hours. Top with green onions if desired.

★★★★★ **READER REVIEW**

"It's the perfect blend of sweet and spicy. My entire family loved it!"

VECTORMOM TASTEOFHOME.COM

SPANISH HOMINY

I received this recipe from a good friend who is a fabulous cook. The colorful side dish gets its zesty flavor from spicy canned tomatoes with green chilies. Hominy makes a great side dish paired with sausage or pork chops.

—**DONNA BROCKETT** KINGFISHER, OK

PREP: 15 MIN. • **COOK:** 6 HOURS
MAKES: 12 SERVINGS

- **4 cans (15½ ounces each) hominy, rinsed and drained**
- **1 can (14½ ounces) diced tomatoes, undrained**
- **1 can (10 ounces) diced tomatoes and green chilies, undrained**
- **1 can (8 ounces) tomato sauce**
- **¾ pound sliced bacon, diced**
- **1 large onion, chopped**
- **1 medium green pepper, chopped**

1. In a 5-qt. slow cooker, combine the hominy, tomatoes and tomato sauce.
2. In a large skillet, cook the bacon until crisp; remove with a slotted spoon to paper towels. Drain, reserving 1 tablespoon drippings.
3. In the same skillet, saute onion and green pepper in the drippings until tender. Stir the onion mixture and bacon into the hominy mixture. Cover and cook on low until heated through, 6-8 hours.

FAST FIX

VEGETABLE-STUFFED PEPPERS

This recipe came with my slow cooker. I fill green peppers with a flavorful combination of cooked rice, kidney beans, corn and onions. I like to fix meatless main dishes for a change of pace, and this one has become a mainstay for my family.

—**SANDRA ALLEN** AUSTIN, TX

PREP: 10 MIN. • **COOK:** 8¼ HOURS
MAKES: 6 SERVINGS

- **2 cans (14½ ounces each) diced tomatoes, undrained**
- **1 can (16 ounces) kidney beans, rinsed and drained**
- **1½ cups cooked rice**
- **2 cups shredded cheddar cheese, divided**
- **1 package (10 ounces) frozen corn, thawed**
- **¼ cup chopped onion**
- **1 teaspoon Worcestershire sauce**
- **¾ teaspoon chili powder**
- **½ teaspoon pepper**
- **¼ teaspoon salt**
- **6 medium green peppers**

1. In a large bowl, combine tomatoes, beans, rice, 1½ cups cheese, corn, onion, Worcestershire sauce, chili powder, pepper and salt. Remove and discard tops and seeds of the green peppers. Fill each pepper with about 1 cup of the vegetable mixture. Place in a 5-qt. slow cooker. Cover and cook on low for 8 hours.
2. Sprinkle with the remaining cheese. Cover and cook until the peppers are tender and the cheese is melted, about 15 minutes longer.

BROWN SUGAR SWEET POTATOES WITH APPLES

FAST FIX

BROWN SUGAR SWEET POTATOES WITH APPLES

This foolproof winner makes a beautiful alternative to traditional sweet potatoes. To save time, make it ahead, allow it to cool, and refrigerate up to two days. On feast day, put it in the slow cooker set to low about two hours before serving, and reheat while the turkey roasts. Add a bit of apple cider or water if needed.

—**JUDY BATSON** TAMPA, FL

PREP: 25 MIN. • **COOK:** 5 HOURS
MAKES: 12 SERVINGS

- 5 pounds sweet potatoes (about 10 medium)
- 3 medium Granny Smith apples, peeled and cut into 1-inch slices
- ¾ cup butter, cubed
- 1 cup packed brown sugar
- 2 teaspoons pumpkin pie spice

1. Peel sweet potatoes and cut lengthwise in half; cut crosswise into ½-in. slices. Place potatoes and apples in a 6-qt. slow cooker. In a small saucepan over medium heat, mix butter, brown sugar and pie spice. Bring to a boil and cook until blended, 1-2 minutes. Pour over potato mixture. Cover and cook on low until potatoes are tender, 5-6 hours.

2. With a slotted spoon, remove potatoes and apples to a bowl, reserving the cooking liquid. Mash the potato mixture, gradually adding enough of the reserved cooking liquid, if necessary, to reach the desired consistency.

TEST KITCHEN TIP

Choose sweet potatoes that are firm with no cracks or bruises. If stored in a cool (under 60°), dark, well-ventilated place, they'll stay fresh for about 2 weeks. Once cooked, sweet potatoes can be stored for up to 1 week in the refrigerator.

SLOW COOKER PUMPKIN YEAST BREAD

SLOW COOKER PUMPKIN YEAST BREAD

Savor the rich flavors of fall with this homey loaf you can bake up in the slow cooker. Butterscotch adds a sweet surprise.

—**ERICA POLLY** SUN PRAIRIE, WI

PREP: 20 MIN. • **COOK:** 2½ HOURS + COOLING
MAKES: 1 LOAF (12 SLICES)

- **⅓ cup packed brown sugar**
- **1 package (¼ ounce) quick-rise yeast**
- **2 teaspoons pumpkin pie spice**
- **¾ teaspoon salt**
- **3½ to 4 cups all-purpose flour**
- **¾ cup 2% milk**
- **2 tablespoons butter, cubed**
- **¾ cup canned pumpkin**
- **1 large egg, lightly beaten**
- **⅓ cup raisins**
- **⅓ cup chopped pecans, toasted**
- **⅓ cup butterscotch chips, optional**

1. In a large bowl, mix brown sugar, yeast, pie spice, salt and 1½ cups flour. In a small saucepan, heat milk and butter to 120°-130°; stir into dry ingredients. Stir in pumpkin, egg and enough of the remaining flour to form a soft dough (dough will be sticky).
2. Turn dough onto a floured surface; knead until smooth and elastic, about 6-8 minutes. During the last few minutes of kneading add raisins, pecans and, if desired, chips. Shape into a 6-in. round loaf; transfer to a greased piece of double-thickness heavy-duty foil (about 12 in. square). Lifting with foil, place loaf in a 6-qt. slow cooker. Press the foil against the bottom and sides of the slow cooker.
3. Cook, covered, on high until a thermometer reads 190°-200°, 2½-3 hours. Remove to a wire rack and cool completely before slicing.

POTLUCK CANDIED SWEET POTATOES

To make it easier to take this traditional southern staple to a potluck, I updated it for the slow cooker. It's hard to go wrong with candied sweet potatoes when it comes to pleasing a crowd!

—**DEIRDRE COX** KANSAS CITY, MO

PREP: 20 MIN. • **COOK:** 5 HOURS
MAKES: 12 SERVINGS

- **1 cup packed brown sugar**
- **1 cup sugar**
- **8 medium sweet potatoes, peeled and cut into ½-inch slices**
- **¼ cup butter, melted**
- **2 teaspoons vanilla extract**
- **¼ teaspoon salt**
- **2 tablespoons cornstarch**
- **2 tablespoons cold water**
- **Minced fresh parsley, optional**

1. In a small bowl, combine sugars. In a greased 5-qt. slow cooker, layer a third of the sweet potatoes; sprinkle with a third of the sugar mixture. Repeat layers twice. In a small bowl, combine the butter, vanilla and salt; drizzle over the potatoes. Cover and cook on low until the sweet potatoes are tender, 5-6 hours.
2. Using a slotted spoon, transfer the potatoes to a serving dish; keep warm. Pour the cooking juices into a small saucepan; bring to a boil. In a small bowl, combine cornstarch and water until smooth; stir into the pan. Return to a boil, stirring constantly; cook and stir until thickened, 1-2 minutes. Spoon over the sweet potatoes. Sprinkle with minced parsley if desired.

TRULY TASTY TURNIP GREENS

These savory greens are a hit at every church dinner and potluck. Adjust the seasonings as you please to make this recipe your own.

—**AMY INMAN** HIDDENITE, NC

PREP: 20 MIN. • **COOK:** 5 HOURS
MAKES: 14 SERVINGS

- **2¾ pounds turnips, peeled and cut into ½-inch cubes**
- **1 bunch fresh turnip greens (about 12 ounces), chopped**
- **8 ounces cubed fully cooked country ham or 2 smoked ham hocks (about 1½ pounds)**
- **1 medium onion, chopped**
- **3 tablespoons sugar**
- **1½ teaspoons coarsely ground pepper**
- **1¼ teaspoons salt**
- **2 cartons (32 ounces each) chicken broth**

In a greased 6- or 7-qt. slow cooker, combine all ingredients. Cook, covered, on low until vegetables are tender, 5-6 hours, stirring once. If using ham hocks, remove the meat from bones when cool enough to handle; cut ham into small pieces and return to slow cooker. Serve with a slotted spoon.

SLOW COOKER SPINACH & RICE

I started making this in the slow cooker to save oven space during the holidays. It's so convenient, I no longer reserve it for special occasions!

—**ERICA POLLY** SUN PRAIRIE, WI

PREP: 20 MIN. • **COOK:** 3 HOURS + STANDING
MAKES: 8 SERVINGS

- **2 tablespoons butter**
- **1 medium onion, finely chopped**
- **2 garlic cloves, minced**
- **¼ teaspoon dried thyme**
- **4 cups reduced-sodium chicken broth**
- **2 packages (10 ounces each) frozen chopped spinach, thawed and squeezed dry**
- **1 package (8 ounces) cream cheese, softened**
- **1 teaspoon salt**
- **1 teaspoon pepper**
- **2 cups uncooked converted rice**
- **2 cups shredded cheddar cheese**
- **½ cup panko (Japanese) bread crumbs**
- **¼ cup grated Parmesan cheese**

1. In a large saucepan, melt butter over medium heat. Add the onion; cook and stir until tender, 4-6 minutes. Add garlic and thyme; cook 1 minute longer. Add broth; bring to a simmer. Remove from heat. Stir in spinach, cream cheese, salt and pepper until blended. Transfer to a 4-qt. slow cooker. Stir in the rice.

2. Cook, covered, until the rice is tender and the liquid is absorbed, 3-4 hours, stirring halfway through cooking. Remove insert; top with cheddar cheese. Let stand, covered, for 20 minutes. Top with bread crumbs and Parmesan cheese.

FAST FIX

CAJUN CORN

My husband loves corn on the cob. Making it like this is so tasty, and there is no standing over a hot stove on a summer day waiting for the water to boil! You can use any blend of seasoning you like. We like a little spice, so Cajun seasoning works well for us—and when I use it, I don't need any additional salt.

—**AUDRA RORICK** SCOTT CITY, KS

PREP: 15 MIN. • **COOK:** 4 HOURS
MAKES: 4 SERVINGS

- **4 tablespoons butter, softened**
- **2 teaspoons Cajun seasoning, or more to taste**
- **4 medium ears sweet corn, husks removed**
- **¾ cup water**

1. Combine butter and Cajun seasoning until well blended. Place each ear of corn on a double thickness of heavy-duty foil. Spread the butter mixture over each ear. Wrap foil tightly around the corn.

2. Place corn in a 6-qt. slow cooker; add water. Cook, covered, on high until the corn is tender, 4-6 hours.

CAJUN CORN

ROSEMARY BEETS

We're a family of beet eaters. For a simple side dish, I use a slow cooker and let the beets mellow with rosemary and thyme.

—**NANCY HEISHMAN** LAS VEGAS, NV

PREP: 20 MIN. • **COOK:** 6 HOURS
MAKES: 8 SERVINGS

- ⅓ cup honey
- ¼ cup white balsamic vinegar
- 1 tablespoon minced fresh rosemary or 1 teaspoon dried rosemary, crushed
- 2 teaspoons minced fresh thyme or ¾ teaspoon dried thyme
- 1 tablespoon olive oil
- 2 garlic cloves, minced
- ¾ teaspoon salt
- ½ teaspoon Chinese five-spice powder
- ½ teaspoon coarsely ground pepper
- 5 large fresh beets (about 3½ pounds), peeled and trimmed
- 1 medium red onion, chopped
- 1 medium orange, peeled and chopped
- 1 cup crumbled feta cheese

1. In a small bowl, whisk the first nine ingredients until blended. Place beets in a greased 4-qt. slow cooker. Add the onion and orange. Pour the honey mixture over top.

2. Cook, covered, on low until the beets are tender, 6-8 hours. Remove the beets; cut into wedges. Return to slow cooker. Serve warm or refrigerate and serve cold. Serve with a slotted spoon; sprinkle with cheese.

FAST FIX

ORANGE SPICE CARROTS

To get my son to eat veggies, I mix and match flavors and spices. My carrots with orange and cinnamon have him hooked.

—**CHRISTINA ADDISON** BLANCHESTER, OH

PREP: 10 MIN. • **COOK:** 4 HOURS
MAKES: 6 SERVINGS

- 2 pounds medium carrots or baby carrots, cut into 1-inch pieces
- ½ cup packed brown sugar
- ½ cup orange juice
- 2 tablespoons butter
- ¾ teaspoon ground cinnamon
- ½ teaspoon salt
- ¼ teaspoon ground nutmeg
- 4 teaspoons cornstarch
- ¼ cup cold water

1. In a 3-qt. slow cooker, combine the first seven ingredients. Cook, covered, on low until the carrots are tender, 4-5 hours.
2. In a small bowl, mix cornstarch and water until smooth; gradually stir into the carrot mixture until the sauce is thickened.

TEST KITCHEN TIP

Are baby carrots really babies? Not really. They are a hybrid carrot that has been developed for its sweetness and lack of a core. The carrots are harvested and then processed in a machine that peels and cuts them to a uniform size.

FAST FIX

CHEDDAR CREAMED CORN

I took this super easy recipe to a school potluck once and it was gone in no time. I've been asked to bring it to every function since.

—**JESSICA MAXWELL** ENGLEWOOD, NJ

PREP: 10 MIN. • **COOK:** 3 HOURS
MAKES: 9 SERVINGS

- **2 packages (one 16 ounces, one 12 ounces) frozen corn, thawed**
- **1 package (8 ounces) cream cheese, cubed**
- **¾ cup shredded cheddar cheese**
- **¼ cup butter, melted**
- **¼ cup heavy whipping cream**
- **½ teaspoon salt**
- **¼ teaspoon pepper**

In a 3- or 4-qt. slow cooker, combine all ingredients. Cook, covered, on low until cheese is melted and corn is tender, 3-3½ hours. Stir just before serving.

FAST FIX

CHEESY SPINACH

My daughter often serves this cheese and spinach blend at church suppers. Even people who don't usually eat spinach like this flavorful dish once they try it. There is never any left.

—**FRANCES MOORE** DECATUR, IL

PREP: 10 MIN. • **COOK:** 5 HOURS
MAKES: 6-8 SERVINGS

- **2 packages (10 ounces each) frozen chopped spinach, thawed and well drained**
- **2 cups (16 ounces) 4% cottage cheese**
- **1½ cups cubed process cheese (Velveeta)**
- **3 large eggs, lightly beaten**
- **¼ cup butter, cubed**
- **¼ cup all-purpose flour**
- **1 teaspoon salt**

In a large bowl, combine all ingredients. Pour into a greased 3-qt. slow cooker. Cover and cook on high for 1 hour. Reduce heat to low; cook until a knife inserted near the center comes out clean, 4-5 hours longer.

BUTTERNUT SQUASH WITH WHOLE GRAINS

Fresh ingredients shine in this scrumptious slow-cooked side. This is how you spread some holiday cheer!

—***TASTE OF HOME*** **TEST KITCHEN**

PREP: 15 MIN. • **COOK:** 4 HOURS
MAKES: 12 SERVINGS

- **1 medium butternut squash (about 3 pounds), cut into ½-inch cubes**
- **1 cup uncooked whole grain brown and red rice blend**
- **1 medium onion, chopped**
- **½ cup water**
- **3 garlic cloves, minced**
- **2 teaspoons minced fresh thyme or ½ teaspoon dried thyme**
- **½ teaspoon salt**
- **¼ teaspoon pepper**
- **1 can (14½ ounces) vegetable broth**
- **1 package (6 ounces) fresh baby spinach**

1. In a 4-qt. slow cooker, combine the first eight ingredients. Stir in broth.
2. Cook, covered, on low until grains are tender, 4-5 hours. Stir in spinach before serving.
Note: This recipe was tested with RiceSelect Royal Blend Whole Grain Texmati Brown & Red Rice with Barley and Rye.

FAST FIX

SLOW COOKER CRAN-APPLE CHUTNEY

My clan isn't crazy for cranberries, but they can't get enough of this delicious chutney. I recommend it for Thanksgiving since it tastes amazing paired with turkey, but it's also good on its own.

—**RAQUEL HAGGARD** EDMOND, OK

PREP: 10 MIN. • **COOK:** 3 HOURS + CHILLING
MAKES: 3 CUPS

- **1 package (12 ounces) fresh or frozen cranberries, thawed**
- **1 medium Gala apple, peeled and finely chopped**
- **⅔ cup sugar or sugar substitute equivalent to ⅔ cup sugar**
- **⅓ cup honey**
- **2 tablespoons brown sugar**
- **2 tablespoons frozen orange juice concentrate, thawed**
- **1 teaspoon ground cinnamon**
- **1 teaspoon cider vinegar**
- **Dash ground ginger**

1. In a 1½-qt. slow cooker, combine all ingredients. Cook, covered, on low until the cranberries pop and mixture is slightly thickened, 3-4 hours.
2. Transfer to a small bowl; cool slightly. Refrigerate until cold.

BROCCOLI-CHEDDAR HASH BROWNS

Need a new go-to comfort food? Hash browns fit the bill. This gooey combo of tender potatoes and broccoli pairs well with a wide variety of entrees.

—**DEBORAH BIGGS** OMAHA, NE

PREP: 20 MIN. • **COOK:** 4½ HOURS
MAKES: 8 SERVINGS

- **1 package (30 ounces) frozen shredded hash brown potatoes**
- **2 cups frozen broccoli florets**
- **1¼ cups shredded sharp cheddar cheese, divided**
- **2 green onions, chopped**
- **2 tablespoons butter**
- **2 tablespoons all-purpose flour**
- **½ cup whole milk**
- **1 can (10¾ ounces) condensed cream of broccoli soup, undiluted**
- **½ teaspoon salt**
- **½ teaspoon Dijon mustard**

1. In a greased 4- or 5-qt. slow cooker, combine the hash browns, broccoli, ¾ cup of the cheese and the onions.
2. In a small saucepan, melt butter. Stir in flour until smooth; gradually add milk. Bring to a boil; cook and stir for 1 minute or until thickened. Stir in the soup, salt and mustard. Pour over potato mixture; stir to combine.
3. Cover and cook on low until the potatoes are tender, 4-5 hours. Sprinkle with the remaining cheese. Cover and cook until the cheese is melted, about 30 minutes longer.

TEST KITCHEN TIP

Frozen hash browns are a real time-saver when you're making breakfast, brunch or even dinner. To perk up the flavor, try a secret ingredient—add a little dill seed to the potatoes before cooking.

SWEET & SOUR BEANS

This recipe is popular on both sides of the border. It came from a friend in Alaska, then traveled with me to Mexico, where I lived for 5 years, and is now a potluck favorite in my Arkansas community. It's easy to keep the beans warm and serve them from a slow cooker.

—**BARBARA SHORT** MENA, AR

PREP: 20 MIN. • **COOK:** 3 HOURS
MAKES: 20 SERVINGS

- **8 bacon strips, diced**
- **2 medium onions, halved and thinly sliced**
- **1 cup packed brown sugar**
- **½ cup cider vinegar**
- **1 teaspoon salt**
- **1 teaspoon ground mustard**
- **½ teaspoon garlic powder**
- **1 can (28 ounces) baked beans, undrained**
- **1 can (16 ounces) kidney beans, rinsed and drained**
- **1 can (15 ounces) pinto beans, rinsed and drained**
- **1 can (15 ounces) lima beans, rinsed and drained**
- **1 can (15½ ounces) black-eyed peas, rinsed and drained**

1. In a large skillet, cook the bacon over medium heat until crisp. Remove with slotted spoon to paper towels. Drain, reserving 2 tablespoons of the drippings. Saute onions in the drippings until tender. Add brown sugar, vinegar, salt, mustard and garlic powder. Bring to a boil.

2. In a 5-qt. slow cooker, combine the beans and peas. Add the onion mixture and bacon; mix well. Cover and cook on high until heated through, 3-4 hours.

SLOW COOKER MARINATED MUSHROOMS

SLOW COOKER MARINATED MUSHROOMS

Here's a terrific healthy addition to any buffet spread. Mushrooms and pearl onions seasoned with herbs, balsamic and red wine are terrific on their own or alongside a tenderloin roast

—**COURTNEY WILSON** FRESNO, CA

PREP: 15 MIN. • **COOK:** 6 HOURS
MAKES: 20 SERVINGS

- **2 pounds medium fresh mushrooms**
- **1 package (14.4 ounces) frozen pearl onions, thawed**
- **4 garlic cloves, minced**
- **2 cups reduced-sodium beef broth**
- **½ cup dry red wine**
- **3 tablespoons balsamic vinegar**
- **3 tablespoons olive oil**
- **1 teaspoon salt**
- **1 teaspoon dried basil**
- **½ teaspoon dried thyme**
- **½ teaspoon pepper**
- **¼ teaspoon crushed red pepper flakes**

Place mushrooms, onions and garlic in a 5- or 6-qt. slow cooker. In a small bowl, whisk the remaining ingredients; pour over the mushrooms. Cook, covered, on low until the mushrooms are tender, 6-8 hours.

To freeze: Freeze cooled mushrooms and juices in freezer containers. To use, partially thaw in refrigerator overnight. Microwave, covered, on high in a microwave-safe dish until heated through, stirring gently and adding a little broth or water if necessary.

HOLIDAY TURKEY GRAVY

I make this a day or so ahead of the big day and then all I have to do is heat it up. It saves time, and getting the food on the table goes much quicker. The smell while this is cooking permeates the whole house and whets the appetite.

—**ISABELLE ROONEY** SUMMERVILLE, SC

PREP: 30 MIN. • **COOK:** 5 HOURS
MAKES: 6 CUPS

- **2 turkey wings, halved (about 3 pounds)**
- **2 medium onions, halved**
- **1 cup water**
- **8 cups reduced-sodium chicken broth, divided**
- **¾ cup chopped carrots**
- **½ teaspoon dried thyme**
- **2 tablespoons butter**
- **¾ cup all-purpose flour**
- **½ teaspoon coarsely ground pepper**

1. Preheat oven to 425°. Place turkey wings and onions in a roasting pan. Roast, uncovered, until well browned, about 1 hour. Transfer wings and onions to a 5-qt. slow cooker. Add water to roasting pan and stir to loosen browned bits. Add to slow cooker. Stir in 6 cups broth, carrots and thyme. Cook, covered, on low for 4 hours.

2. Remove the wings; discard or save for another use. Strain and discard the vegetables; skim fat. In a 6-qt. stockpot, melt butter over medium-low heat; whisk in flour, pepper and the remaining broth until smooth. Slowly whisk in the stock; bring to a boil, stirring constantly. Reduce heat; simmer and stir until the gravy reaches desired consistency.

SLOW COOKER
CHERRY BUCKLE,
PAGE 231

SLOW-COOKED SWEETS

Dessert from the slow cooker? Absolutely! These sweet, delicous meal-enders will be ready to eat when you're done with your main course—no fuss, no added hassle!

STRAWBERRY-BANANA PUDDING CAKE

STRAWBERRY-BANANA PUDDING CAKE

This luscious pink pudding cake is so easy to put together. Top it with ice cream and fresh fruit, and you have one very happy family.

—**NADINE MESCH** MOUNT HEALTHY, OH

PREP: 15 MIN. • **COOK:** 3½ HOURS + STANDING
MAKES: 10 SERVINGS

- **1 package strawberry cake mix (regular size)**
- **1 package (3.4 ounces) instant banana cream pudding mix**
- **2 cups plain Greek yogurt**
- **4 large eggs**
- **1 cup water**
- **¾ cup canola oil**
- **2 tablespoons minced fresh basil**
- **1 cup white baking chips**
- **Optional toppings: vanilla ice cream, sliced bananas, sliced strawberries and fresh basil**

1. In a large bowl, combine the first six ingredients; beat on low speed for 30 seconds. Beat on medium for 2 minutes; stir in basil. Transfer to a greased 5-qt. slow cooker. Cook, covered, on low until the edges of the cake are golden brown (the center will be moist), 3½ to 4 hours.

2. Turn off the slow cooker; sprinkle the cake with baking chips. Remove insert; let stand, uncovered, for 10 minutes before serving. Serve warm with toppings as desired.

TEST KITCHEN TIP

Don't be tempted to use sugar-free instant pudding mix in recipes that call for regular—the sugar-free variety does not have the same consistency nor does it set up like regular instant pudding. It also gives a recipe less bulk.

WARM ROCKY ROAD CAKE

When it's warm, this reminds me of super-moist lava cake. And until I made this, I didn't think a slow-cooker cake could be so attractive. It's a real winner!

—**SCARLETT ELROD** NEWNAN, GA

PREP: 20 MIN. • **COOK:** 3 HOURS
MAKES: 16 SERVINGS

- **1 package German chocolate cake mix (regular size)**
- **1 package (3.9 ounces) instant chocolate pudding mix**
- **1 cup (8 ounces) sour cream**
- **⅓ cup butter, melted**
- **3 large eggs**
- **1 teaspoon vanilla extract**
- **3¼ cups 2% milk, divided**
- **1 package (3.4 ounces) cook-and-serve chocolate pudding mix**
- **1½ cups miniature marshmallows**
- **1 cup (6 ounces) semisweet chocolate chips**
- **½ cup chopped pecans, toasted**
- **Vanilla ice cream, optional**

1. In a large bowl, combine the first six ingredients; add 1¼ cups milk. Beat on low speed 30 seconds. Beat on medium 2 minutes. Transfer to a greased 4- or 5-qt. slow cooker. Sprinkle cook-and-serve pudding mix over batter.

2. In a small saucepan, heat the remaining milk until bubbles form around the sides of the pan; gradually pour over the contents of slow cooker.

3. Cook, covered, on high for 3-4 hours or until a toothpick inserted in the cake portion comes out with moist crumbs.

4. Turn off slow cooker. Sprinkle marshmallows, chocolate chips and pecans over cake; let stand, covered, 5 minutes or until marshmallows begin to melt. Serve warm. If desired, top with ice cream.

Note: To toast nuts, bake in a shallow pan in a 350° oven for 5-10 minutes or cook in a skillet over low heat until lightly browned, stirring occasionally.

CINNAMON SPICED APPLES

If you're feeling festive, spoon my cinnamon spiced apples over pancakes, waffles or even a bowl of oatmeal. They're homey, aromatic and just plain heavenly.

—**AMIE POWELL** KNOXVILLE, TN

PREP: 15 MIN. • **COOK:** 3 HOURS
MAKES: 6 CUPS

- **⅓ cup sugar**
- **¼ cup packed brown sugar**
- **1 tablespoon cornstarch**
- **3 teaspoons ground cinnamon**
- **⅛ teaspoon ground nutmeg**
- **6 large Granny Smith apples, peeled and cut into eighths**
- **¼ cup butter, cubed**

In a small bowl, mix the first five ingredients. Place apples in a greased 5-qt. slow cooker; add sugar mixture and toss to coat. Top with butter. Cook, covered, on low 3-4 hours or until apples are tender, stirring halfway.

SLOW COOKER FLAN IN A JAR

Here's a cute and fun take on the Mexican dessert classic. Spoil yourself or the people you love with these delightful portable custards. Tuck a jar into your lunch box for a sweet treat.

—**MEGUMI GARCIA** MILWAUKEE, WI

PREP: 25 MIN. • **COOK:** 2 HOURS + COOLING
MAKES: 6 SERVINGS

- **½ cup sugar**
- **1 tablespoon plus 3 cups hot water (110°-115°)**
- **6 canning jars (4 ounces each) with lids and bands**
- **1 cup coconut or whole milk**
- **⅓ cup whole milk**
- **⅓ cup sweetened condensed milk**
- **2 large eggs plus 1 large egg yolk, lightly beaten**
- **Pinch salt**
- **1 teaspoon vanilla extract**
- **1 teaspoon dark rum, optional**

1. Spread sugar over the bottom of a small, heavy saucepan; cook, without stirring, over medium-low heat until the sugar begins to melt. Then, gently drag the melted sugar to the center of pan so sugar melts evenly and cook, stirring constantly, until the melted sugar turns a deep amber color, about 2 minutes. Immediately remove from heat and carefully stir in 1 tablespoon hot water. Quickly pour into jars.

2. In a small saucepan, heat coconut milk and whole milk until bubbles form around sides of pan; remove from heat. In a large bowl, whisk condensed milk, eggs, egg yolk and salt until blended but not foamy. Slowly stir in the hot milk; stir in vanilla and, if desired, rum. Strain through a fine sieve. Pour egg mixture into prepared jars. Center the lids on the jars; screw on the bands until fingertip tight.

3. Add the remaining hot water to a 6-qt. slow cooker; place jars in slow cooker. Cook, covered, on high for 2 hours or until centers are set. Cool 10 minutes on a wire rack. Remove jars to a 13x9-in. baking pan filled halfway with ice water; cool for 10 minutes. Refrigerate until cold, about 1 hour. To serve, run a knife around the sides of jars; invert flans onto dessert plates.

SLOW COOKER MIXED FRUIT & PISTACHIO CAKE

This cake is easy to make on a lazy day and is a guaranteed-delicious dessert for several days—if you can make it last that long! It's wonderful for the fall and even the holidays.

—**NANCY HEISHMAN** LAS VEGAS, NV

PREP: 20 MIN. • **COOK:** 2 HOURS + COOLING
MAKES: 8 SERVINGS

- **1½ cups all-purpose flour**
- **1½ teaspoons ground cinnamon**
- **½ teaspoon baking soda**
- **½ teaspoon baking powder**
- **½ teaspoon ground allspice**
- **¼ teaspoon salt**
- **1 can (8 ounces) jellied cranberry sauce**
- **⅓ cup packed brown sugar**
- **⅓ cup buttermilk**
- **¼ cup butter, melted**
- **2 teaspoons grated orange peel**
- **½ teaspoon orange extract**
- **1 large egg**
- **1 cup mixed dried fruit bits**
- **1 cup pistachios**
- **Sweetened whipped cream, optional**

1. Whisk together the first six ingredients. In another bowl, combine the next seven ingredients. Add the cranberry mixture to the flour mixture; stir until smooth. Add dried fruit and pistachios.
2. Pour batter into a greased 1½-qt. baking dish; place in a 6-qt. slow cooker. Lay a 14x12-in. piece of parchment paper over the top of the slow cooker, under the lid. Cook, covered, on high until a toothpick inserted in center comes out clean, about 2½ hours. Remove dish from slow cooker to a wire rack. Cool for 30 minutes before inverting onto a serving platter.
3. Cut into wedges with a serrated knife; if desired, serve with sweetened whipped cream.

SLOW COOKER CINNAMON ROLL PUDDING

A slow cooker turns day-old cinnamon rolls into a comforting, old-fashioned dessert. It tastes wonderful topped with lemon or vanilla sauce or whipped cream.

—**EDNA HOFFMAN** HEBRON, IN

PREP: 15 MIN. • **COOK:** 3 HOURS
MAKES: 6 SERVINGS

- **8 cups cubed day-old unfrosted cinnamon rolls**
- **4 large eggs**
- **2 cups milk**
- **¼ cup sugar**
- **¼ cup butter, melted**
- **½ teaspoon vanilla extract**
- **¼ teaspoon ground nutmeg**
- **1 cup raisins**

Place cubed cinnamon rolls in a 3-qt. slow cooker. In a small bowl, whisk eggs, milk, sugar, butter, vanilla and nutmeg. Stir in raisins. Pour over the cinnamon rolls; stir gently. Cover and cook on low for 3 hours or until a knife inserted near the center comes out clean.

Note: 8 slices of cinnamon or white bread, cut into 1-inch cubes, may be substituted for the cinnamon rolls.

FAST FIX

SLOW COOKER BANANAS FOSTER

The flavors of caramel, rum and walnut naturally complement fresh bananas in this classic dessert made easy! It's my go-to choice for any family get-together.

—**CRYSTAL JO BRUNS** ILIFF, CO

PREP: 10 MIN. • **COOK:** 2 HOURS
MAKES: 5 SERVINGS

- **5 medium firm bananas**
- **1 cup packed brown sugar**
- **¼ cup butter, melted**
- **¼ cup rum**
- **1 teaspoon vanilla extract**
- **½ teaspoon ground cinnamon**
- **⅓ cup chopped walnuts**
- **⅓ cup sweetened shredded coconut**
- **Vanilla ice cream or sliced pound cake**

1. Cut the bananas in half lengthwise, then widthwise; layer in the bottom of a 1½-qt. slow cooker. Combine brown sugar, butter, rum, vanilla and cinnamon; pour over the bananas. Cover and cook on low for 1½ hours or until heated through.
2. Sprinkle with walnuts and coconut; cook 30 minutes longer. Serve with ice cream or pound cake.

TEST KITCHEN TIP

If flaked coconut has been frozen or becomes dried out, you can make it fresh again by placing the amount you need in a bowl and sprinkling with a few drops of water. Cover and microwave until warm.

NUTTY APPLE STREUSEL DESSERT

Many people don't think of using a slow cooker to make dessert, but I like having this hot, scrumptious apple treat waiting to be served when we finish up our dinner. I start it in the morning and don't think about it all day.

—**JACKI EVERY** ROTTERDAM, NY

PREP: 20 MIN. • **BAKE:** 6 HOURS
MAKES: 6-8 SERVINGS

- **6 cups sliced peeled tart apples**
- **1¼ teaspoons ground cinnamon**
- **¼ teaspoon ground allspice**
- **¼ teaspoon ground nutmeg**
- **¾ cup 2% milk**
- **2 tablespoons butter, softened**
- **¾ cup sugar**
- **2 large eggs**
- **1 teaspoon vanilla extract**
- **½ cup biscuit/baking mix**

TOPPING

- **1 cup biscuit/baking mix**
- **⅓ cup packed brown sugar**
- **3 tablespoons cold butter**
- **½ cup sliced almonds**
- **Ice cream or whipped cream, optional**

1. In a large bowl, toss apples with cinnamon, allspice and nutmeg. Place in a greased 3-qt. slow cooker. In a small bowl, combine the milk, butter, sugar, eggs, vanilla and baking mix. Spoon over the apples.
2. For topping, combine biscuit mix and brown sugar in a large bowl; cut in butter until crumbly. Add almonds; sprinkle over the apples.
3. Cover and cook on low for 6-8 hours or until the apples are tender. Serve with ice cream or whipped cream if desired.

NUTTY APPLE STREUSEL DESSERT

FAST FIX

BURGUNDY PEARS

These warm spiced pears elevate slow cooking to a new level of elegance, yet they're incredibly easy to make. Your friends won't believe this fancy-looking dessert came from a slow cooker.

—**ELIZABETH HANES** PERALTA, NM

PREP: 10 MIN. • **COOK:** 3 HOURS
MAKES: 6 SERVINGS

- **6 medium ripe pears**
- **⅓ cup sugar**
- **⅓ cup Burgundy wine or grape juice**
- **3 tablespoons orange marmalade**
- **1 tablespoon lemon juice**
- **¼ teaspoon ground cinnamon**
- **¼ teaspoon ground nutmeg**
- **Dash salt**
- **Vanilla ice cream**

1. Peel the pears, leaving the stems intact. Core from the bottom. Stand pears upright in a 5-qt. slow cooker. In a small bowl, combine sugar, wine or grape juice, marmalade, lemon juice, cinnamon, nutmeg and salt. Carefully pour over the pears.
2. Cover and cook on low for 3-4 hours or until the pears are tender. To serve, drizzle with sauce and garnish with vanilla ice cream.

CINNAMON-APPLE BROWN BETTY

If I had to define the Betty of Apple Brown Betty, she'd be a smart and thrifty Southern gal with a knack for creating simple, soul-comforting desserts. In this sweet dish, spiced apples are slow-cooked between layers of cinnamon-raisin bread cubes for a twist on the traditional oven-baked classic.

—**HEATHER DEMERITTE** SCOTTSDALE, AZ

PREP: 15 MIN. • **COOK:** 2 HOURS
MAKES: 6 SERVINGS

- **5 medium tart apples, cubed**
- **2 tablespoons lemon juice**
- **1 cup packed brown sugar**
- **1 teaspoon ground cinnamon**
- **¼ teaspoon ground nutmeg**
- **6 tablespoons butter, melted**
- **6 cups cubed day-old cinnamon-raisin bread (about 10 slices)**
- **Sweetened whipped cream, optional**

1. In a large bowl, toss apples with lemon juice. In a small bowl, mix brown sugar, cinnamon and nutmeg; add to the apple mixture and toss to coat. In a large bowl, drizzle butter over bread cubes; toss to coat.
2. Place 2 cups bread cubes in a greased 3- or 4-qt. slow cooker. Layer with half of the apple mixture and 2 cups bread cubes. Repeat layers. Cook, covered, on low for 2-3 hours or until the apples are tender. Stir before serving. If desired, top with whipped cream.

★★★★★ **READER REVIEW**

"This smells wonderful as it bakes, especially when you lift the lid off the slow cooker."

NANZIM TASTEOFHOME.COM

BUTTERSCOTCH-PECAN BREAD PUDDING
Lisa Varner
El Paso, TX

BUTTERSCOTCH-PECAN BREAD PUDDING

Bread pudding fans will absolutely adore this treat. Toppings like whipped cream and a butterscotch drizzle make it irresistible.

—**LISA VARNER** EL PASO, TX

PREP: 15 MIN. • **COOK:** 3 HOURS
MAKES: 8 SERVINGS

- **9 cups cubed day-old white bread (about 8 slices)**
- **½ cup chopped pecans**
- **½ cup butterscotch chips**
- **4 large eggs**
- **2 cups half-and-half cream**
- **½ cup packed brown sugar**
- **½ cup butter, melted**
- **1 teaspoon vanilla extract**
- **Whipped cream and butterscotch ice cream topping**

1. Place bread, pecans and butterscotch chips in a greased 4-qt. slow cooker. In a large bowl, whisk the eggs, cream, brown sugar, melted butter and vanilla until blended. Pour over the bread mixture; stir gently to combine.

2. Cook, covered, on low for 3-4 hours or until a knife inserted in the center comes out clean. Serve warm with whipped cream and butterscotch ice cream topping.

PINK GRAPEGRUIT CHEESECAKE

PINK GRAPEFRUIT CHEESECAKE

Cheesecake from a slow cooker? It's true! I experimented a few times to turn this iconic dessert into a slow-cooker classic. Give it a try—you'll be amazed at the results!

—**KRISTA LANPHIER** MILWAUKEE, WI

PREP: 20 MIN. • **COOK:** 2 HOURS + CHILLING
MAKES: 6 SERVINGS

- **¾ cup graham cracker crumbs**
- **1 tablespoon plus ⅔ cup sugar, divided**
- **1 teaspoon grated grapefruit peel**
- **¼ teaspoon ground ginger**
- **2½ tablespoons butter, melted**
- **2 packages (8 ounces each) cream cheese, softened**
- **½ cup sour cream**
- **2 tablespoons pink grapefruit juice**
- **2 large eggs, lightly beaten**

1. Place a greased 6-in. springform pan on a double thickness of heavy-duty foil (about 12 in. square). Wrap the foil securely around the pan. Pour 1 in. water into a 6-qt. slow cooker. Layer two 24-in. pieces of foil. Starting with a long side, fold up foil to create a 1-in.-wide strip; roll strip into a coil. Place in slow cooker to form a rack for the cheesecake.
2. Mix the cracker crumbs, 1 tablespoon sugar, peel and ginger; stir in butter. Press onto bottom and about 1 in. up sides of prepared pan.
3. In a large bowl, beat cream cheese and the remaining sugar until smooth. Beat in sour cream and grapefruit juice. Add eggs; beat on low speed just until combined.
4. Pour into crust. Place springform pan on coil. Cover slow cooker with a double layer of paper towels; place lid securely over towels. Cook, covered, on high for 2 hours. Do not remove lid; turn off slow cooker and let cheesecake stand, covered, in slow cooker for 1 hour. Center of cheesecake will be just set and top will appear dull.
5. Remove springform pan from slow cooker; remove foil from pan. Cool cheesecake on a wire rack for 1 hour. Loosen sides from pan with a knife. Refrigerate overnight, covering when completely cooled. Remove rim from pan.

SLOW COOKER LAVA CAKE

Because I enjoy chocolate, this decadent slow cooker cake has long been a family favorite. This cake can also be served cold.

—**ELIZABETH FARRELL** HAMILTON, MT

PREP: 15 MIN. • **COOK:** 2 HOURS + STANDING
MAKES: 8 SERVINGS

- **1 cup all-purpose flour**
- **1 cup packed brown sugar, divided**
- **5 tablespoons baking cocoa, divided**
- **2 teaspoons baking powder**
- **¼ teaspoon salt**
- **½ cup fat-free milk**
- **2 tablespoons canola oil**
- **½ teaspoon vanilla extract**
- **⅛ teaspoon ground cinnamon**
- **1¼ cups hot water**

1. In a large bowl, whisk flour, ½ cup brown sugar, 3 tablespoons cocoa, baking powder and salt. In another bowl, whisk milk, oil and vanilla until blended. Add to the flour mixture; stir just until moistened.
2. Spread batter into a 3-qt. slow cooker coated with cooking spray. In a small bowl, mix cinnamon and the remaining brown sugar and cocoa; stir in hot water. Pour over batter (do not stir).
3. Cook, covered, on high for 2 to 2½ hours or until a toothpick inserted in cake portion comes out clean. Turn off slow cooker; let stand for 15 minutes before serving.

TEST KITCHEN TIP
Dutch-process cocoa can be used instead of regular cocoa if the recipe doesn't call for a leavening agent, or if it calls for baking powder. Baking soda needs the acidity of regular cocoa to activate and for the cake or cookie to rise.

FAST FIX

OLD-FASHIONED TAPIOCA

My family loves old-fashioned tapioca, but I don't always have time to make it. So, I came up with this simple recipe. It lets us enjoy one of our favorites without all the hands-on time.

—**RUTH PETERS** BEL AIR, MD

PREP: 10 MIN. • **COOK:** 4½ HOURS
MAKES: 18 SERVINGS

- **8 cups 2% milk**
- **1 cup pearl tapioca**
- **1 cup plus 2 tablespoons sugar**
- **⅛ teaspoon salt**
- **4 large eggs**
- **1½ teaspoons vanilla extract**
- **Sliced fresh strawberries and whipped cream, optional**

1. In a 4- to 5-qt. slow cooker, combine the milk, tapioca, sugar and salt. Cover and cook on low for 4-5 hours.
2. In a large bowl, beat the eggs; stir in a small amount of the hot tapioca mixture. Return all to the slow cooker, stirring to combine. Cover and cook 30 minutes longer or until a thermometer reads 160°. Stir in vanilla.
3. Serve with strawberries and whipped cream if desired.

VERY VANILLA SLOW COOKER CHEESECAKE

Cinnamon and vanilla give this cheesecake so much flavor, and making it in the slow cooker creates a silky, smooth texture that's hard to resist.

—**KRISTA LANPHIER** MILWAUKEE, WI

PREP: 40 MIN. • **COOK:** 2 HOURS + CHILLING
MAKES: 6 SERVINGS

- **¾ cup graham cracker crumbs**
- **1 tablespoon sugar plus ⅔ cup sugar, divided**
- **¼ teaspoon ground cinnamon**
- **2½ tablespoons butter, melted**
- **2 packages (8 ounces each) cream cheese, softened**
- **½ cup sour cream**
- **2 to 3 teaspoons vanilla extract**
- **2 large eggs, lightly beaten**

TOPPING

- **2 ounces semisweet chocolate, chopped**
- **1 teaspoon shortening**
- **Miniature peanut butter cups, toasted sliced almonds, or topping of your choice**

1. Grease a 6-in. springform pan; place on a double thickness of heavy-duty foil (about 12 in. square). Wrap foil securely around pan.
2. Pour 1 in. water into a 6-qt. slow cooker. Layer two 24-in. pieces of foil. Starting with a long side, roll up the foil to make a 1-in.-wide strip; shape strip into a circle. Place circle in the bottom of the slow cooker to make a rack.
3. Mix cracker crumbs, 1 tablespoon sugar and cinnamon; stir in butter. Press onto bottom and about 1 in. up the sides of the prepared pan.
4. In a large bowl, beat cream cheese and the remaining sugar until smooth. Beat in sour cream and vanilla. Add eggs; beat on low speed just until combined. Pour into crust.
5. Place springform pan on the foil circle without touching the slow cooker sides. Cover slow cooker with a double layer of white paper towels; place lid securely over towels. Cook, covered, on high for 2 hours.
6. Do not remove lid; turn off slow cooker and let cheesecake stand, covered, in slow cooker 1 hour.
7. Remove springform pan from slow cooker; remove foil around pan. Cool cheesecake in pan on a wire rack for 1 hour longer. Loosen sides from pan with a knife. Refrigerate overnight, covering when completely cooled.
8. For topping, in a microwave, melt chocolate and shortening; stir until smooth. Cool slightly. Remove rim from springform pan. Pour the chocolate mixture over cheesecake; sprinkle with miniature peanut butter cups or almonds, or decorate with the topping of your choice.

Note: Cheesecake may be stored in the refrigerator for 4-6 days before serving. Wrap securely before chilling; add topping just before serving.

VERY VANILLA SLOW
COOKER CHEESECAKE

MINTY HOT FUDGE SUNDAE CAKE

The best part about dessert from the slow cooker is that when dinner's done, a hot treat is all ready to serve—no last-minute fuss. In this case, it's a chocolaty, gooey, minty treat!

—**TERRI MCKITRICK** DELAFIELD, WI

PREP: 15 MIN. • **COOK:** 4 HOURS
MAKES: 12 SERVINGS

- **1¾ cups packed brown sugar, divided**
- **1 cup all-purpose flour**
- **5 tablespoons baking cocoa, divided**
- **2 teaspoons baking powder**
- **½ teaspoon salt**
- **½ cup evaporated milk**
- **2 tablespoons butter, melted**
- **½ teaspoon vanilla extract**
- **⅛ teaspoon almond extract**
- **1 package (4.67 ounces) mint Andes candies**
- **1¾ cups boiling water**
- **4 teaspoons instant coffee granules**
- **Vanilla ice cream, whipped cream and maraschino cherries**

1. In a large bowl, combine 1 cup brown sugar, flour, 3 tablespoons cocoa, baking powder and salt. In another bowl, combine milk, butter and extracts. Stir into the dry ingredients just until moistened. Transfer to a 3-qt. slow cooker coated with cooking spray. Sprinkle with candies.

2. Combine water, coffee granules and the remaining brown sugar and cocoa; pour over the batter (do not stir). Cover and cook on high for 4 to 4½ hours or until a toothpick inserted near the center of the cake comes out clean. Serve with ice cream, whipped cream and cherries.

SLOW COOKER STRAWBERRY-RHUBARB SAUCE

We recently started growing our own rhubarb, and we live in a part of Oregon where strawberries are plentiful. I created this to drizzle over ice cream and filled a crisp with the rest.

—**KIM BANICK** SALEM, OR

PREP: 15 MIN. • **COOK:** 4½ HOURS
MAKES: 5 CUPS

- **4 cups sliced fresh or frozen rhubarb, thawed (about 10 stalks)**
- **4 cups fresh strawberries (about 1¼ pounds), halved**
- **1½ cups sugar**
- **¼ cup water**
- **3 tablespoons butter**
- **1 teaspoon vanilla extract**
- **¼ cup cornstarch**
- **3 tablespoons cold water**
- **Vanilla ice cream**

1. In a 3-qt. slow cooker, combine the first six ingredients. Cook, covered, on low for 4-5 hours or until the rhubarb is tender.

2. In a small bowl, mix cornstarch and cold water until smooth; gradually stir into the sauce. Cook, covered, on low for 30 minutes longer or until thickened. Serve with ice cream.

Note: If using frozen rhubarb, measure rhubarb while still frozen, then thaw completely. Drain in a colander, but do not press liquid out.

SLOW COOKER TEQUILA POACHED PEARS
Nancy Heishman
Las Vegas, NV

SLOW COOKER TEQUILA POACHED PEARS

Bring out this creative sweet when you want to impress dinner guests. The deliciously refreshing fresh pears and mint get a distinctive new twist with the addition of tequila.

—**NANCY HEISHMAN** LAS VEGAS, NV

PREP: 20 MIN. • **COOK:** 4 HOURS
MAKES: 8 SERVINGS

- **2 cups water**
- **1 can (11.3 ounces) pear nectar**
- **1 cup tequila**
- **½ cup sugar**
- **2 tablespoons lime juice**
- **2 teaspoons grated lime peel**
- **1 cinnamon stick (3 inches)**
- **¼ teaspoon ground nutmeg**
- **8 whole Anjou pears, peeled**
- **Sweetened whipped cream**
- **Fresh mint leaves**

1. In a large saucepan, combine the first eight ingredients. Bring to a boil over medium-high heat; boil for 2 minutes, stirring constantly.
2. Place pears in a 4- or 5-qt. slow cooker; add liquid. Cook, covered, on low until pears are tender, 4-5 hours. Remove cinnamon stick and discard. Pour 3 cups of the cooking liquid in a small saucepan. Bring to a boil; cook, uncovered, until liquid is reduced to 1 cup, about 20 minutes.
3. Halve pears lengthwise and core them. Serve with sauce, whipped cream and mint leaves.

PUMPKIN CRANBERRY
BREAD PUDDING

PUMPKIN CRANBERRY BREAD PUDDING

Savor your favorite fall flavors with this scrumptious bread pudding, served warm with a sweet vanilla sauce.

—**JUDITH BUCCIARELLI** NEWBURGH, NY

PREP: 15 MIN. • **COOK:** 3 HOURS
MAKES: 8 SERVINGS (1⅓ CUPS SAUCE)

- **8 slices cinnamon bread, cut into 1-inch cubes**
- **4 large eggs, beaten**
- **2 cups 2% milk**
- **1 cup canned pumpkin**
- **¼ cup packed brown sugar**
- **¼ cup butter, melted**
- **1 teaspoon vanilla extract**
- **½ teaspoon ground cinnamon**
- **¼ teaspoon ground nutmeg**
- **½ cup dried cranberries**

SAUCE

- **1 cup granulated sugar**
- **⅔ cup water**
- **1 cup heavy whipping cream**
- **2 teaspoons vanilla extract**
- **Vanilla ice cream, optional**

1. Place bread in a greased 3- or 4-qt. slow cooker. Combine next eight ingredients; stir in cranberries. Pour over bread cubes. Cook, covered, on low until a knife inserted near the center comes out clean, 3-4 hours.

2. For sauce, bring granulated sugar and water to a boil in a large saucepan over medium heat. Cook until the sugar is dissolved and the mixture turns golden amber, about 20 minutes. Gradually stir in cream until smooth. Remove from heat; stir in vanilla. Serve warm with bread pudding. If desired, add a scoop of vanilla ice cream to each serving.

AMARETTO CHERRIES WITH DUMPLINGS

Treat everyone to a dessert of comfort food—warm tart cherries drizzled with amaretto and topped with fluffy dumplings. A scoop of vanilla ice cream is the perfect finishing touch.

—***TASTE OF HOME*** **TEST KITCHEN**

PREP: 15 MIN. • **COOK:** 7¾ HOURS
MAKES: 6 SERVINGS

- **2 cans (14½ ounces each) pitted tart cherries**
- **¾ cup sugar**
- **¼ cup cornstarch**
- **⅛ teaspoon salt**
- **¼ cup amaretto or ½ teaspoon almond extract**

DUMPLINGS

- **1 cup all-purpose flour**
- **¼ cup sugar**
- **1 teaspoon baking powder**
- **½ teaspoon grated lemon peel**
- **⅛ teaspoon salt**
- **⅓ cup 2% milk**
- **3 tablespoons butter, melted**
- **Vanilla ice cream, optional**

1. Drain cherries, reserving ¼ cup juice. Place cherries in a 3-qt. slow cooker.

2. In a small bowl, mix sugar, cornstarch and salt; stir in reserved juice until smooth. Stir into cherries. Cook, covered, on high 7 hours. Drizzle amaretto over the cherry mixture.

3. For dumplings, in a small bowl, whisk flour, sugar, baking powder, lemon peel and salt. In another bowl, whisk milk and melted butter. Add to the flour mixture; stir just until moistened.

4. Drop by tablespoonfuls on top of the hot cherry mixture. Cook, covered, for 45 minutes or until a toothpick inserted in center of dumplings comes out clean. If desired, serve warm with ice cream.

BREAD PUDDING WITH BOURBON SAUCE

There's nothing I like better on a cold, wintry day than this soothing bread pudding. The bourbon sauce makes the dessert taste special, but you wouldn't believe how easy it is to prepare.

—**HOPE JOHNSON** YOUNGWOOD, PA

PREP: 20 MIN. • **COOK:** 3 HOURS.
MAKES: 6 SERVINGS

- **3 large eggs**
- **1¼ cups 2% milk**
- **½ cup sugar**
- **3 teaspoons vanilla extract**
- **½ teaspoon ground cinnamon**
- **¼ teaspoon ground nutmeg**
- **⅛ teaspoon salt**
- **4½ cups cubed day-old brioche or egg bread**
- **1¼ cups raisins**

BOURBON SAUCE

- **¼ cup butter, cubed**
- **½ cup sugar**
- **¼ cup light corn syrup**
- **3 tablespoons bourbon**

1. In a large bowl, whisk the first seven ingredients; stir in bread and raisins. Transfer to a greased 4-qt. slow cooker. Cover and cook on low for 3 hours.
2. In a small saucepan, heat butter. Stir in sugar and corn syrup; bring to a boil. Reduce heat; cook and stir until sugar is dissolved. Remove from the heat; stir in bourbon. Serve warm with bread pudding.

CHOCOLATE MALT PUDDING CAKE

When I make this warm, comforting cake, I chop the malted milk balls by putting them in a plastic bag and pounding it with a rubber mallet. It completely eliminates the mess.

—**SARAH SKUBINNA** CASCADE, MT

PREP: 25 MIN. • **COOK:** 2 HOURS + STANDING
MAKES: 8 SERVINGS

- **½ cup 2% milk**
- **2 tablespoons canola oil**
- **½ teaspoon almond extract**
- **1 cup all-purpose flour**
- **½ cup packed brown sugar**
- **2 tablespoons baking cocoa**
- **1½ teaspoons baking powder**
- **½ cup coarsely chopped malted milk balls**
- **½ cup semisweet chocolate chips**
- **¾ cup sugar**
- **¼ cup malted milk powder**
- **1¼ cups boiling water**
- **4 ounces cream cheese, softened and cubed**
- **Vanilla ice cream and sliced almonds**

1. In a large bowl, combine milk, oil and extract. Combine flour, brown sugar, cocoa and baking powder; gradually beat into milk mixture until blended. Stir in milk balls and chocolate chips.
2. Spoon into a greased 3-qt. slow cooker. In a small bowl, combine sugar and milk powder; stir in water and cream cheese. Pour over batter (do not stir).
3. Cover and cook on high for 2-3 hours or until a toothpick inserted in center of cake comes out clean. Turn off heat. Let stand 15 minutes. Serve warm with ice cream; sprinkle with almonds.

SLOW COOKER CHERRY BUCKLE

FAST FIX

SLOW COOKER CHERRY BUCKLE

I saw this recipe on a cooking show and came up with my own version. When the comforting aroma of this homey dessert drifts around the house, it's hard not to take a peek inside.

—**SHERRI MELOTIK** OAK CREEK, WI

PREP: 10 MIN. • **COOK:** 3 HOURS
MAKES: 6 SERVINGS

- **2 cans (15 ounces each) sliced pears, drained**
- **1 can (21 ounces) cherry pie filling**
- **¼ teaspoon almond extract**
- **1 package yellow cake mix (regular size)**
- **¼ cup old-fashioned oats**
- **¼ cup sliced almonds**
- **1 tablespoon brown sugar**
- **½ cup butter, melted**
- **Vanilla ice cream, optional**

1. In a greased 5-qt. slow cooker, combine the pears and pie filling; stir in extract. In a large bowl, combine cake mix, oats, almonds and brown sugar; stir in melted butter. Sprinkle over the fruit.

2. Cook, covered, on low 3-4 hours or until topping is golden brown. If desired, serve with ice cream.

MAPLE CREME BRULEE

The slow cooker is a surprisingly great way to cook a classic creme brulee. The crunchy brown sugar topping is wonderful, and the custard is smooth and creamy.

—***TASTE OF HOME* TEST KITCHEN**

PREP: 20 MIN. • **COOK:** 2 HOURS + CHILLING
MAKES: 3 SERVINGS

- **1⅓ cups heavy whipping cream**
- **3 large egg yolks**
- **½ cup packed brown sugar**
- **¼ teaspoon ground cinnamon**
- **½ teaspoon maple flavoring**

TOPPING

- **1½ teaspoons sugar**
- **1½ teaspoons brown sugar**

1. In a small saucepan, heat cream until bubbles form around the sides of the pan. In a small bowl, whisk the egg yolks, brown sugar and cinnamon. Remove cream from the heat; stir a small amount of hot cream into the egg mixture. Return all to the pan, stirring constantly. Stir in maple flavoring.
2. Transfer to three 6-oz. ramekins or custard cups. Place in a 6-qt. slow cooker; add 1 in. of boiling water to slow cooker. Cover and cook on high for 2 to 2½ hours or until the centers are just set (the mixture will jiggle). Carefully remove the ramekins from slow cooker; cool for 10 minutes. Cover and refrigerate for at least 4 hours.
3. For topping, combine sugar and brown sugar. If using a creme brulee torch, sprinkle custards with sugar mixture. Heat sugar with the torch until caramelized. Serve immediately.
4. If broiling the custards, place ramekins on a baking sheet; let stand at room temperature for 15 minutes. Sprinkle with sugar mixture. Broil 8 in. from the heat for 3-5 minutes or until sugar is caramelized. Refrigerate for 1-2 hours or until firm.

CARIBBEAN BREAD PUDDING

A completely unexpected dessert from the slow cooker, this bread pudding is moist and sweet with plump, juicy raisins and wonderful tropical flavors of pineapple and coconut.

—**ELIZABETH DOSS** CALIFORNIA CITY, CA

PREP: 30 MIN. • **COOK:** 4 HOURS
MAKES: 16 SERVINGS

- **1 cup raisins**
- **1 can (8 ounces) crushed pineapple, undrained**
- **2 large firm bananas, halved**
- **1 can (12 ounces) evaporated milk**
- **1 can (10 ounces) frozen non-alcoholic pina colada mix**
- **1 can (6 ounces) unsweetened pineapple juice**
- **3 large eggs**
- **½ cup cream of coconut**
- **¼ cup light rum, optional**
- **1 loaf (1 pound) French bread, cut into 1-inch cubes**
- **Whipped cream and maraschino cherries, optional**

1. In a small bowl, combine raisins and pineapple; set aside. In a blender, combine the bananas, milk, pina colada mix, pineapple juice, eggs, cream of coconut and, if desired, rum. Cover and process until smooth.
2. Place two-thirds of the bread in a greased 6-qt. slow cooker. Top with 1 cup of the raisin mixture. Layer with the remaining bread and raisin mixture. Pour banana mixture into slow cooker. Cover and cook on low for 4-5 hours or until a knife inserted in the center comes out clean. Serve warm with whipped cream and cherries if desired.

CARIBBEAN BREAD PUDDING

MESQUITE RIBS, PAGE 238

BONUS: INSTANT POT®

Meet the newest addition to the essential kitchen tool list! The electric pressure cooker cuts cooking times down drastically, making convenient, tasty and tender meals in record time.

EASY RIGATONI WITH SAUSAGE & PEAS

EASY RIGATONI WITH SAUSAGE & PEAS

With a tomato-y meat sauce and tangy goat cheese, this weeknight wonder is my version of comfort food. You just want to have bowl after bowl.

—**LIZZIE MUNRO** BROOKLYN, NY

START TO FINISH: 30 MIN.
MAKES: 6 SERVINGS

- **1 pound bulk Italian sausage**
- **4 garlic cloves, minced**
- **¼ cup tomato paste**
- **12 ounces uncooked rigatoni or large tube pasta**
- **1½ cups frozen peas (about 6 ounces)**
- **1 can (28 ounces) crushed tomatoes**
- **½ teaspoon dried basil**
- **¼ to ½ teaspoon crushed red pepper flakes**
- **4 cups water**
- **½ cup heavy whipping cream**
- **½ cup crumbled goat or feta cheese**
- **Thinly sliced fresh basil, optional**

1. Select saute setting and adjust for high heat in a 6-qt. electric pressure cooker. Cook and crumble sausage until no longer pink, 4-6 minutes. Add garlic; cook 1 minute longer. Add tomato paste; cook and stir until the meat is coated, 1-2 minutes. Stir in the next five ingredients; pour in water. Lock lid; make sure the vent is closed. Select manual setting; adjust pressure to low and set time for 6 minutes. When finished cooking, quick-release pressure according to manufacturer's directions.
2. Stir in cream; heat through. Top with cheese and, if desired, fresh basil.

SUNDAY BRUNCH BROCCOLI EGG CUPS

Serving brunch? This delicious egg dish is filled with crunchy bites of broccoli and served in ramekins. Your company will love it!

—**EDNA HOFFMAN** HEBRON, IN

START TO FINISH: 25 MIN.
MAKES: 4 SERVINGS

- **7 large eggs**
- **1½ cups half-and-half cream**
- **3 tablespoons shredded Swiss cheese**
- **2 teaspoons minced fresh parsley**
- **1 teaspoon minced fresh basil**
- **¼ teaspoon salt**
- **⅛ teaspoon cayenne pepper**
- **1 to 1½ cups frozen broccoli florets, thawed**
- **1 cup water**

1. Whisk three of the eggs with the next six ingredients; pour into four greased 8-ounce ramekins. Divide broccoli among the ramekins; top each with one of the remaining eggs.
2. Add 1 cup water and the trivet insert to a 6-qt. electric pressure cooker. Place the ramekins on the trivet, offset-stacking as needed; cover loosely with foil. Lock lid; make sure the vent is closed. Select steam setting; adjust pressure to high, and set time for 6 minutes. When finished cooking, quick-release pressure according to manufacturer's directions. Remove the lid; using tongs, remove ramekins. Let stand 3 minutes before serving.

FAST FIX

MESQUITE RIBS

When we're missing the grill during winter, these tangy ribs give us that same smoky barbecue taste we love. They're so simple, and fall-off-the-bone delicious, too.

—**SUE EVANS** MARQUETTE, MI

PREP: 10 MIN. • **COOK:** 35 MIN. + RELEASING
MAKES: 8 SERVINGS

- **1 cup water**
- **2 tablespoons cider vinegar**
- **1 tablespoon soy sauce**
- **4 pounds pork baby back ribs, cut into serving-size portions**
- **2 tablespoons mesquite seasoning**
- **½ cup barbecue sauce**

1. Combine water, vinegar and soy sauce in a 6-qt. electric pressure cooker. Rub ribs with mesquite seasoning; add to the pressure cooker.
2. Lock lid in place; make sure vent is closed. Select manual setting; adjust pressure to high, and set time to 35 minutes. When finished cooking, naturally release pressure for 10 minutes, then quick-release any remaining pressure according to manufacturer's directions.
3. Remove ribs to a foil-lined baking sheet; preheat broiler. Brush with barbecue sauce. Broil 4-6 in. from heat until ribs are glazed.

CHICKEN TIKKA MASALA

The flavors of this Indian-style dish keep me coming back for more—it's a simple dish spiced with garam masala, cumin and gingerroot that's simply amazing.

—**JACLYN BELL** LOGAN, UT

PREP: 20 MIN. • **COOK:** 20 MIN.
MAKES: 8 SERVINGS

- **2 tablespoons olive oil**
- **½ large onion, finely chopped**
- **4½ teaspoons minced fresh gingerroot**
- **4 garlic cloves, minced**
- **1 tablespoon garam masala**
- **2½ teaspoons salt**
- **1½ teaspoons ground cumin**
- **1 teaspoon paprika**
- **¾ teaspoon pepper**
- **½ teaspoon cayenne pepper**
- **¼ teaspoon ground cinnamon**
- **2½ pounds boneless skinless chicken breasts, cut into 1½-inch cubes**
- **1 can (29 ounces) tomato puree**
- **1 jalapeno pepper, halved and seeded**
- **1 bay leaf**
- **1 tablespoon cornstarch**
- **1½ cups (12 ounces) plain yogurt**
- **Hot cooked basmati rice**
- **Chopped fresh cilantro, optional**

1. Select saute setting and adjust for medium heat in a 6-qt. electric pressure cooker; heat oil. Cook onion until tender. Add ginger and garlic; cook for 1 minute. Stir in seasonings and cook 30 seconds. Add chicken, tomato puree, jalapeno and bay leaf.
2. Lock lid; make sure vent is closed. Select manual setting; adjust the pressure to high and set time for 10 minutes. When finished cooking, quick-release pressure according to manufacturer's directions. Discard the bay leaf.
3. Select saute setting and adjust for medium heat; bring the mixture to a boil. In a small bowl, mix the cornstarch and yogurt until smooth; gradually stir into the sauce. Cook and stir until the sauce is thickened, about 3 minutes. Serve with rice. If desired, sprinkle with cilantro.

FAST FIX

SOUTH CAROLINA-STYLE VINEGAR BBQ CHICKEN

I live in Georgia but I appreciate the tangy, sweet and slightly spicy taste of Carolina vinegar chicken.

—**RAMONA PARRIS** CANTON, GA

START TO FINISH: 25 MIN.
MAKES: 6 SERVINGS

- **2 cups water**
- **1 cup white vinegar**
- **¼ cup sugar**
- **1 tablespoon reduced-sodium chicken base**
- **1 teaspoon crushed red pepper flakes**
- **¾ teaspoon salt**
- **1½ pounds boneless skinless chicken breasts**
- **6 whole wheat hamburger buns, split, optional**

1. In a 6-qt. electric pressure cooker, mix first six ingredients; add chicken. Lock lid; make sure vent is closed. Select manual setting; adjust pressure to high, and set time for 5 minutes.
2. When finished cooking, allow the pressure to naturally release for 8 minutes, then quick-release the remaining pressure according to the manufacturer's directions.
3. Remove chicken; cool slightly. Reserve 1 cup cooking juices; discard the remaining juices. Shred chicken with two forks. Combine with the reserved juices. If desired, serve chicken mixture on buns.

TEST KITCHEN TIP

Vinegar should be kept in a cool dark place. Unopened, it will keep indefinitely; once opened, it can be stored for up to 6 months.

MEXICAN CARNITAS

Carnitas are easy-to-make pork crisps that are popular in Mexico. The secret to this recipe is the citrus and quick frying. Be sure the meat is well drained before it's placed in the oil, or it will splatter and pop.

—**PATRICIA COLLINS** IMBLER, OR

PREP: 15 MIN. • **COOK:** 40 MIN. + RELEASING
MAKES: 12-16 SERVINGS

- **1 boneless pork shoulder roast (3 to 4 pounds), cut into 2-inch cubes**
- **1 teaspoon salt**
- **1 teaspoon pepper**
- **6 large garlic cloves, minced**
- **½ cup fresh cilantro leaves, chopped**
- **3 large navel orange**
- **1 large lemon**
- **Canola oil or bacon drippings**
- **16 flour tortillas (8 inches), warmed**
- **Optional toppings: chopped tomatoes, shredded cheddar cheese, sliced green onions, sour cream and sliced avocado**

1. Place pork in a 6-qt. electric pressure cooker. Season with salt and pepper; sprinkle with garlic and cilantro. Squeeze juice from the oranges and lemon over the meat.

2. Lock lid; make sure vent is closed. Select manual setting; adjust the pressure to high and set time for 25 minutes. When finished cooking, allow pressure to naturally release for 10 minutes, then quick-release according to manufacturer's directions. With a slotted spoon, remove the meat and drain well on paper towels. Pour the cooking liquid into a glass measuring cup and let the fat rise to the surface. Skim fat from surface and place in the cooker insert; discard remaining cooking liquid.

3. Select saute setting and adjust for high heat. Add enough canola oil or bacon drippings to measure ½-in. depth. When hot, add pork, in batches, and fry until dark golden brown and crisp. Remove and keep warm. Repeat with the remaining pork.

4. Serve warm in tortillas with toppings of your choice.

Freeze option Freeze cooled pork mixture in freezer containers. To use, partially thaw in refrigerator overnight. Fry meat as directed until crisp and brown. Serve as directed.

GARLIC-DILL DEVILED EGGS

I like to experiment with my recipes, and was pleasantly pleased with how the fresh dill really perked up the flavor of these irresistible appetizers.

—**KAMI HORCH** CALAIS, ME

PREP: 20 MIN. • **COOK:** 10 MIN. + CHILLING
MAKES: 2 DOZEN

- **1 cup cold water**
- **12 large eggs**
- **⅔ cup mayonnaise**
- **4 teaspoons dill pickle relish**
- **2 teaspoons snipped fresh dill**
- **2 teaspoons Dijon mustard**
- **1 teaspoon coarsely ground pepper**
- **¼ teaspoon garlic powder**
- **⅛ teaspoon paprika or cayenne pepper**

1. Pour water into 6-qt. electric pressure cooker. Place trivet in cooker; set eggs on the trivet. Lock lid; make sure the vent is closed. Select manual setting; adjust the pressure to high, and set time to 8 minutes. When finished cooking, quick-release the pressure according to manufacturer's directions. Immediately place the eggs in a bowl of ice water to cool.

2. Cut the eggs lengthwise in half. Remove yolks, reserving whites. In a bowl, mash the yolks. Stir in all the remaining ingredients except paprika. Spoon or pipe into the egg whites.

3. Refrigerate, covered, for at least 30 minutes before serving. Sprinkle with paprika.

TEST KITCHEN TIP
For a handy way to serve deviled eggs, set them in paper cupcake liners in a muffin tin. They stay upright and neat, and the eggs in the paper cups won't slide around on people's plates.

GARLIC-DILL
DEVILED EGGS

FAST FIX

SWEET & SMOKY BBQ CHICKEN & SAUSAGE

My party-ready barbecue recipe works well on weeknights, too. With just a few minutes of prep time, you still get that low-and-slow flavor everybody craves (thanks, pressure cooker!). Throw in minced jalapenos for extra oomph.

—**KIMBERLY YOUNG** MESQUITE, TX

PREP: 10 MIN. • **COOK:** 25 MIN.
MAKES: 8 SERVINGS

- **1 medium onion, chopped**
- **1 large sweet red pepper, cut into 1-inch pieces**
- **4 bone-in chicken thighs, skin removed**
- **4 chicken drumsticks, skin removed**
- **1 package (12 ounces) smoked sausage links, cut into 1-inch pieces**
- **1 cup chicken broth**
- **1 cup barbecue sauce**
- **Sliced seeded jalapeno pepper, optional**

1. Place the first six ingredients in a 6-qt. electric pressure cooker; top with barbecue sauce. Lock the lid; make sure the vent is closed. Select manual setting; adjust pressure to high, and set time for 12 minutes. When finished cooking, quick-release pressure according to the manufacturer's directions (a thermometer inserted in chicken should read at least 170°-175°). Remove chicken, sausage and vegetables from cooker; keep warm.
2. Select saute setting and adjust for high heat; bring liquid to a boil. Reduce heat; simmer until thickened, 12-15 minutes, stirring occasionally.
3. Serve chicken, sausage and vegetables with sauce. If desired, top with jalapeno.

POTATO-CHEDDAR FRITTATA

I like to serve this protein-packed frittata with toasted rustic bread. You can also use leftovers instead of the refrigerated potatoes with onions.

—**DONNA-MARIE RYAN** TOPSFIELD, MA

PREP: 15 MIN. + STANDING
COOK: 30 MIN. + RELEASING
MAKES: 4 SERVINGS

- **1 tablespoon canola oil**
- **1½ cups refrigerated diced potatoes with onion**
- **1 cup water**
- **8 large egg whites**
- **4 large eggs**
- **½ cup fat-free milk**
- **2 green onions, chopped**
- **2 teaspoons minced fresh parsley**
- **¼ teaspoon salt**
- **¼ teaspoon pepper**
- **½ cup shredded cheddar cheese**

1. In a large skillet, heat oil over medium-high heat. Add potatoes; cook and stir until lightly browned, 4-6 minutes. Transfer to a greased 1½-2½ qt. souffle or round baking dish. Pour water into 6-qt. electric pressure cooker. Place trivet in cooker.
2. Whisk next seven ingredients; stir in the shredded cheese. Pour egg mixture over potatoes. Loosely cover baking dish with foil and set on the trivet in the cooker. Lock lid; make sure the vent is closed. Select manual setting; adjust pressure to high, set time to 30 minutes.
3. After cooking, let the pressure release naturally for 10 minutes, then quick-release any remaining pressure according to manufacturer's directions. Remove the lid and remove the baking dish. Let stand for 10 minutes before serving.

SWEET & SOUR BEET SALAD

My husband loves, loves pickled beets. I paired them with a little citrus for an Eastery salad. It has such a great color combination!

—**MICHELLE CLAIR** SEATTLE, WA

PREP: 15 MIN. **COOK:** 20 MIN.
MAKES: 8 SERVINGS

- **6 medium fresh beets (about 2 pounds)**
- **1½ cups water**
- **¼ cup extra virgin olive oil**
- **3 tablespoons lemon juice**
- **2 tablespoons cider vinegar**
- **2 tablespoons honey**
- **¼ teaspoon salt**
- **¼ teaspoon pepper**
- **2 large ruby red grapefruit, peeled and sectioned**
- **2 small red onions, halved and thinly sliced**

1. Scrub beets, trimming tops to 1 in. Place beets on trivet of a 6-qt. electric pressure cooker. Add 1½ cups water. Lock lid; make sure vent is closed. Select manual setting; adjust pressure to high and set time to 20 minutes.
2. When finished cooking, let pressure release naturally before opening; remove the beets, and cool completely before peeling, halving and thinly slicing them. Place in a serving bowl. Whisk together the next six ingredients. Pour over the beets; add grapefruit and onion. Toss gently to coat.

FAVORITE PEPPER STEAK

Pepper steak is one of my favorite dishes but I was always disappointed with beef that was too tough. This recipe solves that problem! I've stored leftovers in one big resealable bag and also in individual portions for quick lunches.

—**JULIE RHINE** ZELIENOPLE, PA

PREP: 15 MIN. • **COOK:** 1 HOUR
MAKES: 12 SERVINGS

- **1 beef top round roast (3 pounds)**
- **1 cup water, divided**
- **½ cup reduced-sodium soy sauce**
- **4 garlic cloves, minced**
- **1 large onion, halved and sliced**
- **1 large green pepper, cut into ½-inch strips**
- **1 large sweet red pepper, cut into ½-inch strips**
- **⅓ cup cornstarch**
- **2 teaspoons sugar**
- **2 teaspoons ground ginger**
- **8 cups hot cooked brown rice**

1. In a 6-qt. electric pressure cooker, combine roast, ½ cup water, soy sauce and garlic. Lock lid; make sure vent is closed. Select manual setting; adjust pressure to high, and set time for 1 hour. When finished cooking, quick-release pressure according to manufacturer's directions. Add onion and peppers. Lock lid; make sure the vent is closed. Select manual setting; adjust pressure to high, and set time for 2 minutes. When finished cooking, quick-release the pressure. Remove beef to a cutting board.
2. Select saute setting, and adjust for high heat; bring liquid to a boil. In a small bowl, mix cornstarch, sugar, ginger and remaining water until smooth; gradually stir into the vegetable mixture. Cook and stir until sauce is thickened, 1-2 minutes.
3. Cut the beef into slices. Stir gently into sauce; heat through. Serve with rice.

Freeze option Freeze cooled beef mixture in freezer containers. To use, partially thaw in refrigerator overnight. Heat through in a saucepan, stirring occasionally and adding a little water if necessary.

QUICK & EASY HOISIN MEATBALLS

I love the start of fall because that means it's football season! Meatballs are filling and hearty and great for a tailgate. I served this for the first time at the OSU home opener. My best friend, who hates meatballs, couldn't get enough of them! If you are serving children and prefer not to add the wine, substitute beef broth instead.

—**LISA DE PERIO** DALLAS, TX

PREP: 20 MIN. • **COOK:** 10 MIN. + RELEASING
MAKES: ABOUT 2 DOZEN

- **1 cup dry red wine or beef broth**
- **3 tablespoons hoisin sauce**
- **2 tablespoons soy sauce**
- **1 large egg, lightly beaten**
- **4 green onions, chopped**
- **¼ cup finely chopped onion**
- **¼ cup minced fresh cilantro**
- **2 garlic cloves, minced**
- **½ teaspoon salt**
- **½ teaspoon pepper**
- **1 pound ground beef**
- **1 pound ground pork**
- **Sesame seeds**

1. In a 6-qt. electric pressure cooker, whisk the wine, hoisin and soy sauce.
2. In a large bowl, combine the next seven ingredients. Add beef and pork; mix lightly but thoroughly. Shape into 1½-in. meatballs; place in cooker. Lock lid; make sure the vent is closed. Select manual setting; adjust the pressure to high, and set the time for 10 minutes. When finished cooking, quick-release pressure according to manufacturer's directions. Sprinkle with sesame seeds.

Freeze option Freeze cooled meatball mixture in freezer containers. To use, partially thaw in refrigerator overnight. Microwave, covered, on high until heated through, about 8 minutes, gently stirring halfway through.

FAST FIX

PUMPKIN & BROWN SUGAR OATMEAL

There's nothing like a warm cup of oatmeal in the morning, and my spiced version works in an electric pressure cooker. Store leftovers in the fridge.

—**JORDAN MASON** BROOKVILLE, PA

START TO FINISH: 30 MIN.
MAKES: 6 SERVINGS

- **1 can (15 ounces) solid-pack pumpkin**
- **1¼ cups steel-cut oats**
- **3 tablespoons brown sugar**
- **1½ teaspoons pumpkin pie spice**
- **1 teaspoon ground cinnamon**
- **¾ teaspoon salt**
- **3 cups water**
- **1½ cups 2% milk**
- **Optional toppings: toasted chopped pecans, ground cinnamon, additional brown sugar and 2% milk**

1. Stir together all ingredients in a 6-qt. electric pressure cooker. Lock lid; make sure vent is closed. Select manual setting; adjust pressure to high, and set time for 10 minutes.
2. When finished cooking, allow the pressure to naturally release for 10 minutes, then quick-release any remaining pressure according to manufacturer's directions. Stir; let stand 5-10 minutes to thicken. Serve, if desired, with toppings of choice.

Note Steel-cut oats are also known as Scotch oats or Irish oatmeal.

PUMPKIN & BROWN SUGAR OATMEAL
Jordan Mason
Brookville, PA

LORA'S ZESTY RED BEANS & RICE

LORA'S ZESTY RED BEANS & RICE

My dear mother-in-law passed this simple recipe to me. With meats, beans and savory veggies, it's tasty, easy and economical, too!

—**CAROL SIMMS** MADISON, MS

PREP: 15 MIN. + SOAKING • **COOK:** 30 MIN.
MAKES: 10 SERVINGS

1 package (16 ounces) dried kidney beans (about 2½ cups)
2 cups cubed fully cooked ham (about 1 pound)
1 package (12 ounces) fully cooked andouille chicken sausage links or flavor of choice, sliced
1 medium green pepper, chopped
1 medium onion, chopped
2 celery ribs, chopped
1 tablespoon hot pepper sauce
2 garlic cloves, minced
1½ teaspoons salt
Hot cooked rice

1. Rinse and sort beans. Soak overnight according to package directions. Drain, discarding water; rinse with cool water.
2. In a 6-qt. electric pressure cooker, combine ham, sausage, vegetables, pepper sauce, garlic and salt. Lock lid; make sure the vent is closed. Select manual setting; adjust pressure to high, and set time for 30 minutes. When finished cooking, quick-release pressure according to manufacturer's directions. Serve with rice.

FAST FIX

CHEESY BACON SPAGHETTI SQUASH

This quick casserole is called cheesy for a reason. Stir in any kind of cheese you've got!

—**JEAN WILLIAMS** STILLWATER, OK

START TO FINISH: 30 MIN.
MAKES: 4 SERVINGS

1 large spaghetti squash (3½ pounds)
1 cup water
4 bacon strips, chopped
3 tablespoons butter
1 tablespoon brown sugar
½ teaspoon salt
¼ teaspoon pepper
½ cup shredded Swiss cheese

1. Halve squash lengthwise; discard seeds. Place squash, cut side down, on the trivet of a 6-qt. electric pressure cooker. Add water to cooker; insert trivet. Lock lid; make sure vent is closed. Select steam setting; adjust pressure to high, and set time to 7 minutes. When finished cooking, quick-release pressure according to manufacturer's directions. Set aside; remove water from cooker.
2. Select saute setting, and adjust for high heat; add bacon, stirring occasionally, and cook until crisp. With a slotted spoon, remove the bacon to paper towels; reserve drippings. Stir in butter, brown sugar, salt and pepper. Separate squash strands with a fork and add to cooker; toss and heat through. Remove from heat. Stir in cheese, and place in a serving bowl. Top with bacon and serve.

GENERAL RECIPE INDEX

Find every recipe by food category and major ingredient.

SOUTHWESTERN PULLED PORK CROSTINI PAGE 14

THAI CHICKEN NOODLE SOUP PAGE 75

POLYNESIAN PULLED CHICKEN PAGE 145

SLOW COOKER JERKED SHORT RIBS PAGE 103

ASIAN BBQ PORK BUNS PAGE 172

SWEET & SMOKY BBQ CHICKEN & SAUSAGE PAGE 242

ALPHABETICAL RECIPE INDEX

STRAWBERRY-BANANA PUDDING CAKE PAGE 215

NUTTY APPLE STREUSEL DESSERT PAGE 218

Q

R

S

T

U

V

W

Z